D0941417

CONTEMPORARY PROBLEMS
OF
PAKISTAN

INTERNATIONAL STUDIES

IN

SOCIOLOGY AND SOCIAL ANTHROPOLOGY

General Editor

K. ISHWARAN

VOLUME XV

CONTEMPORARY PROBLEMS
OF PAKISTAN

LEIDEN

E. J. BRILL

1974

CONTEMPORARY PROBLEMS
OF
PAKISTAN

EDITED BY

J. HENRY KORSON

LEIDEN
E. J. BRILL
1974

ISBN 90 04 03942 2

CONTENTS

J. HENRY KORSON, Introduction. 1

CRAIG BAXTER, The People's Party vs. the Punjab "Feudalists" . . . 6

FAZLUR RAHMAN, Islam and the New Constitution of Pakistan. 30

HAFEEZ MALIK, The Emergence of the Federal Pattern in Pakistan . . 45

LAWRENCE ZIRING, Bhutto's Foreign Policy, 1972–73 56

W. ERIC GUSTAFSON, Economic Reforms under the Bhutto Regime . . 81

LEE L. BEAN and A. D. BHATTI, Pakistan's Population in the 1970's:
Problems and Prospects 99

J. HENRY KORSON, Bhutto's Educational Reform 119

Biographical Notes 147

Index 149

Introduction

J. HENRY KORSON

University of Massachusetts, Amherst, U.S.A.

Perhaps the most important development on the world scene during the last generation has been the achievement of national independence by dozens of former colonial territories. The striving for nationhood is rarely smooth, and frequently is attained only after great political and even military struggle.

Pakistan is only one of the nations in South Asia which achieved independence from Great Britain in the early post-war years, and its trials in achieving and maintaining nationhood have been almost unparalleled. The one factor which distinguishes Pakistan from almost all other newly-established nations is its commitment to the religious ideology of Islam, a commitment which was a foundation stone for the new nation. This commitment a generation after independence is no less today, as can be ascertained by a close reading of the new constitution inaugurated in August, 1973. In fact, the nation has from the start referred to itself as "The Islamic Republic of Pakistan."

The problems which the young nation faced in the early years of independence were, indeed, monumental. Since the nation was founded on the ideology of Islam, various political leaders have, from time to time, raised the slogan of "Islamic Socialism." Yet as an agrarian society the concepts of private property and the ownership of land have been, and continue to be the most cherished values.

As has been the case in many other newly-founded nations, the first leaders of Pakistan had no experience in self government and used the model of the Indian Civil Service to establish their own Civil Service of Pakistan. Both, of course, followed the British pattern which had been long established on the subcontinent. Since many Pakistani leaders had served in the Indian Civil Service at various levels of administration, it was not too difficult to establish the Government Administrative Staff College to train additional members to serve the nation. Political parties began to function, and men who had served as leaders of the Pakistan movement in India became the leaders of the new nation.

The Muslim separatist movement before independence was led by unorthodox men like Mohammad Ali Jinnah who had in mind a secular state, but he did not oppose the pressures of the sectarians provided there was freedom for the religious minorities. And this freedom of worship has been maintained. Leadership in a political movement is not to be equated with experience in national leadership and its responsibilities, so that the earliest leaders didn't even have the opportunity to survive their apprenticeships. For eleven years the nation's leadership wallowed in uncertainty and ineffectiveness – perhaps no worse than the leadership of most other newly-formed nations. As is also frequently the case where one unsuccessful regime is followed by another, the military came to the fore, and in 1958 General Mohammad Ayub Khan assumed the presidency.

Every new administration takes the reins of government with high hopes for the resolution of the major problems of its people, and such was the case eleven years later when Ayub Khan stepped down for still another military leader, General Yahya Khan. When the latter assumed office he made it clear that his personal preference was to continue in his military career and that he considered his political role as president to be that of caretaker until national elections could be held. The election of December, 1970, and the disastrous war in East Pakistan that followed left Zulfikar Ali Bhutto, leader of the People's Party of Pakistan (which had won the majority of West Pakistan's seats in the National Assembly) as the man who not only had to carry the burdens of office under "normal" circumstances, but was challenged to retrieve the nation's dignity. By many observers the economy was considered to be in considerable disrepair, and the election campaign promises of the PPP had to be considered by Bhutto and his party leaders as something far more serious than ordinary campaign rhetoric.

When Bhutto assumed the presidency on December 20, 1971 following the cease-fire in East Pakistan/Bangladesh, he wasted little time in organizing his cabinet and setting about instituting many of the reforms he and his party had promised. This brief statement cannot hope to explore all the problems of the nation in those dark days, nor the solutions promised by Bhutto and his administration, because at its birth and since, Pakistan was a nation with exceedingly limited resources, and this enormous handicap presented almost insuperable barriers to the achievement of rapid economic development.

As in the case of so many ex-colonial nations, foreign aid at the start became a *sine-qua-non* not only for the economic development of the nation, but for its very survival. Aid soon became available from many of the western nations, both in the form of outright grants as well as loans and technical assistance. This economic assistance to Pakistan has continued over the years, which has helped spur the development and growth of the economy. Beginning in 1947 and the years following, some of the immigrants from India were able to bring some of their resources, while others with business experience were able to obtain sufficient credit to undertake various enterprises. The leaders of the new nation opted for private enterprise, although the theme of egalitarianism within the framewerk of Islam was frequently propounded.

Following the disastrous war in East Pakistan, and with the economy in a shambles, the problems that confronted Bhutto were, indeed, monumental and of long standing. Although the PPP won the majority of West Pakistan's seats in the national assembly in the 1970 election, Bhutto lost no time in instituting reforms—many of which had appeared in the party's platform during the campaign. Unlike the previous Five Year Plans, almost all the reforms were outlined to be achieved by the end of the decade. For example, within three months of taking office, in December, 1971, the Educational Policy for 1972–1980 was announced under that very title.

In this brief introduction, it is impossible to discuss at length the many and varied problems that face the Bhutto regime during the balance of this decade, but the chapters that follow in this small volume are by scholars who have written widely on various aspects of the nation and people of Pakistan since its inception. It should be kept in mind, however, that the chapters that follow were completed in August/September, 1973, and that although they were "contemporary" as of that time, it is never possible in a work of this kind to make the efforts of the contributors as timely as the daily newspaper. Nevertheless, it is hoped that the reader will profit from the perspectives and insights offered.

The Punjab has not only been the most heavily populated province, but all too often has been considered the power center of the four provinces that constitute contemporary Pakistan. The landholders have always been the major center of political power, and in his chapter "The People's Party Vs. the Punjab Feudalists," Professor Baxter offers some deep insights into some of the long-standing problems of power politics in what was (and perhaps still is) an essentially feudal society.

We are fortunate to have as the contributor of the second chapter, Professor Fazlur Rahman, assess the new Constitution of Pakistan, which was inaugurated on August 14, 1973. In this chapter Professor Rahman makes comparisons with the Interim Constitution of May, 1972, and points up Bhutto's efforts to compromise with the traditionalists. The new constitution does lay greater stress on the basic philosophy of Islam. Furthermore, although the "Islamic Republic of Pakistan" has been the official name used, not until the new Constitution was written has Islam been recognized as the official state religion. One of the compromises Bhutto and the PPP apparently had to make with the opposition was to grant the Islamic Council veto power over the National Assembly. This point has not been widely publicized, and its effect will be interesting to observe.

All too frequently some of the major political problems of newly established nations are internal ones based on ethnic, tribal, and/or regional differences. Since nationhood is a concept rarely found among a people striving for political independence, self interest is usually found to be the overriding element in the difficulties that confront political leaders as they attempt to resolve the young nation's problems. Regionalism, then, can be readily understood from the point of view of self-interest. But when the greatest concentration of population is combined with the concentration of the most productive land in a primarily agricultural society, the result equates with the concentration of political power. The Punjab, then, in [West] Pakistan has played that role since independence, and will undoubtedly continue to do so in the future. Prof. Malik assesses some of the problems of regionalism that the government has attempted to resolve.

In his chapter on Bhutto's foreign policy in the course of his first eighteen months in office, Professor Ziring reviews the background of Bhutto's experience in the nation's foreign affairs, – which had been the Prime Minister's almost total experience and preoccupation in his nation's government. Bhutto served as Ayub Kahn's minister of foreign affairs before their falling out, and, in the intervening years appears to have been largely concerned with Pakistan's relations with India, – and only secondarily with other nations. How successful his stewardship will be will have to await the time when he has completed his service to the nation.

Operating from an essentially weak position at the end of the war in December, 1971, Bhutto has won the admiration of foreign leaders for his astuteness in handling both the nation's foreign policy as well as reaching a working accommodation with the leaders of the minority parties on the nation's most pressing domestic problems.

The status and character of a nation's economic organization is a fairly accurate indicator of that society's economic and social welfare, and, as one of the numerous newly organized nations of the post World war II period, Pakistan has had its difficulties, but also its share of successes. As with so many underdeveloped nations, foreign aid in a variety of forms has been crucial to the development of its economy, and this aid continues to play a vital role today.

With exceedingly limited natural resources and the desire to encourage rapid economic development, successive administrations offered attractive inducements to the entrepreneurial class which not only resulted in high annual economic growth rates, but also resulted in the concentration of great wealth in the hands of relatively few people – the renowned "22 families." Since the election platform of the People's Party of Pakistan laid considerable stress on "Islamic Socialism" and egalitarianism as goals to be achieved for the nation, Professor Gustafson reviews the government's major accomplishments to date: nationalization of [some] of the basic industries; labor reforms, which are aimed largely at the larger companies; land reforms, the results of which are open to question; and the devaluation of the rupee, which Professor Gustafson considers the most fruitful move to date. The loss of East Pakistan, the major source of foreign exchange earnings, has evidently not had the disastrous effects on the economy of Pakistan that had been predicted. Instead, the resurgence of the economy and annual growth rate has surprised many observers.

Although the economic problems that confront the many underdeveloped nations of the world command the major attention of their leaders, all too often the most serious factor that contributes to the continued economic difficulties of these nations is the unabated population increase. With the relatively rapid adoption of modern public health measures the reduction in mortality rates for many of these nations has been quite dramatic. Unfortunately, the same cannot be claimed for efforts to reduce fertility rates on a comparable basis. The result has almost invariably been a sharp and continued net increase in the population, and Pakistan is no exception. Although the official government position has favored the introduction of family planning, the optimistic results that have been reported in the past have evidently been exaggerated. In their paper devoted to Pakistan's population problems, Bean and Bhatti point up some of the difficulties of the governmentally sponsored fertility control program in a traditional society and discuss the prospects for the future.

In this age of rising expectations, perhaps no other item has greater emotional appeal to the masses in the less-developed nations than universal literacy and free education. It is no accident of history that the ex-colonial nations have, as a rule, the weakest systems of education and the highest rates of illiteracy. It doesn't take much imagination on the part of men who seek high office in such nations to attack illiteracy and promise universal (and frequently free) education. And such has been the case in Pakistan. Previous regimes have proclaimed and promised much, but they can show only an erratic record of accomplishment, and one far below the expectations and hopes of either the people or today's leaders.

That Bhutto was serious about educational reform can be judged by the fact that within three months of taking office the *Education Policy, 1972–1980*, was announced and widely published. Although wide-ranging, its major goals were the nationalization of private schools and colleges without compensation; the universalization of free primary (and, later, secondary) education, and a major attack on the problem of illiteracy. Of these three goals, the first has been largely achieved within the first eighteen months; considerable progress has been made toward the second, while universal literacy will undoubtedly take many years to achieve. In the chapter "Bhutto's Educational Reform," I have tried to assess the new education policy and the progress made in the first eighteen months since it was announced.

Four of the chapters: those by Professors Ziring, Gustafson, Malik and Korson, are revised and expanded versions of papers presented at the annual meeting of the Association of Asian Studies in March, 1972, in Chicago.

The People's Party Vs. the Punjab "Feudalists"

CRAIG BAXTER

U.S. Department of State and the United States Military Academy, West Point, U.S.A.

IN ITS MANIFESTO issued prior to the 1970 elections, the Pakistan People's Party (PPP) led by Zulfiqar Ali Bhutto reiterated one of its "programmatic principles" by declaring "the party stands for elimination of feudalism and will take concrete steps in accordance with the established principles of socialism to protect and advance the interests of the peasantry" (1970:29). The manifesto reviewed the land reforms of the Ayub era and criticized them: "Since it was legally permitted, the feudal landowner divided the excess [i.e., land above the permissible ceiling] among the members of his family…in most parts of West Pakistan the feudal owners live in a social system of castes, caste-clans and surviving traditions of joint families. Thus even with his estate divided in this manner, the feudal lord retains his power" (1970:28). To the PPP the "feudal lords constitute a formidable obstacle to progress. Not only by virtue of their wealth, but on account of their hold over their tenants and the neighbouring peasantry, they wield considerable power and are, even at present, a major political force" (1970:28).

The words "even at present" assume, at least in the eyes of the PPP, the existence of feudal political power in the past. It is the purpose of this article to explore the importance of the major landlords in the Punjab in the political system of the province since the introduction of reforms in 1919 and to look at the impact of the PPP on them in the 1970 election. In the pre-independence period the study will be limited to the Muslim seats in the territory which became part of Pakistan after the partition of 1947. The use of the essentially perjorative terms "feudalism", "landlordism" and similar words and their derivatives by opponents of the traditional leadership of the rural areas will not be challenged here, although the present writer does not subscribe fully to such use. An alternative term might well be "squirearchy", under which the local squires performed political roles in which they both protected and defended their own high estate and legislated, perhaps paternalistically, to improve the conditions of the agrarian population in general, or at least those who owned the land they tilled.

What ever may be the correct term the PPP call for land reform was not original. The party which has been credited with furthering the interests of large landlords, the Unionist Party of pre-partition Punjab, was itself founded to protect the samall as well as the large landowner, primarily against the urban (and largely Hindu) commercial and money lending groups. The Muslim League, following closely the program of the Congress Party, called for the break up of large *zamindari* holdings and a moderate program of land reform in both the 1936 and 1946 elections. More equitable distribution of land was again in the Muslim League manifesto in the 1951 Punjab election. And as we have already noted the 1958 revolution of Ayub Khan included among its basic tenets a revision of the land holding patterns in West Pakistan. The 1951 Muslim League received and the 1958 revolution seized a mandate for reform but neither carried out a program to the extent demanded by the PPP. The party of President Bhutto now has that mandate. Its exercise of the mandate is beyond the scope of this article but it can be noted that, using continuing martial law powers. the new president has announced a land reform program.

Unionist Domination

The Government of India Act, 1919, usually known as the Montagu-Chelmsford reforms, introduced major changes in the administration of the provinces of British India. Now a majority of the members of the provincial Legislative Council would be elected and, while the principle of executive responsibility to the Council was not granted, the Council would have expanded control over the acts of the executive. Additionally, the executive departments were divided into two categories: one group, concerned with fiscal and law and order matters, would remain under the jurisdiction of the Governor and would be administered by officially appointed executive councillors; the second, concerned primarily with "nation-building" subjects, would be transferred to ministers appointed by the Governor from among the elected members of the Council. The new system, "dyarchy", would almost inevitably lead to the formation of parties, informally or formally, either within or outside of the Council. The ambiguous position of the Congress on "council entry" meant that in most provinces parties other than the Congress took the lead and these parties generally were formed first within the Council and later extended their activities outside by organizing in order to present a common electoral front. The franchise was severely restricted with eligibility based primarily on property ownership and income qualifications. Constituencies were divided into general (i.e., territorial) and special, the latter including seats for such groups as landholders, university graduates and industrial and commercial interests. The territorial constituencies were divided in two manners: first, seats were assigned to various communities in a system of separate electorates in accordance with the Lucknow Pact between the Muslim League and the Congress in 1916; and, secondly, within the communal allotments seats were assigned to urban and rural electorates.

In the Punjab a total of 64 members of the Council were to be elected from territorial constituencies and seven more from special constituencies. The 64 general seats were divided into twenty non-Muhammadan (seven urban and

13 rural), 32 Muhammadan (five urban and 27 rural) and twelve Sikh (one urban and eleven rural). The seven special constituencies included four for landholders (one for each community plus a separate seat for the Baluch *tumandars*), one for university graduates and two to represent commercial and industrial groups.

Despite the widening of the franchise under the Montagu-Chelmsford reforms the number of eligible voters in the general constituencies was only 3.4 percent of the population (1921) in the 1926 election (Gr. Brit., 1930: 41–43). In this article we are concerned primarily with the Muhammadan rural constituencies in the territory which was to become part of Pakistan. There were nineteen such seats located in fifteen districts lying east of the Ravi and Sutlej rivers. In 1921 these had a Muslim population of 7,191,140 of which 189,157 were eligible to vote in 1926, a percentage of 2.63, which is significantly lower than that of the province as a whole. It can be assumed that virtually all the electors achieved that designation through the property ownership qualification and from the lower percentage of the Muslim population meeting the standard that the land holdings were perhaps larger than in other districts. There was considerable regional variation in the percentage, ranging from about 5 percent in Rawalpindi, Jhelum and Lyallpur districts down to less than 1 percent in Dera Ghazi Khan and Muzaffargarh (Gt. Brit., 1930: 41–43). Generally the ratio of eligible voters was higher in districts containing canal colonies than in non-colony districts, i.e., those districts in which Darling reports the average land holding to be higher (1947: 127 and *passim*).

Elections were held for the Council in 1920, 1923, 1926 and 1930, with the term of the last Council being extended pending the election of members of the new Assembly created under the 1935 Act. In the nineteen seats together with the Muhammadan landholders and the Baluch tumandars, 21 seats in all, only 51 different persons were elected, an average of 2.43 per seat. Only two seats were won by different persons in each election, Lyallpur South and Gujranwala, but in the latter two of the occupants were from the same family. Four members were elected in each of the four elections, Nawab Chaudhury Fazl Ali of Gujrat, Malik Sir Muhammad Firoz Khan Noon of Shahpur, Makhdum Syed Reza Shah Gilani of Multan and Nawab Sir Muhammad Jamal Khan Leghari of the Baluch tumanders seat. Seven more were elected three times, although like those elected four times not necessarily from the same seat on each occasion. Another 13 were elected twice.

Many of those elected, thirteen, were from among those families listed in the compilation of Punjab chiefs sanctioned by the provincial government (Griffin 1940). Many more are included among such notable categories as provincial and divisional *darbaris*. The names form a listing of the squirearchy of Punjab. Extending the time from 1919 to the end of parliamentary government in 1958 – not all listed had members in the 1921–36 Council – one can note the Arain Mians of Baghbanpura (Sir Muhammad Shafi, Mian Muhammad Shah Nawaz, Begum Jahanara Shah Nawaz, Mian Iftikharuddin, Mian Bashir Ahmad), the Mokul family (Sardar Habibullah), and the Qizilbash clan (Nawab Sir Muzaffar Ali Khan Qizilbash) of Lahore District; the Chathas (Riasat Ali, Salahuddin, Nasiruddin) of Gujranwala; the Janjuas of Darapur (Talib Mehdi Khan, Khair Mehdi Khan, Lahrasab Khan), Pirs of Jalalpur (Nawab Sir Syed Mehr Shah) and Khokars (Raja Ghazanfar Ali Khan) of Jhelum; the Pirs of Makhad, the Kot Ghebas (Sir Muhammad Shah Nawaz Khan), the Hayats of Wah (noted below), and the Shamasabad Awans (Nawab Muhammad Amin Khan) of Attock (now Campbellpur); the Noons and Tiwanas (both noted below), the Qureshis (Nawab Muhammad Hayat, Mian Saeed, Mian Zakir), Pirachas (Sheikh Fazle Haq, Sheikh Fazal Ilahi) and the Pirs of Jahanian Shah (Syed Ghulam Muhammad) of Shahpur (now Sargodha); the Wanbachran (Malik Muzaffar Khan) and Kalabagh (Malik Amir Muhammad Khan) families of Mianwali; the Pirs of Rajoa (Syed Ghulam Abbas) and of Shah Jiwana (Syed Mubarik Ali, Syed Abid Husain) and Sials (Nawazish Ali Khan) of Jhang; the Daultanas (see below), Gilanis (eight have held seats from 1921 through 1958), Dahas (Khan Haibat Khan), Qureshis (Murid Hussain, Ashiq Hussain), Gardezis (Syed Ali Husain Shah) and Khaggas (Pir Budhan Shah) of Multan; Gurmanis (Mushtaq Ahmad, Ghulam Jilani) and Dastis (Abdul Hamid Khan) of Muzaffargarh and Legharis (Sir Jamal Khan), Drishaks (Allan Khan, Bahadur Khan), Mazaris (Balakh Sher, Sher Baz) and Pirs of Taunsa Sharif in Dera Ghazi Khan. The listing is long but incomplete as the unravelling of family connections is a difficult task. However, the families noted above held at least 42 of the 84 seats for which elections were held to the Council and at least 53 of the 116 seats for which elections were held in 1936 and 1946 for the Assembly in the districts under study (i.e., four elections at 21 seats each for the Council and two elections at 58 seats each for the Assembly). If the districts of Sialkot, Gujrat, Sheikhupura, Montgomery, and Lyallpur – largely Jat and small holdings – are eliminated the key families won 70 percent of the Council elections and 68 percent of the pre-independence Assembly elections. With almost no exceptions all those elected to the Council and those elected to the first Assembly were associated with the Unionist Party. The 1945–46 contest between the Unionists and the Muslim League will be discussed below.

The founder and principal mover behind the Unionist Party was Mian Sir Fazli Husain (1877–1936). He has been the subject of an excellent biography by his son (Husain, 1946) and an appreciation by an experienced journalist (Ahmad, 1936). Fazli Husain had been a member of the Legislative Council as it existed prior to the Montagu-Chelmsford reforms and was elected in 1920 to the Muhammadan landholders seat. Under dyarchy he was one of two ministers chosen by the Governor, the other being an urban Hindu, Lala Harkishen Lal (Gauba). He remained a minister until he was oppointed an Executive Councillor in 1926. In 1930 he was appointed a member of the Viceroy's Executive Council in New Delhi where he remained until 1935. He again became a minister in the Punjab in 1936 just prior to his death.

In the first Council Fazli Husain was clearly the most prominent and experienced among the Muslim members and it was to him that they looked for leadership. The informal organization of a rural bloc began in the first Council and drew support not only from Muslims but also from rural Hindus under the leadership of Chaudhury Lal Chand and later Chaudhyry Sir Chhotu Ram, who became the leader of the Unionist Party when Fazli Husain joined the Executive Council. The rural Sikh members, while retaining a separate organization, also gave support to the rural bloc; prior to Fazli Husain's appointment to the Executive Council, one of the two members was the Sikh leader Sardar Sir Sundar Singh Majithia (1872–1941). In 1923 the rural grouping formally constituted itself the Punjab National Unionist Party "intended [as] a mass organization of the Punjab peasant proprietors" (Husain 1964: xi). While the party gained support only from rural members of the Hindu and Sikh communities, and not by any means all of the former, it did gain the adherance of the bulk of the urban Muslim members including such prominent members as Dr. Sir Muhammad Iqbal (1877–1938) (Malik 1971: 82–83), Sir Abdul Qadir and Mir Maqbool Mahmud.

The party adopted a sixteen point program which included the constitutional attainment of dominion status and the "statesmanlike" working of the Montagu-Chelmsford reforms to that end. The latter was a rebuff to the Congress of Gandhi and clearly showed a moderate stance as behooved those with property interests. Underlying the operative points was the urban-rural conflict: the achievement of a balance between urban and rural taxation with the clear implication that the land revenue was a greater burden on the rural population that those taxes laid on city dwellers were on them; the checking of "exploitation of economically backward classes by economically dominant classes," and the continuation of the Punjab Land Alienation Act to protect agriculturist against money lenders (Husain 1946: 154–5). Although there were occasional breaks in the ranks on matters which were specifically communal, it was a program on which the rural elite of the Punjab could agree and carry out cooperatively and inter-communally (Ahmad 1967: 57–64).

Three Families

Sir Fazli Husain's immediate family did not continue in electoral politics. One son, Azim, is a high official in the Indian Foreign Service and another, Nasim, served in the Pakistan Foreign Service as did a nephew and son-in-law, Mian Arshad Husain, who became for a short period a Foreign Minister under Ayub Khan. Another son-in-law, Sheikh Manzur Qadir, son of Sir Abdul Qadir, has been prominent in legal affairs and has served as both Chief Justice and Law Minister of Pakistan, while still another is a member of the Noon family but has not been active in politics. Thus there is no lineal continuation of Fazli Husain's political activity, although Azim Husain's book remains perhaps the best single work on the Unionist Party up to 1936.

There are however three other families who were important in the Unionist period and which have members of the family still active in legislative bodies in Pakistan. These are the Hayats of Wah, the Noon-Tiwana group of Sargodha and the Daultanas of Mailsi in Multan District. These are not the only ones of the key families which survived the People's Party onslaught in 1970. There are others but they do not meet the qualification of being among the highest echelon of the Unionists in the past as well as sitting today. These include the Legharis of Dera Ghazi Khan (Sardar Ata Muhammad Khan, Sardar Mahmud Khan), the Pir of Makhad from Campbellpur, Pirachas (Sheikh Fazal Ilahi, a senator), Kalabagh (Malik Muzaffar Khan), Gilani (Faiz Mustafa Shah), Multan Qureshis (Nawab Sadiq Hussain) and Dastis (Amjad Hamid Khan), the names in parentheses being those who sit today in legislative bodies. Several of these were either elected on the People's Party ticket or were elected as independents and joined the PPP later. Thanks to indirect elections for women's seats the Arain Mians of Baghbanpura (Begum Nasim Jehan) and Pirs of Shah Jiwana (Begum Abida Fakr Imam) have also been seated in legislative bodies.

The *Hayats of Wah* have been represented in legislative bodies continuously since 1921 with the exception of late 1921 to 1923 and of 1955–1958, up to the time of the Ayub revolution, and are again represented in the National Assembly. The principal member of the family was Sardar Sir Sikandar Hayat Khan (1892–1942). Sikandar was elected to the Council in 1921, but was soon unseated in an election petition. In 1923 he was returned again from the Attock seat and in 1926 won the Muhammadan landholders seat previously held by Sir Fazli Husain. Sikandar again followed in Fazli Husain's steps when he became a member of the Executive Council in 1930 at the time Sir Fazli was promoted to the Viceroy's Council in Delhi. In early 1935 Sikandar resigned to become Deputy Governor of the Reserve Bank of India but a year later returned to his position in Punjab. The Hayats, however, were not without a voice in the Council chamber as Sikander was replaced in Lahore by his cousin and brother-in-law, Nawab Muzaffar Khan (1879–1951). Muzaffar Khan, as a government official, had several times been a nominated official member of the Council. After the introduction of further reforms and provicial autonomy under the Government of India Act, 1935, and following the death of Sir Fazli Husain, Sikandar became leader of the Unionist Party and first premier of the Punjab. Muzaffar Khan also became a member of the Legislative Assembly and remained so until 1943. Upon Sikandar's death in 1942 his son, Sardar Shaukat Hayat Khan (b. 1915) was elected to the Assembly and made a member of the new cabinet under Sir Khizr Hayat Khan Tiwana. Shaukat was re-elected on a Muslim League ticket in 1946 and also became a member of the Constituent Assembly where he remained until 1954. In 1970 he was elected to the National Assembly as a candidate of the Council Muslim League of which he is now the leader. A younger brother of Sikandar, Sardar Barkat Hayat Khan, was a member of the Legislative Assembly, 1946–1948. One of Sikandar's daughters, Mahmuda Salim Khan, although not involved in electoral politics, was a minister in the West Pakistan cabinet of the Nawab of Kalabagh from 1962 to 1965. Mumtaz Ali Khan, a nephew of Muzaffar Khan, also was an M.L.A. both in the 1946–1948 assembly and in the 1951–55 assembly.

The elder brother of Sikandar, Nawab Sir Liaquat Hayat Khan (1887–1948), was a member of the Indian Police Service and was detailed to the princely state of Patiala in 1923, where he became prime minister in 1930. He was connected by marriage with the Sadiq family of Amritsar which has contributed several members of legislative bodies: Sheikh Muhammad Sadiq was a member of the Council from 1924 to 1936 and the Assembly, 1938–1939; Sheikh Sadiq Hassan was a member of the Central Legislative Assembly, 1923–1926 and 1930–1934, of the provincial Assembly, 1939–1948, and of the Constituent Assembly, 1951–1954; and Sheikh Masood Sadiq was a member of provincial Assembly, 1951–1958, and later a member of the cabinet of the Nawab of Kalabagh. Liaquat also connects the Hayat family with Mir Maqbool Mahmud (d. 1948), whose wife's uncle Liaquat was. Maqbool Mahmud was a member of the Council, 1923–1930, and of the Assembly, 1937–1945, and served a chief parliamentary secretary to Sikandar during the latter period. When not in the legislature Maqbool Mahmud was active in administrative and judicial positions in princely India, notably in Patiala, and at the time of partition he was director of the secretariat of the Chamber of Princes. He was closely tied to the Hayats by marriage: two of his sisters were married to Sikandar, two of his wife's siblings were married to children of Liaquat, and his daughter is the wife of Shaukat Hayat Khan. Maqbool Mahmud also married a daughter of the Sind political leader, Sir Abdullah Haroon.

The collaterals of the Hayat family are numerous as the family did not frequently follow the cross-cousin marriage pattern adopted by many leading Punjab Muslim families. Without detailing the relationships the family is connected through marriages with the Haroons of Karachi; the Amir of Bahawalpur; S. Osman Ali, several times an ambassador of Pakistan; the Baghbanpura Mians; the Quereshis of Multan; author Herbert Feldman; Shakir Durrani, former director of Pakistan International Airlines; Ahmad Bakhsh Khan (M.L.A., 1937–1938); Syed Fida Hasan, a principal adviser to Ayub Khan; Hakim Ahmad Shuja, for years the secretary of the Council and the Assembly; B. A. Kureshi, former chief secretary of West Pakistan – and even Mian Saeed, the star of Pakistan's cricket efforts in the early days of independence. Today, however, the only legislative representative of the direct line of the family is Shaukat.

The *Noons and Tiwanas* of Sargodha District might more correctly be called a "family group" rather than a single family. They have generally worked in political harmony, expecially prior to independence, and have numerous interconnections through marriage. Griffin (1940: I: 191–235) details four branches of the Tiwanas in addition to the Noons. The Noons alone have been represented in legislative bodies continuously since 1921 with an interruption only when Ayub Khan governed without a legislature from 1958 to 1962. One or more Tiwanas occupied seats in Lahore, New Delhi, London (as a member of the Council of the Secretary of State for India), Karachi or Islamabad almost continuously with only brief gaps in 1934–1937 and 1962–1965 in addition to the Ayub martial law period.

The record for longevity in senior positions for Punjabis belongs to Malik

Sir Muhammad Firoz Khan Noon (1893–1970). He was a member of the Council from its inception in 1921 until just before its close in 1936. During that period he served as Minister of Local Government from 1927 to 1931, succeeding Mian Fazli Husain as Unionist representative in the cabinet, and as Minister of Education from 1931 until 1936, when he resigned to become High Commissioner for India in London, an office created under the 1935 Act. However, Noons were not absent from Lahore. Firoz's father Nawab Malik Sir Muhammad Hayat Khan Noon (1875–1943), who had been a nominated member of the Council of State, 1935–1937, was returned from a landholder's constituency in 1936, and a cousin, Malik Sardar Khan Noon, was elected from another landholder's seat in 1943. In 1941 Firoz returned to India to become a member of the Viceroy's Council, holding first the labor portfolio and in 1942 the defense portfolio, the first Indian to be so designated. He was also a member of the Imperial War Cabinet in 1944. He left the Viceroy's Council in September, 1945, to return to the Punjab to campaign as a Muslim Leaguer for the impending election to the Legislative Assembly. He was elected from the Rawalpindi Division Towns urban seat and was also elected to the Constituent Assembly. In 1950 he was appointed Governor of East Bengal and remained in Dacca until 1953 when he was called back to Lahore to become Chief Minister of the province. He was elected to the second Constituent Assembly in 1955 and left office as Chief Minister the same year, pending the creation of the single province of West Pakistan. In 1956 and 1957 he was Foreign Minister in the cabinet of H. S. Suhrawardy and in January, 1958, became Prime Minister of Pakistan. He was in office when the coup led by General Ayub Khan took place in October, 1958. Firoz Khan Noon was barred from electoral politics by the Elective Bodies Disqualification Order (EBDO) of 1959. In the 1962 indirect elections under the Ayub constitution and again in 1965, his eldest son, Malik Nur Hayat Khan Noon (b. 1927) was elected to the National Assembly. Nur Hayat contested the 1970 election for the National Assembly on the ticket of the Pakistan Muslim League (Qayyum) but was defeated by a relative, Malik Anwar Ali Khan Noon (b. 1924) who contested on the People's Party ticket.

Nawab Malik Sir Umar Hayat Khan Tiwana (1874–1944) of the Mitha Tiwana branch held various offices for almost thirty years. He was named to the pre-reform Legislative Council of Punjab in 1904 and to the Imperial Legislative Council in 1909 where he remained until 1920. He was elected to the Council of State, the upper house of the legislature in Delhi, in 1920, but yielded his elective seat in 1925 to Nawab Sir Mehr Shah. Umar Hayat Khan was then nominated to the Council of State in 1926. In 1929 he was appointed to the Council of the Secretary of State for India in London and completed his term in 1934. His son, Nawab Malik Sir Khizr Hayat Khan Tiwana (b. 1900) was elected to the Assembly in 1937 and became Minister of Public Works in the cabinet headed by Sir Sikandar Hayat Khan. On Sikandar's death, Khizr succeeded him as Prime Minister of the Punjab. Running as the titular head of the Unionist Party and against the tide of the Muslim League, Khizr was re-elected in 1946 and briefly headed a coalition ministry including Unionists,

Akalis and Congressmen. Since the fall of his ministry in 1947, prior to partition, Khizr has not taken an active part in politics.

The Mitha Tiwana branch of the Tiwana clan is not the only one which has
been active in politics. The Hamoka branch has four members who have held
seats in legislatures. Nawab Malik Sir Khuda Baksh Khan (d. 1930) was a
member of the Council, 1925–1926, occupying through a by-election the seat
vacated by Fazli Husain when he joined the Executive Council (the next
general election saw the seat go to Sikandar Hayat Khan unopposed). Khuda
Bakhsh's son, Sir Allah Bakhsh Khan (1887–?), followed a civil service career
with an appointment to the Central Legislative Asssembly in 1931 and election
to the Punjab Legislative Assembly in 1936 and again in 1946. He was considered to be one of the closest advisers of his nephew, Khizr. Also from the
Hamoka branch, Malik Fateh Muhammad Khan (b. 1895), was a member of
the Assembly 1951–1958, and his son, Malik Muhammad Anwar Khan
(b. 1934) was a member of the second National Assembly under Ayub Khan
(1965–1969) and was defeated in the 1970 National Assembly election, fin-
ishing third behind nominees of the Council Muslim League and the People's
Party. The Mundial Tiwanas of Jahanabad have been represented by Nawab
Malik Mumtaz Muhammad Khan, member of the Council, 1923–1926, and
his son, Nawabzada Malik Muhammad Habibullah Khan (b. 1907), who was
a member of the Assembly, 1937–1945 and 1951–1955. Mumtaz Muhammad
Khan opposed Khizr in the 1946 election in an intra-clan contest. A Lyallpur
branch of the family has been represented by Malik Nadir Ali Khan, who was
a member of the National Assembly, 1968–1969. The strong tendency toward
inter-marriage among the Tiwanas and the Noons limits the number of
politically important collaterals. A relative of the Hamoka branch, Malik
Khuda Bakhsh Bucha, was a career civil servant, including a tour as private
secretary to Khizr in the forties, and was elevated to the cabinet as Minister of
Agriculture by the Nawab of Kalabagh in 1966. He is now special adviser to
President Bhutto for agricultural affairs.

Possibly even more intertwined with other political families than the Hayats
are the *Daultanas* of Multan District. Among the family itself and its close collaterals only during the period of Ayub's martial law and the time of the second
Ayub National Assembly and the Yahya period are Daultanas missing from the
legislatures. For immediate family members (those actually named Daultana)
the gaps are 1923–1926 and 1958–1970.

Four Daultanas have sat in legislative bodies. The first was Nawab Mian
Ahmad Yar Khan Daultana (d. 1940), along with Mir Maqbool Mahmud one
of the closest political associates of Sikandar. He was a parliamentary secretary
and chief whip of the Unionist Party in the Assembly. Ahmad Yar was a
member of the Council, 1921–1923 and 1926–1936, and of the Assembly from
1937 until his death. His cousin and brother-in-law, Mian Allah Yar Khan,
won the seat in a by-election in 1940 and was re-elected in 1946, reamining in
the Assembly until his death in 1947. At that time Allah Yar's son, Mian Riaz
Ahmad Khan, occupied the seat until the Assembly was dissolved in 1948.

The principal member of the family, however, has been Mian Mumtaz Muhammad Khan Daultana (b. 1916). Returning to Lahore after an academic career in England, Mumtaz was elected to the Assembly in the by-election for the West Punjab Landholders seat following the death of Muhammad Hayat Khan Noon. He was elected as a Muslim Leaguer in 1946 from the seat formerly held by his maternal uncle, Chaudhury Sir Shahabuddin, in Sialkot District, leaving the family's home constituency for Allah Yar. He was also elected a member of the Constituent Assembly and was re-elected in 1955. In 1951 he was elected to the provincial Assembly from Multan District and became Chief Minister of the Punjab, holding that post for two years. He was briefly a member of the first Khan Sahib cabinet in West Pakistan and was Defense Minister in the short lived Chundrigar cabinet in 1957. Like Sir Firoz Khan Noon he was disqualified from electoral politics under EBDO, but within the limitations imposed acted as a principal adviser to the Council Muslim League when that party was reorganized. He became president of the party when the EBDO restrictions were removed in 1967 and held office until after the 1970 election in which he was returned to the National Assembly from his home constituency. Daultana remains a member of the Assembly but has accepted an appointment as Ambassador of Pakistan in the United Kingdom.

Ahmad Yar and Chaudhury Sir Shahabuddin, a Jat from Sialkot District, were married to sisters. Shahabuddin was a member of the Council from 1923 until its termination in 1936 and became president (i.e., speaker) of the Council in 1927. He also was briefly a minister. On 1936 he was elected a member of the Assembly and when the new body convened in 1937 he became speaker. Childless, Shahabuddin in a sense "adopted" Mumtaz, who now lives in the Shahabuddin house in Lahore. On his maternal side, Mumtaz is related to a number of political figures including Yusuf Khattak of the Frontier, the Dahas of Multan, and Chaudhury Salahuddin Chatha of Gujranwala (1912–1970), a member of the Assembly, 1951–1958, and of the National Assembly, 1962–1965. One of Mumtaz's susters is married to Nawabzada Mian Muhammad Saeed Qureshi of Sargodha. Saeed Qureshi was a member of the Assembly, 1951–1958. His father, Nawab Mian Muhammad Hayat Qureshi, was an opponent of the Noon-Tiwana group in Sargodha and a member of the Council, 1926–1936. Having defeated a Tiwana in 1926, he was himself defeated in an Assembly contest by Sir Allah Bakhsh Khan Tiwana in 1936 and by another Unionist candidate in 1946. His son, Saeed, as mentioned, won in 1951, and in 1962 another son, Mian Muhammad Zakir, was elected to the National Assembly, and was defeated in 1965 by Muhammad Anwar Khan Tiwana. In 1970, Zakir was elected to the National Asembly as a candidate of his relative Daultana's Council Muslim League. The rivalry between Daultana and the Noon-Tiwana group has been played locally on the Sargodha electoral scene.

Provincial Autonomy

The Government of India Act of 1935, which went into effect in the provinces in 1937, brought substantial changes. Dyarchy was ended and all subjects were transferred to a responsible ministry subject only to limited reserved powers which could be used by the Governor in emergency circumstances. All members of the provincial legislatures were to be elected by a franchise which was substantially enlarged, although it fell far short of universal suffrage. The membership of nominated officials was ended and those special interests which were represented by nominated non-official members would now elect their spokesmen. The division of seats among the three major communities in the Punjab was governed by the Communal Award made by the British following the inability of Indians to agree on a formula at the Round Table Conferences in the early thrities. The Punjab Legislative Assembly, as the new body was denominated, would have 175 members of which 157 would be elected from territorial communal constituencies. General (i.e., Hindu) constituencies would elect 42 (eight urban and 34 rural); Muslim constituencies 84 (nine urban and 75 rural); and Sikhs 31 (two urban and 19 rural). Four seats were allocated to women, two Muslim and one each Hindu and Sikh. Indian Christians were to have two seats; Europeans and Anglo-Indians, one each. Special interests were alloted one seat for university graduates, one for commerce and industry, three for labor and five for landholders (including one for the Baluch tumandars). Muslims were thus guaranteed 87 seats (84 in territorial constituencies, two women's seats and the tumandar seat as all electors in that seat were Muslim) which was one seat short of a majority. In practice they could also expect two additional landholders seats and one (1936) or two (1946) of the labor seats, for a total of 90 or 91. The first election under the new system was held in the winter of 1936–1937 and resulted in a Unionist sweep of the Muslim seats. Two Muslim Leaguers were elected, one leaving the party the day the result was announced. Including Hindu seats won in Haryana by the Chhotu Ram group the Unionists won 96 seats and could count on the support of twenty Sikh members elected on the Khalsa Nationalist ticket (Coupland 1943: 42).

As noted earlier the families identified as dominant in rural areas in the fifteen districts which became part of Pakistan won 53 of the 58 seats at stake. Six of the 21 sitting members of the last Council chose not to contest and eleven of the fifteen who did contest were elected to the Assembly. One, Chaudhury Asadullah, a brother of Chaudhury Sir Muhammad Zafrullah Khan, may have lost as anti-Ahmadi feeling was more clearly expressed with the wider franchise. Another, Sardar Habibullah of the Mokal family, lost to Mian Muhammad Iftikharuddin, who was elected as a Congress candidate. Another lost to Raja Ghazanfar Ali Khan, but the Raja, elected on the Muslim League ticket, defected to the Unionists immediately and became a parliamentary secretary. (His notes form the basis of Ahmad, 1967.)

When Sir Fazli Husain returned to Lahore from New Delhi in 1935 he immediately set about the task of organizing the Unionist Party to wage an electoral battle. He was not unaware of factional alignments in the party and set about to try to end them. Sikandar was off in Bombay as Deputy Governor of the Reserve Bank but his lieutenants, especially Nawab Muzaffar Khan, Mir Maqbool Mahmud and Ahmad Yar Khan Daultana, were active on his behalf.[1] Sikandar felt himself to be, and in many ways, was, the senior person in the party after Sir Fazli Husain and were Fazli to remain out of active politics he pictured himself as the leader and prime minister-presumptive under the new reforms.[2] He was not without a serious rival in Sir Firoz Khan Noon who had since 1927 been a minister. In early 1936 Noon was dispatched to London as High Commissioner, leaving a vacancy in the ministry. To forestall a scramble, Sir Fazli himself filled the vacancy in June, 1936. At the same time urban supporters of the Unionists wished to have the party more closely associated with the Muslim League. Among them were Iqbal, Malik Barkat Ali (who was the only Muslim Leaguer elected in 1936 who stayed with the party), and Mian Abdul Aziz Marwada, a former member of the Council who was to come in to the Assembly as an independent. At a meeting with Jinnah at the home of Abdul Aziz, the League leader was told in effect to stay out of the Punjab and not to interfere with the multi-communal politics of the province. In addition to heading off Jinnah, Fazli made strides in reorganization, in financing and in allocation of tickets for the party. He had, however, returned from New Delhi in poor health and the burden resulted in his death in July, 1936. The Unionists would go to the election without their founder (Husain 1946: 297–346; Ahmad 1967: 158–162; Malik 1971: 94–100).

With Noon in England, and with the support of the factional organization led by his close associates, Sir Sikandar Hayat Khan became without challenge the leader of the Unionist Party and first Prime Minister of the Punjab. In his cabinet he included Malik Sir Khizr Hayat Khan Tiwana of the rival group and urban Unionist Mian Abdul Haye as well as the leader of the Hindu Unionists of Haryana, Chaudhury Sir Chhotu Ram. The Sikh member was Sardar Sir Sundar Singh Majithia and Sir Manohar Lal, an urban non-Congress Hindu who had been a minister in the Council period, completed the ministry. At the junior level, parliamentary secretaries and parliamentary private secretaries, eight Muslims (of a total of 16) were appointed and all but one came from the principal families identified earlier.

Space does not permit the detailing of the political developments in the

---

1 As mentioned earlier both Mir Maqbool Mahmud and Nawab Muzaffar Khan were brothers-in-law of Sikandar. A story is told, which may not be correct in detail, that Sikandar and Ahmad Yar Daultana exchanged turbans in order to symbolize their becoming brothers. Sikandar did occasionally refer to Ahmad Yar as "*bhaijan*" in correspondence. Thus far the story seems credible. It is then said that the two men suggested that one of Sikandar's daughters marry Ahmad Yar's son, Mumtaz, to cement further the relationship between the two families. In any event, either she (the daughter), he (Mumtaz) or they did not go along with the plan, if indeed such a plan existed.

2 Actually the leader of the party was Chaudhury Sir Chhotu Ram, but it was inconceivable that a Hindu would be selected as Prime Minister.

province prior to Sikandar's death in December, 1942. The election had shown the Muslim League to be strong in Muslim minority provinces but weak in Muslim majority provinces. At the 1937 session of the League in Lucknow a pact was signed between Jinnah and Sikandar. Ostensibly on the national level it strengthtened the League, as did similar agreements with A. K. Fazlul Haq of Bengal and Sir Muhammad Saadullah of Assam, by bringing the Muslim members of the Unionist Party into the League and gaining the support of the Unionists on *national* issues of concern to the Muslim community. On the other hand it was agreed that the Punjab Muslim League would be reconstituted in accordance with the new membership. And this would give Sikandar and his associates control over the provincial League. Iqbal and others who were in the League prior to the pact were opposed but Jinnah, to gain national support, was willing to yield local control (Iqbal 1942: *passim*; Batalvi 1967: *passim*). Nawab Sir Shah Nawaz Khan of Mamdot (1883–1946) became the president of the provincial league and the Unionists controlled the party rather closely.

At the 1940 session of the Muslim League in Lahore the "Pakistan" Resolution was passed. Among those who seconded the resolution was Sikandar. But it is evident that the "Pakistan" envisioned by Sikandar was a vastly different thing than that which emerged in 1947. Sikandar had published in 1939 his own proposal for a united India in which the highest possible level of provincial autonomy would be part of the scheme and the central government would have limited powers in defense and foreign affairs (Jafri 1967: II: 247–253). The Nawab of Mamdot either wrote or caused to be written another pamphlet, by "A Punjabee", which opposed Pakistan and proposed sub-federations between the provinces and the central government, with the separation of eastern Punjab from the rest of the province (Jafri 1967: II: 263–265). If there were any doubts that old line Unionists were still Unionists and not proponents of Pakistan, the speech by Sikandar in the Assembly on March 11, 1941, would remove them: "...we in the Punjab stand united and will not brook any interference from whatever quarter it may be attempted... [we will tell] meddling busybodies from the ouside, 'Hands off the Punjab'." (Coupland 1943: 252). The "busybody" in question was Jinnah.

The tide, however, was turning against those who supported an economically based, multi-communal party in the Punjab. Reports of Congress inter ference in Muslim customs in Uttar Pradesh (the Pirpur report) and Bihar (the Sharif report), the failure of the Congress to work with the League especially in Uttar Pradesh and the growing antagonism between the two major communities – these had their effect even in the Punjab. The death of Sikandar removed the strong hand of the Prime Minister. He was replaced by the junior rural Muslim in the cabinet, Sir Khizr Hayat Khan Tiwana, only 42 years old when he took office. It is a matter of conjecture why the Unionists did not turn to its then seniormost member, Nawab Muzaffar Khan, who by his relationship to Sikandar and his political skill in the party might have been able to command a measure of respect, both provincially and nationally, approaching that of Sikandar. Such a move would have precluded a second step taken, the bringing into the cabinet of Sikandar's son, Sardar Shaukat Hayat Khan. (Chhotu Ram, Abdul Haye, and Manohar Lal continued in the cabinet and Sardar Baldev Singh became the Sikh member, replacing Sardar Dasaundha Singh, who in turn had replaced Majithia on the latter's death in 1941.)

Tiwana and Partition

Shaukat, who had been released from the Army to join the cabinet, lost little time before he quarreled with Khizr. While much of the debate was personal, it served as the first major open split in Unionist ranks and, therefore, among the Muslim rural elite. Shaukat soon found allies, especially in Nawab Iftikhar Husain Khan of Mamdot (1906–1969) who was to succeed his father as provincial League president in 1946 and who was not to be a stand-in for Unionist control, and in Mumtaz Daultana, returned from England and soon to become an M.L.A. and general secretary of the provincial League. Khizr attempted to maintain the Sikandar-Jinnah pact and separate national Muslim matters from provincial concerns (Tiwana 1944). Khizr then, and still, does not accept the two nation theory and felt that, in essence, a Muslim majority government in the Punjab would be an important guarantee of the rights of Muslims in a minority province, the reverse being similarly true. Shaukat, the younger Mamdot, Mumtaz Daultana and others felt that the unity of India was not capable of preservation and that the Muslims of the Punjab should stand firmly with their co-religionists throughout the country in the demand for Pakistan. Unionist control eroded, although the party maintained its majority in the Assembly with little difficulty. It is to be noted, however, that neither the Unionists nor the new Leaguers wished to destroy the rural elite control of the province. It was an internecine battle, not one which would have transferred control to the Muslim masses.

By the end of the war and the signal for new provincial elections it appeared that Jinnah's firmness would lead to the realization of his goal of Pakistan, possibly not fully independent but certainly a rearrangement in which the north-east and north-west would be separated from the main central stem of Hindu majority provinces. With this there was an increasing rush of Muslims in the Punjab to join the band-wagon, that is to join the League and desert the cause of Unionism. Of the 79 Muslim Unionists elected in 1936 from the territorial, women's and landholders constituencies (their successors in the case of by-elections) 34 chose not to run in 1946. Of the remaining 45, seventeen took the Muslim League ticket and all won. Those contesting again as Unionists were 26, and only eight of them won. The remaining two contested as independents and one won. In the districts which were very soon to become part of Pakistan 58 rural seats were contested. The Unionists had won all but two in 1936. Of the 56 incumbents, 23 chose not to contest, leaving 33 in the electoral picture. Ten took the ticket of the Muslim League and all won. The Unionist Party nominated 21, of whom eight won. As had been noted earlier the leading families won 27 of the 58 seats in the Pakistan districts. Of these nine were returned as Unionists, seventeen as Muslim Leaguers and one as an independent. It would seem that this split, even with the strong popular tide among Muslims in favor of the Pakistan concept, shows that the traditional leaders even when retaining their Unionist designation were not routed completely, and were able to maintain considerable support. District results for the Unionists in terms of popular vote in 1946 are shown in Table I and serve to reinforce the conclusion that Unionism was not entirely dead.

There has been much controversy over the events following the election of 1946. The official return (GOI 1948: 153–172) gives the following party breakdown. The Muslim League was the largest with 73 seats. The Congress won 51, of whom 42 were Hindus and nine Sikhs. The Unionist Party won 21, all Muslims except for one Indian Christian. The Panthic Party (Akalis) won twenty. Independents won ten seats (one Hindu, two Muslims, two Sikhs, one European, one Anglo-Indian, one Indian Christian and two labor seats, the occupants of which were one Hindu and one Muslim). There was some post-election shifting, the extent of which is a matter of controversy. Nonetheless the Muslim League, now under the leadership of Nawab Iftikhar Husain Khan of Mamdot, did not have a majority nor was it likely to be able to coalesce with any other party in order to attain a majority. At the same time the other three parties were willing to work together to form a majority government. The coalition may have received official blessing. It did fit the Congress strategy of denying the Muslim League a provincial government at the time of important negotiations with the British on the future of India (Azad 1959: 128–129; Sayeed 1968: 217–218).

The Khizr ministry included Nawab Sir Muzaffar Ali Khan Qizilbash and Mian Muhammad Ibrahim Barq of the Unionists, Lala Bhim Sen Sachar and Chaudhury Lehri Singh of the Congress and Sardar Baldev Singh of the Akali Dal. Before its short career was ended Sardar Swaran Singh replaced Baldev Singh, who became Defense Member in New Delhi. Almost immediately the Unionist ministry was beset with a civil disobedience movement launched by the Muslim League. Disturbances grew to such proportions that the government was unable to contain them. In March, 1947, Khizr submitted the resignation of the ministry and the province was placed under the direct rule of the Governor. Rioting, however, continued as the disturbances surrounding the partition of India and of the Punjab began almost as the anti-Khizr movement ended. The partition tragedy has been described elsewhere (see especially Moon 1961: 71 ff).

Mamdot and Factionalism

Following partition the Muslim League assumed the government of that part of the Punjab which went to Pakistan. Iftikhar Hussain Khan of Mamdot was appointed Chief Minister and included in his cabinet Mumtaz Daultana,

Shaukat Hayat Khan, Mian Muhammad Iftikharuddin, and Sheikh Karamat Ali. Three of the five were from leading rural families and Mamdot himself was included in Griffin (1940: I: 229–233) but not included in this study as his home district, Ferozepur, went to India.

Quarrels hit the cabinet almost immediately. Iftikharuddin left the ministry over a disagreement on refugee policy, a part of his portfolio. Neither Daultana nor Shaukat was prepared to accept cabinet discipline and both looked toward the Muslim League organization. Daultana succeeded in capturing the party from its titular leader, the Chief Minister. Shaukat eventually left the League for a time to join with Iftikharuddin in forming the Azad Pakistan Party, a forerunner of the present National Awami Party. The factionalism grew to such an extent that Mamdot was unable to carry on and he resigned in 1948. As no one was then able to form a new ministry, the Governor once again assumed the powers of the ministry and the Assembly.

During the period preceding the 1951 election Daultana acquired virtually complete control of the League. Noon was in East Bengal as Governor although he had hoped for leadership in his home province. Khizr had retired from politics and had spent much of the post-independence period abroad. Shaukat was out of the League. Daultana now isolated Mamdot and caused him also to leave the League and form a separate party, the Jinnah Muslim League (fragments of which joined later with H. S. Suhrawardy's Awami League). The advisors appointed by the Governor to assist him in his work were increasingly nominees of Daultana. The stage was set for the 1951 election.

From Daultana to Ayub

In 1951 Mumtaz Daultana reached one goal he had set for himself: he became Chief Minister of the Punjab. In the election the Muslim League had won 143 of the 197 seats, to 35 for the Mamdot led Jinnah Awami League (actually an alliance of the Jinnah Muslim League and the Awami League) and one each for the Azad Pakistan Party and the orthodox Jama'at-i-Islami; seventeen others were independents. The organization built by Daultana produced the victory in what was the only unified effort by the League after the formation of Pakistan. Among the key families the proportion elected decreased, both as a result of the increased number of seats and of the granting of universal franchise, which perhaps diluted the power of the traditional leadership. It is, of course, not clear how many of those elected were propelled to victory through the support of local leaders from among the elite. Of the 197 seats, 191 were clearly designated for Muslims (including five set aside for women). The others were four for Christians, one "general" (i.e., Hindu) and one for university graduates, which was won by a Muslim. However, of the 191 Muslim seats, 44 were reserved for refugees in double member constituencies. Thus only 147 seats were available to pre-partition residents of West Punjab. Of these at least 31 (21.1 percent) were won by members of elite families. The Muslim League won 28 of these including a representative each of the Tiwana and Hayat families, the Jinnah Awami League won one (a Tiwana) and one, Nawab Qizilbash, was returned as an independent.

In forming his cabinet, Daultana included four from the principal families (Sardar Abdul Hamid Khan Dasti, Sardar Muhammad Khan Leghari, Sheikh Fazal Ilahi Piracha and Syed Ali Husain Shah Gardezi) in addition to himself. Outside this category were only two: Soofi Abdul Hamid Khan, a refugee, and Chaudhury Muhammad Husain Chatha. The story of the ministry must be curtailed here. It fell in 1953 largely as a result of the anti-Ahmadi riots which rent the city of Lahore and other areas and resulted in a short period of martial law (Munir 1954: *passim*).

Daultana was replaced by Malik Sir Firoz Khan Noon who achieved the position he felt he had been denied in 1947. Noon again drew on members of the elite for his cabinet retaining Dasti and Leghari and adding, among others, the controversial Nawab Muzaffar Ali Khan Qizilbash. The Daultana faction of the League had not forgiven Qizilbash his association with the unpopular Khizr ministry in 1946. Noon remained Chief Minister until shortly before the institution of one-unit in West Pakistan. He then yielded to Dasti who made few changes other than dropping Qizilbash.

Under the one-unit plan the Punjab agreed to accept a severe reduction in its membership in the Provincial Assembly. It would have only 40 percent of the members rather than the nearly 60 percent to which it was entitled on a population basis. This led to a complicated electoral process. The relative population had changed since the influx of refugees and the beginnings of urban development. Thus the number of seats from the Punjab was reduced from 197 to 124 but the reduction was unevenly spread. As an interim measure the incumbent M.L.A.'s were to choose, from among themselves or from outside the group, district by district, the members of the new unified Assembly, with some districts choosing more and some fewer than the present membership. Most of those who belonged to the rural elite were returned, some from districts other than their home. It was clear, however, that in most districts Daultana and his associates were able to control the vote.

The first Chief Minister, Dr. Khan Sahib, was from the Frontier and not a member of the Muslim League. In a broad based and short lived cabinet he included members from all factions, including both Daultana and Mamdot. Daultana and others pressed for the formation of a Muslim League party in the Assembly with the clear implication that only the leader of that party could be Chief Minister. Khan Sahib stoutly refused to join the League. Matters were brought to a head with a threat of a no confidence motion being carried against Khan Sahib. Karachi did not wish to upset a carefully constructed arrangement under which the Frontier would retain the West Pakistan chief ministership, Karachi in this case meaning especially President Iskander Mirza. Aisle crossing became a regular part of the legislative proceedings in Lahore until overnight a new party was created, the Republican Party, pledged to support Khan Sahib. Care was taken by the Republicans to avoid frequent votes of confidence and by this means and the probability that at many times they could actually command a majority permitted Khan Sahib and his Republican successors, Sardar Abdur Rashid and Nawab Qizilbash to retain office until October, 1958, when martial law was imposed (Ahmad 1967: 444–451). A 1958 compilation of Republicans and Muslim Leaguers in the West Pakistan Assembly showed that among the rural elite there was about an even split between the two parties, roughly a dozen each. After the departure of Daultana and his associates from the Khan Sahib cabinet the leading family membership in the ministry was (subject to frequent changes of membership) on the order of three of six Punjabis in the Khan Sahib ministry, five of six in Rashid's, and five of seven in Qizilbash's.

On October 7, 1958, President Mirza proclaimed martial law, abrogated the constitution, abolished legislative bodies and appointed General Muhammad Ayub Khan to be chief martial law administrator. Three weeks later Ayub abolished Mirza and assumed the presidency himself. For our purposes here two events are of special importance. One was the Elective Bodies Disqualification Order under which Ayub moved to bar from politics those political figures who, in his view, were responsible for the situation in Pakistan which led to martial law. Twenty leading Punjabi politicians were "EBDOed" of which twelve, including Mamdot, were from among the leading families and most of the others were close political associates of them. Among those barred from political activity (party as well as electoral) were Daultana, Noon, Qizilbash, Iftikharuddin, Dasti and a member each of the Shah Jiwana, Gilani, Gardezi, Sargodha Qureshi, Leghari and Gurmani families. The ban lasted until January 1, 1967.

The second step was the introduction of basic democracies both for local government functions and as an electoral college to select the president and members of the national and provincial assemblies (Ziring 1971: 15–16). The first exercise of the electoral function came in 1962 when those basic democrats elected in 1959 were called upon to choose members of the legislatures. Ayub's was to be a partyless government so all candidates ran as independents and with little interference from above. Not surprisingly a large number of persons who had been elected earlier to legislative bodies, or relatives of them, were chosen to sit in both Rawalpindi and Lahore. At least eighteen, nine to Rawalpindi and nine to Lahore, were elected from among the leading families.

The lack of political organization prior to the election did not preclude the formation of parties inside the assemblies after the election. In the National Assembly an almost equal balance between supporters and opponents of the President resulted. Ayub recognized the need for a party committed to the support of his program. In 1962, after the Assembly opened, a convention of the Muslim League was called. Ayub consented to become president of the Pakistan Muslim League (Convention). Those Leaguers who opposed the President formed the Council Muslim League, claiming direct inheritance from pre-independence days. The elite split again. Daultana, Shaukat and their associates supported, indeed ran from behind the scenes, the Council League. Noon,

Qizilbash, Nawab Malik Amir Muhammad Khan of Kalabagh (d. 1967), by this time Governor of West Pakistan, and others of the elite supported and campaigned for the Convention League. The 1965 elections for both assemblies saw a tightening of political control from above on the basic democrats and the returning to Rawalpindi and Lahore of an overwhelming majority of Convention Leaguers. Noon's son, Qizilbash's brother, Kalabagh's son and others of the old chief families were among those returned, while those who belonged to the Council League were, with very few exceptions defeated. Ayub found that in the Punjab he needed to rely on those whose past was Republican, Muslim League and Unionist in reverse chronological order.

The events of 1969, 1970 and 1971 have been related in many places and need not be repeated here. With Ayub out of office in March, 1969, and Yahya Khan installed as president and chief martial law administrator a new epoch began in Pakistan. Yahya Khan promised that elections would be held and they were in December, 1970.

The Elections of 1970

The ground rules of the election, the conduct of the campaigning, the nature of the participating parties and the results have been discussed elsewhere (Baxter 1971: 197–218). Here we will look specifically at the interaction between the traditional rural elite families and clans and the PPP. The discussion is handicapped to a degree in that no official return of the elections to the National and Provincial Assembly has been published by the Government of Pakistan. Hence, reliance on press reports of results is necessary and these are in some cases incomplete and, even in cases where figures are given for all contestants, may be inaccurate. Nonetheless figures of reasonable acceptability for purposes here can be obtained and used; that is, even with final corrections the magnitude of the PPP vote is not likely to be altered significantly. A further handicap is that there has so far been no definitive "who's who" of new legislators prepared, and identification of all successful contestants is not possible from published sources, especially for the provincial seats.

The results of the two elections are given in Table I, which lists, by district, the percentage of eligible voters who participated, the percentage of seats and votes received by the PPP and the percentage of votes received by the three Muslim Leagues. In the latter the votes of the Pakistan Muslim League (Conventionist), Pakistan Muslim League (Qayyum) and Council Muslim League are accumulated. This papers over differences in program details among the three parties, but it is useful as many of the rural elite ran on one of the three tickets and it is a rough measure of the strenth of this group. It is only rough as some of the elite ran as independents and, as we shall see, some ran on the PPP ticket. Another column gives the percentage of votes polled by a group here labelled "Islamic". Indeed it also papers over differences as it accumulates the votes of the Jama'at-i-Islami, Jamiat-ul-Ulema-i-Islam (both Hazarvi and

Thanvi groups), Markazi Jamiat-ul-Ulema-Pakistan and Jamiat-i-Ahl-i-Hadith. Programmatic differences among these parties are great but each has underlying an appeal based on Islamic principles, albeit differently stated and interpreted (Baxter 1971: 204–206). It is useful especially in those districts near the Indus where the appeal of Islamic sentiments was greater than in other areas of the province. As mentioned earlier, the 1946 Unionist and Muslim League votes are also listed, although these are for rural seats only.

The order in which the districts are listed is according to an index of modernization developed by Shahid Javid Burki (1972: 204–205). While the details can be obtained from the reference just cited, Burki summarizes as follows: "This index was based on a weighting in equal proportions of three characteristics: urbanization, industrialization and education. Urbanization was defined in terms of the proportions of each district in the total urban population, similarly for industrial output and literate population for the entire region." He classified districts as advanced, intermediate and backward, all of the districts in the Punjab falling into one or the other of the first two categories.

The polling for the National Assembly was held on December 7, 1970. The result in the Punjab was a startling victory for the PPP which won 62 of the 82 seats alloted to the province. The Council Muslim League won seven; the Markazi Jamiat, four; the Convention League, two; the Qayyum League, one; the Jama'at-i-Islami, one and independents, five. On December 20, the voters again went to the polls to select members of the provincial assemblies. Of the 180 seats in the Punjab, the PPP won 113. The Council Muslim League with 15 was the only other party to win more than ten seats.

At least 23 candidates from the rural elite can be identified in National Assembly contests. The Council League accounted for eight of these and four won seats (Daultana, Shaukat, the Pir of Makhad and Zakir Qureshi of Sargodha). Each of the three accepting the PPP label were winners (Anwar Ali Noon, Sadiq Husain Qureshi of Multan, and Abbas Husain Gardezi, also of Multan). The other two winners were independents: Malik Muzaffar Khan of Kalabagh and Sardar Sher Baz Khan Mazari of Dera Ghazi Khan. Noted among those who lost were Nur Hayat Khan Noon (Qayyum League), Anwar Tiwana (Convention League), Zulfiqar Qizilbash (Independent), Alamdar Husain Gilani (Qayyum League), Arif Iftikhar (Bhashani group of the National Awami Party) and Sardar Mahmud Khan Leghari (Independent). Winning only nine of the 82 seats (11 percent) the elite slumped to the lowest level ever. In the indirect election for women's seats, the PPP named a member of the Baghbanpura family to one of the seats.

Identification is particularly difficult with candidates for the Provincial Assembly. Among winners ten can be identified as belong to the families listed at the beginning of this article. Five of them were independents (two Legharis and a Mazari from Dera Ghazi Khan being the most prominent), two were from the Council Muslim League and one each from the Pakistan Democratic Party (a Dasti), the Qayyum League (a Gilani) and the PPP (a Gardezi). The Gardezis of Multan who were shut out of pre-independence seats seem to

Table I

The Punjab: Election Data for 1946 and 1970*

| 1946 Vote | | | 1970 National Assembly | | | | | 1970 Provincial Assembly | | | | |
NUP	ML	Advanced Districts	Part.	PPP Seats	PPP Vote	MLs Vote	Islam Vote	PPP Seats	PPP Vote	MLs Vote	Islam Vote	Part.
29.5	67.6	1. Lahore	68.6	100	51.9	14.0	20.6	82	55.5	7.0	8.5	59.3
35.4	62.4	2. Lyallpur	60.0	100	56.4	12.1	20.8	84	51.6	10.0	10.4	60.6
28.2	67.4	3. Multan	69.0	78	47.4	25.5	17.4	79	48.6	24.7	12.0	63.2
11.1	74.7	4. Rawalpindi	57.9	100	48.9	19.9	16.9	88	45.3	35.8	4.2	46.7
22.8	77.2	5. Sahiwal	63.7	100	54.9	29.8	10.0	93	50.8	27.7	3.2	62.1
41.7	58.3	6. Gujranwala	72.6	60	49.7	30.4	10.0	78	42.4	29.3	4.1	69.9
52.5	47.4	7. Sargodha	67.5	100	38.6	35.4	9.7	60	41.1	23.1	16.7	58.0
19.1	65.8	8. Sialkot	70.2	75	57.0	12.8	17.2	100	49.4	20.7	3.2	64.9
40.0	60.0	9. Gujrat	63.0	100	30.2	46.0	12.3	50	27.9	35.8	7.6	62.0
22.6	77.3	10. Jhelum	77.0	100	40.9	30.3	11.2	60	35.2	27.3	3.7	71.9
30.3	69.7	11. Sheikhupura	68.9	100	55.0	31.3	4.7	75	45.4	17.9	8.7	63.6
		Intermediate Districts										
—	—	12. Rahim Yar Khan	66.8	33	20.7	31.8	32.1	14	17.7	40.9	16.2	65.4
43.9	56.1	13. Mianwali	63.1	0	5.8	32.9	43.3	0	9.6	48.6	20.9	64.4
19.9	80.0	14. Jhang	68.0	0	17.0	—	46.4	13	14.0	—	17.8	63.6
56.7	42.8	15. Campbellpur	60.7	0	23.7	67.5	8.7	40	35.4	35.8	3.4	53.8
—	—	16. Bahawalpur	67.8	0	8.6	30.7	16.7	20	21.4	6.6	9.4	62.8
—	—	17. Bahawalnagar	47.6	67	35.7	22.8	14.0	67	31.2	42.5	5.4	49.7
22.8	38.7	18. Dera Ghazi Khan	52.0	0	12.0	—	38.1	0	15.5	—	18.4	52.5
33.9	55.2	19. Muzaffargarh	64.8	67	27.0	9.3	46.1	0	14.7	29.9	23.8	62.3
33.6	62.6	*Total*	65.1	76	41.7	24.0	22.8	63	39.3	22.5	9.9	61.1

Sources: For 1946, COI, 1948. For 1970, press reports. Figure for participation in Bahawalnagar presumably is in error.

* Election results by district; the percentage of eligible voters who participated; the percentage of seats and votes received by the PPP, and the percentage of votes received by the three Muslim Leagues. For fuller explanation see text. NUP—National Unionist Party. Sahiwal formerly Montgomery; Sargodha formerly Shahpur; Campbellpur formerly Attock. For 1946, only rural seats are included. Participation is based on valid votes, not on total votes cast including invalid votes.

have been more ready to associate with the PPP although both Gilanis and Qureshis have also joined the party. In the polling for women's seats, the PPP elected Begum Abida Fakr Imam, a member of the Shah Jiwana family of Jhang.

To return to the Burki index and the material in Table I, some general conclusions can be drawn. The PPP performed better in the advanced districts than it did in the intermediate both for the National and the Provincial Assembly. The party won 92 percent of the National Assembly seats in the advanced districts and only 25 percent in the intermediate. For the Provincial Assembly the figures were 79 percent and 18 percent. In vote data as opposed to seat data it can be noted that for National Assembly contests only one district in the advanced group gave fewer votes to the PPP than the highest PPP district among the intermediate group. For provincial contests the picture is less clear but generally the advanced districts gave more support to the PPP than the intermediate. Sargodha appears to be a problem in correlation and this is perhaps explained by the division within the district in which the more highly developed eastern *tehsils* supported the PPP more than the less developed western *tehsils*. The votes for the Islamic group of parties appears very much to follow the course of the Indus River: Mianwali, Jhang, Muzaffargarh and Dera Ghazi Khan, the four highest districts all lie in the western reaches of the province. Campbellpur is an exception, but the leading religio-political figure in the district, the Pir of Makhad, ran on the Council Muslim League ticket. The vote for the three Muslim Leagues tended to be higher in the intermediate districts, especially for the provincial seats where the constituencies are smaller and more susceptible to traditional leadership than to broad appeals.

The appeal of the PPP was not rooted in traditional leadership in the Punjab, with a few exceptions. It was rooted in an economic and social appeal for better housing, more food, improved education and increased health facilities. Although the "confrontation" with India theme was part of the manifesto, reports seem to indicate that as the campaign progressed it receded to the background and the economic and social issues were stressed. The PPP mobilized the youth, Bhutto projected a charismatic personality to this group, and as college students who had learned the PPP program in the cities and towns returned to rural areas (colleges were closed during the final part of the campaign) they acted as missionaries for the PPP. This may indicate a major change in rural politics if the college youth can replace the traditional landed aristocracy and the religious *mullahs* as guides to voting behavior. The Islamic parties often ran on – to use the words of a keen Pakistani observer to the writer – a straight "heaven or hell" platform and only those near the Indus seemed to be greatly concerned. In Jhang, especially, the Markazi Jamiat exploited the Shi'a – Sunni split. The expected strength of the Jama'at-i-Islami in urban areas did not materialize despite that party's reputation for a strong organization. The failure of the Muslim Leagues to unite – although numerous abortive talks were held – no doubt affected those parties' ability to win seats at a rate approaching the rate at which they won votes, but this can be exaggerated. A close look at the seats shows that even if they had united on a single candidate and that candidate were able to poll the combined votes the result would seldom have been changed. In short, a few more seats but probably not to the extent of denying the PPP a majority in both Islamabad and Lahore. The Leagues ran on outdated program of "Islam in danger," a package which does not sell in the more highly developed areas where the issues have become economic rather than religious. One defeated Conventionist told the writer that he lost because he ran on the 1937 and 1946 platform rather than the 1970 issues.

Conclusion

No member of the rural elite can find much pleasure in the results of the 1970 elections. Perhaps individuals, Daultana, Shaukat, those who jumped to the PPP, might find their own picture not clouded but as a group the rural elite was badly beaten and this by a group largely comprising unknowns.

Two points might be made. First, the rural elite needs an "enforcer" of unity. Sir Fazli Husain and after him Sir Sikandar Hayat Khan performed this role. Their successors, Khizr, Mamdot, Daultana, Noon, Qizilbash, Kalabagh, have not been able to suppress personal differences to an extent that unity can be achieved. Programatic differences also entered as Daultana's views on socio-economic issues differ greatly from, say, Qizilbash. Secondly, the rural elite, obviously, does better in limited or controlled elections, as in those prior to independence or those during the Ayub period.

But the changes in the Punjab since the thirties have been great. Agricultural income is higher, education is more widely spread, urbanization and industrialization have increased – perhaps not in each case to the extent desired by Pakistani leaders but the change has nonetheless been vast based on the pre-independence or even 1951 data. The ballot is now available to all and, in 1970, less susceptible to control. One might conclude that the day of the rural elite control of government in the Punjab has ended, but one caution must be noted. The PPP has promised in its manifesto many changes and in another election it may be judged on its performance. Possibly, should the judgment be adverse to the PPP, the electorate might turn again to those groups which have governed in the past. Only another election held on the terms of those in 1970 can determine the future of the landed aristocracy – and whether the PPP has redeemed its pledge to end "feudal" power in politics.

BIBLIOGRAPHY

Ahmad, Nur, Syed
    1936   Mian Fazl-i-Husain, a Review of His Life and Work, Lahore, Punjab Education Press.
    1967   Martial Law-se Martial Law-tak, Lahore.

Azad, Abul Kalam, Maulana
   1959   India Wins Freedom, Bombay, Orient Longmans.
Batalvi, Ashiq Husain
   1967   "Iqbal and the Pakistan Movement", addresses in Lahore, April, 1967, in Urdu.
Baxter, Craig
   1971   "Pakistan Votes—1970", Asian Survey XI: 3 (March): 197–218.
Burki, S. J.
   1972   "Ayub's Fall, a Socio-Economic Explanation". Asian Survey XII: 3 (March):
       201–212.
Coupland, Reginald
   1943   Indian Politics, 1936–1942. London, Oxford.
Darling, Malcolm
   1947   The Punjab Peasant in Prosperity and Debt. Oxford, Oxford. Fourth edition.
Government of India
   1948   Return Showing the Results of Elections to the Central Legislative Assembly and
       the Provincial Legislatures in 1945–46. New Delhi, Manager of Publications.
Great Britain
   1930   Indian Statutory Commission. Volume X. Memorandum Submitted by the
       Government of the Punjab. London, HMSO.
Griffin, Lepel H.
   1940   Chiefs and Families of Note in the Punjab. Revised by G. L. Chopra. Lahore,
   Superintendent of Government Printing.
Husain, Azim
   1946   Fazl-i-Husain, a Political Biography. Bombay, Longmans.
Iqbal, Muhammad, Dr. Sir
   1942   Letters of Iqbal to Jinnah. Lahore, Ashraf.
Jafri, Rais Ahmad, Syed
   1967   Rare Documents. Lahore, Mohammad Ali Academy.
Malik, Hafeez, editor
   1971   Iqbal: Poet-Philosopher of Pakistan. New York, Columbia.
Moon, Penderel
   1961   Divide and Quit. London, Chatto and Windus.
Munir, Muhammad
   1954   Report of the Court of Inquiry ... to Enquire into the Punjab Disturbances of
       1953. Presided over by Justice M. Munir. Lahore, Superintendent, Government
       Printing.
Pakistan People's Party
   1970   Election Manifesto, Karachi, n. pub.
Sayeed, Khalid B.
   1968   Pakistan: The Formative Years. London, Oxford. Second edition.
Tiwana, Khizr Hayat Khan, Malik Sir
   1944   Statement on the Sikandar-Jinnah Pact. Manuscript.
Ziring, Lawrence
   1971   The Ayub Khan Era. Syracuse, Syracuse University Press.

Islam and the New Constitution of Pakistan[1]

FAZLUR RAHMAN

University of Chicago, Chicago, U.S.A.

THE NEW CONSTITUTION of Pakistan, adopted by the National (also Constituent) Assembly on the 10th of April, 1973, and enforced on the 14th of August, is the third constitution in Pakistan's brief history. The first constitution (1956), of a parliamentary type, was enacted by a Constituent Assembly about nine years after its election and was abrogated in October 1958 by a military coup. The second, a presidential-type constitution, was promulgated by a military ruler, Mohammad Ayub Khan, in 1962, and was abrogated in March 1969 by General Yahya Khān, to whom Ayub Khan entrusted power on his own resignation. The new constitution, enacted after the dismemberment of Pakistan in December, 1971, is once again of the parliamentary type, is the first bicameral constitution, and, since it is the result of a freshly elected Assembly, may be said to represent more genuinely the will of the people. Since Mr. Bhutto, in the present delicate situation of Pakistan – both internal and external – wanted the constitution to be based on a consensus of the Assembly, the constitution reflects some heavy compromises with the religious right, a fact which cannot have pleased many extreme leftists in the People's Party of which Mr. Bhutto is not only the unquestioned leader but finally, the sole decision-maker.

But it is not only the compromises on Islam that are in sight in the constitution; what is also concretely present there is a new socio-economic orientation of economic justice and social progressivism. If the constitution can state and reiterate in various contexts woman's essential role in the future development of Pakistan, perhaps it can afford to repeat, along with the previous constitutions, the confused and confusing statement, at the opening of the Preamble, about the Sovereignty of Allah in the Universe, and linking it directly with the delegated sovereignty of the people of Pakistan in Pakistan; or, if it can declare that parliament may enact laws fixing a ceiling on private property or nationalizing industry or other sources of production, it can also afford to drop the word "socialism" or "Islamic socialism" to appease the opposition. We shall examine these issues in somewhat closer detail below; procedurally, it seems convenient to divide the field of Islam under three titles: economics, society, and Islamic propositions including law-making.

---

1 It would be useful if an earlier article of mine titled "Islam and the Constitutional Problem of Pakistan" is read along with the present one (*Studia Islamica*, XXXII, 4 (December 1970), pp. 275–87.

A. Economics – Islamic Socialism

In the summer of 1966, an intense debate erupted in West Pakistan over the question of the compatibility of socialism with Islam and whether the term "Islamic Socialism" was a meaningful expression or an absurd juxtaposition of contradictories, and has continued ever since. Earlier, this subject had attracted a number of writers in the Middle East and a Syrian scholar and member of the Muslim Brotherhood, Dr. Muṣṭafā al-Sibāʿī, had written a fairly comprehensive work in Arabic in 1959 entitled "The socialism of Islam,"[1] which became widely influential in the Middle East and pioneered a spate of other works, particularly after Nasser's promulgation of "Arab Socialism" in 1962. Judging from their writings, the "Islamic Socialists" of Pakistan were apparently quite unaware of this rich literature and did not exploit it.[2] Much earlier, in the subcontinent, Iqbāl had vigorously denounced Western capitalism, had praised Lenin in a famous poem, "Lenin's Petition to God," had even advocated the abrogation of all traditional religion, if it did not give the peasant and the worker his full due, in a poem "God's Command to Angels," and had roundly proclaimed in a poem "It Is God's Earth" that the earth and its resources cannot become the property of a few. But Iqbāl was equally critical of the materialistic philosophy of Communism and in one of his last poems, "Satan's Advisory Council," decisively repudiated it: He thought that Communism had planted an excellent egalitarian economic system (which is identical with or close to Islam) in the barren soil of materialism. In a letter to Sir Francis Younghusband in 1930 Iqbāl wrote, "If Bolshevism can accept God, it will come very close to Islam. I will not, therefore, be surprised if at some future time Islam overwhelms Russia or Russia overwhelms Islam."[3] Such themes are also given full vent in his letters to Jinnah, where the "atheistic socialism of Jawaharlal [Nehru]" is rejected but the Muslim League's attitude of indifference to the improvement of the lot of the Muslim masses is strongly repudiated as un-Islamic.[4]

In the Pakistani debate of 1966 and since, Iqbal has been heavily invoked by both sides, the socialists appealing to his numerous positive statements in favor of an Islam-based socialism, and anti-socialists to his repudiation of atheistic socialism and communism. Jinnah and Liaqat Ali Khan had both explicitly used the term "Islamic Socialism" (which had actually been used by the pioneer of Muslim Modernism, Jamāl al-Dīn al-Afghānī in Istanbul in the

---

1 *Ishtirākiyat'l-Islām* (Damascus, 1959).

2 For a short survey of the development of Islamic Socialism in the Middle East, cf. my article "Sources and Meaning of Islamic Socialism," in Donald Smith, ed., *Religion and Political Modernization* (to be published by Yale University Press, Spring, 1974); for some literature in English translation, Hanna, Sāmī and Gardner, G.: *Arab Socialism* (Leiden, 1969).

3 Quoted by Safdar Mīr in the Urdu monthly *Nusrat* (ed. Haneef Ramay), September-October 1966, p. 90.

4 Aziz Ahmad and G. E. Von Grunebaum, *Muslim Self-Statement in India and Pakistan* (1970), pp. 151–52.

1890's). Ayub Khan had proclaimed "Islamic Socialism" to be the goal of state policies in his Introduction to the Guidelines of the Third Five-Year Plan. But the subject had become so controversial and so much pressure was exerted by big business (whose prominent spokesman in the debate was A. K. Sumar, himself a businessman), which found ready allies in the representatives of traditionalism in the Jamā'at-i-Islami and the majority of the 'Ulama (whose very religion Iqbal wanted to be abrogated!) that when the Third Five Year Plan was actually published, the term "Islamic Socialism" was not there. This is not the place to give the details of this debate, of which the most important single epitome is the Urdu monthly "Nusrat" of Lahore, in its September-October issue of 1966. Some highly interesting material was yielded by the debate, and some ingenious interpretations of the Quar'an. On the anti-socialist side, while much of what the religious right said was little more than obscurantism, nevertheless some genuine points were made (just as they had been made earlier in the Middle East) – that is, they express the worry that the term "Islamic Socialism" had been cleverly popularized by the surreptitious voice of the Communists, that should things not work out successfully for, say, a period of two decades or if there are setbacks, this voice will then say, "You see, the adjunct 'Islamic' is responsible for your failures; why can't you just be 'socialist' and forget about Islam."[1] This is exactly what this Voice said to Nasser after the Arab-Israeli war of June, 1967. But this is, after all, a relatively minor point and no socialist ideology consciously based in Islam need worry about it unduly.

When Mr. Bhutto launched his socialist campaign in 1966 after his ouster from the Ayub Government, he seems gradually to have realized that, to get popular support, he must include Islam as an integral part of socialism, even though Mr. J. A. Rahim, a Communist and his chief party ideologue, did not like this, and when he appointed Mawlana Kawsar Niazi, who had risen from the rightist ranks, as the Propaganda Secretary of the Party, Mr. Rahim strongly protested. Nevertheless, in its election manifesto, the People's Party stood squarely on the platform of Islamic Socialism and the very next day after elections in December, 1970, which gave his party an overwhelming majority in the center, Mr. Bhutto hailed the election result as a "great victory for Islam."[2] The fact is that, in any developing country, promises to the masses of an approaching millennium through a liquidation of the exploitative upper classes and vested interests bring favorable results, and, in a country like Pakistan, when this is coupled with an appeal to Islam, the results are assured. It is, indeed, a comment on the stupidity of the right which, in *this* climate, did not show enough perception and continued to harp on the unique Islamicity of private property and the traditional concepts of the relationship between employers and employees.

---

1   Sumār, A. K., in *Nusrat*, op. cit., p. 54, lines 18–21.
2   My paper "The Islamic Experience of Pakistan," in *Islam and the Modern Age* (New Delhi), II, No. 4, p. 1 ff.

But it is relatively easy to be swept atop by a flood of aroused hopes, it is a different story when one assumes reins of affairs of the state. Indeed, at election time the People's Party was not a party but a movement of vast dimensions, a veritable ground-swell, and so there gathered together in its fold elements of all sorts – from Communists through socialists and Islamic Socialists to people of vested interests, even landlords. Whereas this highly mixed character yields a certain flexibility, it obviously makes it difficult to find a firm basis for clear-cut directives. Secondly, and importantly, with the departure of East Pakistan, although Pakistan may have lost some political strength in international affairs, economically this has resulted in sheer gain. For Pakistan, as it stands now, is economically the best part of the subcontinent and has a bright future for development, provided its big neighbor would allow it (and itself) to develop in peace; the direst need of the subcontinent is to re-orient itself from a politico-militaristic stance to a socio-economic development posture. Granted this, Pakistan does not *need* any drastic form of socialism (as, for example, Bangladesh does), but certain necessary adjustments. Thirdly, as we said earlier, since Mr. Bhutto took over power under conditions of severe disadvantage, he felt the need for national consensus and has,therefore, heavily compromised. Finally, an Islamic Socialist state obviously requires a systematic and well-worked-out ideology, and that on an Islamic basis, and also an ideologically-geared governmental structure to implement it. Neither of these is available to Mr. Bhutto.

Despite all this, however, the total omission of "Islamic Socialism" from the Constitution remains a mystery, since the battle-cry of the People's Party for election was precisely this; and, after all, there was nothing wrong with the term; on the contrary, it was pregnant with new possibilities of working the state policies progressively towards a goal where Islamic egalitarianism in a modern setting could be effectively realized. What went wrong? I can only surmise that the two other socialistically oriented parties, the National Awami Party of Walī Khan and the Jamʿīyat ul-ʿUlama of Hazārvī have become so uncompromisingly entrenched in opposition to Mr. Bhutto that he felt it easier to compromise with his ideological opponents – the moribund rightists. And so, while the Constitution has received heavy doses of *formal* Islam – much heavier than either of the two previous constitutions – as we shall see in the third section of this paper, the essence of Islam was incredibly diluted. Indeed, with the exception of three or four provisions, this Constitution differs little from its predecessors.

These provisions, though they are also general and indirect, are nonetheless important and, when viewed in the light of Mr. Bhutto's initial policies, lend support to genuine optimism. The first is a hint in the penultimate clause of the Preamble that the people of Pakistan have resolved "to protect our national and political unity and solidarity by creating an egalitarian society *through a new order.*" Here was a proper place to add the phrase "based on Islamic Socialism," and the omission hits the eye. Nevertheless, the phrase "new order" does clearly imply that the existing order (i.e., the traditional order) is undesirable.

Further, this statement means that only a new, progressive, and just order is the final guarantee for the survival and solidarity of Pakistan, not primarily the defense in mere military terms or the outworn cliches about "Islam in danger."

The second major economic provision is enunciated in Article 3, which says, "The State shall ensure the elimination of all forms of exploitation and the gradual fulfilment of the fundamental principle, from each according to his ability, to each according to his work." The elimination of exploitation was also contained in the two previous constitutions, but the latter half of the article is entirely new. It is obviously a modification of the principle of classical Communism, "From each according to his capacity, to each according to his *need*." But the Communist formula means that those persons who can work more or perform duties meriting higher reward would be denied part of that reward in order to meet the needs of the less fortunate members of society. This idealistic principle was given up in Russia, which, in 1956, expressly admitted "the profit motive." But, apparently, the Pakistani formula cannot mean this, although it has a conscious verbal affinity with it, since, if "ability" meant the ability to work, the formula would become nonsensical and would be translated "those who can work more or perform duties meriting higher rewards will be denied part of that reward in order to pay those who work"! What it presumably does mean is that if, for example, an industrialist increases his capital through the surplus value created by the workers' labor, he will not be allowed to keep all that increase in capital but must share it with workers who will be rewarded according to their work. The phrasing of the formula, therefore, seems to be misleading and it would have been much better to put the matter in simple and direct terms. What the principle does state is, however, a great step in the direction of Islamic Socialism and a clear-cut advance over the two previous Constitutions.

Further, according to Article 38(a), the State shall raise the standard of living of all the people by preventing the *concentration of wealth and means of production and distribution* in the hands of a few... "and by ensuring equitable adjustment of rights between employers and employees, and landlords and tenants." This may be regarded as a commentary on the principle cited in the preceding paragraph, if our interpretation of that principle is correct. The previous constitutions spoke not of "concentration of wealth" but "*undue* concentration of wealth," for one thing. The words "means of production and distribution" are entirely new. This means, first, that means of production and distribution, i.e., the economic base, will be made as broad as possible, but it also means, secondly, that, whenever public interest so demands, any industry, service, or source of production or distribution may be nationalized. Immediately after taking over power, Mr. Bhutto *did* nationalize, i.e., put the management under government control, several basic utilities like gas and insurance. This is, indeed, a basic feature of the constitution in the economic field. Article 18(c) states that nothing shall prevent "the carrying on, by the Federal Government or a Provincial Government, or by a corporation controlled by any such government, of any trade, business, industry or service, to the exclusion, complete or partial, of other persons." In Article 253 (b), it is said that Parliament may make laws to authorize such nationalization.

But the upshot of all this is in Article 253 (a), according to which "Parliament may by law prescribe the maximum limits as to property or any class thereof which may be owned, held, possessed, or controlled by any person." Mr. Bhutto had already, through what the Constitution calls "Economic Reforms," promulgated by ordinances, put a ceiling of 150 acres on irrigated agricultural land. But attempts to lay his hands on the industrialists were unsuccessful. They withheld their investments, locked up their factories, and some of them are even said to have stealthily taken their installations out of Pakistan. The government had ultimately to give in and the then Minister of Industries had to resign. This capital provision rejects the extremist opinions of both the right and the left, yet accepts the basic principle of social justice, i.e., the interference by the State in private wealth, should it become detrimental to the interests of the society as a whole, which is undoubtedly a great achievement.

But two quite basic and closely allied criticisms are to be made of these economic propositions. First, they do not appear as a compact whole but are of a desultory and rambling nature. They appear from the Preamble, through the Principles of Policy, to the "Miscellaneous" provisions. Indeed, so isolated is their character that fundamental questions like the organization of *Zakāt* and the elimination of *Ribā* appear in the Principles of Policy in Articles 2(c) and 38(f) respectively, as though they had little to do with the positive economic policy. The reason is obviously that these two are regarded as "uniquely Islamic" phenomena since they appear in the Qur'ān and are seen as apparently fundamentally different from other economic propositions. Also, their interpretation has become controversial in modern times. As for *Zakāt*, this was the only permanent tax levied by the Qur'ān and the Prophet. The Qur'ān envisages it as a comprehensive tax for all the needs of the society as well as social welfare.[1] But during later Muslim history other taxes appeared without being integrated into *Zakāt* and under colonial domination *Zakāt* disappeared altogether and became a mere private and voluntary charity. It would appear that *Zakāt* has now to be interpreted as a principle of interference in private wealth to satisfy public needs, but this is precisely what the religious right as a whole resists strenuously, clinging to the economic values of the Prophet's time! *Zakāt* in fact is nothing but a blueprint for policies of social justice, and yet the present Constitution – just like its predecessors – puts it in an isolated corner as though it had little to do with the rest of economic life. This leaves the positive economic enunciations of the Constitution as purely secular; they obey an established tradition rather than Islam. And a still greater irony is that these very rightists are always hankering after the restoration of *Zakāt* to its proper position! As for *Ribā*, it was a system of usurious exploitation in the Prophet's Arabia; the Qur'ān, after a series of warnings, banned it altogether. Medieval Muslim lawyers, generally speaking, took this to mean that all

---

1 Qur'ān, IX, 60.

increments on loans are banned, although it continued in practice, thanks to various "legal fictions." Muslim Modernists have contended that *Ribā* meant usury, not interest in the modern banking system, which is development-oriented, but the traditionalists have stuck to their guns, and, ironically, have unwittingly sought to reinforce their position by Marxism! It is to the credit of Ayūb Khan's Constitution that it interpreted *Ribā* as usury (1964 edition, Article 18). But the framers of the present Constitution were apparently afraid and were content with the ambiguous statement that they will "eliminate *ribā* as early as possible."

In the light of the foregoing, it cannot be said that the economic principles of the Constitution are Islamic. The hope undoubtedly is that this procedure will be shielded by the "Repugnancy Clause" (Article 227), which has been enshrined in all Constitutions since 1956, and which states that no law shall be enacted which is repugnant to Islam or injunctions of Islam. But that clause is productive of secular law, *not* of Islamic Law, since in order for a law to be Islamic it is obviously not sufficient that it not be "repugnant to Islam" but that it be derived from Islamic principles. The Repugnancy Clause is inherently incapable of producing a legal system like that of classical Fiqh law (which is genuinely Islamic Law), but a legal system promulgated by the various Sultans in the later medieval period, particularly the Qānūn-law of the Ottomans, which is a secular body of law. It is this fundamental fact which makes all social and economic enunciations of these three constitutions both desultory and non-Islamic. The right procedure would have been to set out all political, economic, and social policies as compact sections and linked organically with the general principles of Islam. This is why in a previous paper I had characterized both the 1956 and 1964 Constitutions as an "Islamic Fetish,"[1] and I am afraid the present Constitution has exactly the same format.

B. Social Provisions

In the social sphere, a major feature of the Constitution is the encouragement it gives to women to enter public life and take on professional careers. The locus classicus (besides equality clauses, inherited from the previous constitutions, in all manner of conduct of life "irrespective of race, color, creed and sex") for this is Article 34: "Steps shall be taken to ensure full participation of women in all spheres of national life," which is an entirely new and highly welcome principle. Some steps the Constitution itself has taken. Ten seats, *in addition to* the two hundred seats for members of the National Assembly (the Constitution is silent on this point concerning the Senate) are reserved for women, while women are also eligible to run for other seats as well (Article 51[4]). In the previous Constitution the number was six, but these six seats were part of the normal number of seats in the legislature, although women could run for

---

1   Fazlur Rahman, *op. cit.* in note 1, p. 285.

other seats as well. But a bold step on this subject is taken in Article 221 (2) where it is laid down that *at least one woman* shall be a member of the Islamic Council, whose minimal strength shall be eight.

The major, indeed, pioneering thrust in this direction, however, was made by Ayūb Khan's Muslim Family Laws Ordinance of January, 1961. That Law not only gave a regular share of inheritance to the orphaned grandchildren against the traditional Muslim practice, but put restrictions on polygyny and regulated the procedure of divorce, abolishing the notorious traditional repudiation of a wife by her husband by the simple utterance of a formula. But Ayūb Khan was, at that time, a military ruler, and it is more than doubtful if a democratically elected ruler in Pakistan can repeat that masterly stroke in the foreseeable future. Indeed, it will be to the credit of the present government if it can protect that Law. For while Ayūb Khan's 1964 Constitution had given absolute protection, the present one apparently does not. It does give initial protection (Article 8[3][b]) to a number of laws included in the First Schedule (pp. 143–47), including the Muslim Family Laws Ordinance of 1961, but says ([4]), "Within a period of two years from the commencement day, the appropriate legislature shall bring the laws specified in the First Schedule – not being a law which relates to or is connected with economic reforms – into conformity with the rights conferred by this chapter." Mr. Bhutto himself and many of his party men are undoubtedly progressive; yet a very large number of Pakistanis not only consider the Muslim Family Laws repugnant to Islam, but look upon them as abridging the rights of Muslim males (although the new census of Pakistan has revealed a preponderance of males over females!) and may well institute proceedings in the National Assembly for the repeal of these Laws.

Of equal importance is the stress on education. In the previous constitution, achievement of universal literacy and of universal, free, and compulsory primary education were envisaged "as soon as is practicable" (1966 Constitution, No. 7 of the Principles of Policy). The present Constitution is much more emphatic and advanced to secondary education, since the State shall "remove illiteracy and provide free and compulsory secondary education within the minimum possible period" (Article 37[b]). It is well-known, however, that in Ayūb Khan's Second Five Year Plan, enforced in 1965, funds provided for education were drastically reduced in favor of economic development. So far as the present government is concerned, not only has it given high priority to education in its actual policies but has laid down a plan in stages, according to its policy statement on education,[1] for completing universal primary education and for the take-over by the government of all private and foreign educational institutions. The government will not only endeavor to make Islamic Studies compulsory – this was also present in the previous Constitution – but will facilitate the learning of the Arabic language (Article 31[2]). This meets a very fundamental desideratum since an adequate knowledge of Arabic is a *sine*

---

1   Government of Pakistan, Ministry of Education, Islamabad *The Educational Policy, 1972–1980.*

qua non of understanding Islam from its primary sources – the Qur'ān and the Prophetic Sunna. Indeed, the main malady of those who, in Pakistan, have tried to learn Islam has been that most of them do not know Arabic and have been "free-landing" with Islam. But, of course, Arabic is necessary, but not enough: what is equally important is to cultivate a sense of history of the development of Islam over the past fourteen centuries and to compare this development with what the Qur'ān and the Prophet said, and the entire sociologico-historical background which renders the Qur'ān and the Prophet *intelligible*.

The most basic trouble with education in Pakistan and some other Muslim countries, however, is its dichotomy: two systems of education are running side by side, one modern and the other the traditional *madrasas*, untouched by any modern outlook. The former is government-funded, while the latter is privately financed. They are producing men of quite different and incongruous outlooks on life, and incompatible world-views. It would be no exaggeration to say that *two nations* are being produced. No government with the nation's interests at heart can simply go on looking at this fundamentally injurious state of affairs. In Turkey, the impatient Ataturk abolished the old *madrasa* system with one stroke. In Egypt, the famous al-Azhar University experienced a series of reforms in the present century, which widened its curriculum and changed its outmoded methods of instruction. Under Nasser, al-Azhar has been given even a medical and an agricultural college. In Tunisia, President Bourguiba simply lifted the age-old Zaitūna Seminary from the Zaitūna Mosque and replanted it in the University of Tunisia. The Indonesian Government is currently making strenuous efforts to streamline the *madrasas* and in some meaningful way integrate the two educational systems. It is very much to be hoped that the Islamic Republic of Pakistan will, in due course, take steps to improve this grave situation, even though it has found it necessary to state in its educational policy statement referred to above – no doubt with a political end in view – that "status quo shall be maintained" with regard to the *madrasas*. It is also not clear why, in view of the nationalization of education, the Constitution tells so much in the Principles of Policy. None of these institutions, to my knowledge, teaches even Islamic history, let alone general history, philosophy, any modern Western language, economics, or political science.

C. Islamic Propositions and Law-Making

So far as Islam is concerned, the most formidable difficulty faced by the Constitution-makers of Pakistan at the very outset was the location of sovereignty in the new State and whether democracy was Islamic or not. Already before the creation of Pakistan, the leader of the Jamā'at-i-Islamī, Alu'l-A'la Mawdūdī had forcefully contended that Islam could not accept modern democracy since in a democracy people are law-makers, whereas in

---

1 *Ibid.*, p. 37, clause 14.5.

Islam God is the law-giver.[1] Twisting the purely religious sense in which the Qur'ān speaks of God as "sovereign in heaven and earth,"[2] into a modern political sense, Mawdūdī and, following him, the traditionalist 'ulamā, insisted that the Constitution must recognize the sovereignty of Allāh. The idea behind this was, of course, to accept the sovereignty of the Sharī'a Law. The Modernist should have stood firm on the principle of the political sovereignty of the people, because otherwise one would have to admit the ludicrous conclusion that in officially atheistic countries God had set up governments-in-exile! The Modernist, instead, compromised. Hence the opening clause of the Preamble: "Whereas sovereignty over the entire Universe belongs to Almighty Allah alone and the authority to be exercised by the people of Pakistan, within the limits prescribed by Him, is a sacred trust." One would like to know how and through which instrument God had delegated this trust to the people of Pakistan. However, by this compromise, the Modernist managed to avoid a headlong conflict with the traditionalist, and to his own satisfaction, obtained a sanction for *working* democracy. The traditionalist, for his part, thought that *he* had gained what he wanted, viz., a restriction on the will of the people through God's sovereignty. That is where the crux lies in all the three Constitutions.

The Preamble then goes on to say that the State shall establish an order – "wherein the principles of democracy, freedom, equality, tolerance, and social justice, *as enunciated by Islam*, shall be fully observed." In the light of what has been said, the italicized words mean for the Modernist one thing, for the Traditionalist quite another. For the Modernist, democracy, etc., are understood in their modern meaning, for the Conservative, these words serve as a limitation on freedom. For otherwise, these words have no function, since, if the Modernist view is correct (and all Muslim Modernists since the latter half of the last century have been arguing this case with a great deal of plausibility), then Islam apparently enjoined democracy, social justice, etc., not *Islamic* democracy, social justice, etc. These words are, therefore, again a concession to the traditionalists. This is why, in the eyes of the present writer, the form in which Islam has been treated in all these Constitutions is unfortunate. They give the decisive impression of Islam being an artificial adjunct attached to some propositions, while most of the rest of substantive propositions are without any mention of Islam at all. The proper way to produce an authentic Islamic Constitution would have been to write a brief but comprehensive Introduction (or Preamble) where the relevance of Islam to political democracy, social philosophy, economic policies of social justice, treatment of minorities, and international behavior of the State would be set out. Then, one by one, each of these fields would have been treated in a compact and logical manner. Instead, all these fields have been treated in a diffuse and fragmentary manner.

On the subject of Islamization of the society, the Constitution (Preamble, paragraph 5) reaffirms the dicta of the previous constitution that the Muslims

---

1 Mawhūdī, *The Political Theory of Islam*, translated into English by M. Siddiqui (Lahore, n.d.).
2 For example, Qur'ān, III, 26; LVII, 2; III, 14; XXIII, 88, etc.

of Pakistan will be enabled to order their lives in the individual and collective spheres in accordance with the teachings and requirements of Islam "as set out in Holy Quran and Sunnah." In Ayūb Khan's original constitution of 1962, the term "Sunnah" had been dropped but was restored under public pressure through the First Amendment Act of 1964. The "Sunnah of the Prophet" means the example of the Prophet handed down through *Ḥadīth*-reports or traditions collected in the third century of Islam by the Sunnis and in the fourth century by the Shī'a. This Ḥadīth literature is quite amorphous and often self-contra-dictory and modern scholarship has shown that, by and large, it represents, not the Prophet's sayings but the opinions of the very early generations of Islam. Moreover, Shī'a Ḥadīth collections are different from the Sunnī ones. How-ever, it would be unwise to repudiate the Sunnah, for without it the meaning of the Qur'ān itself would often become difficult to settle. What is really re-quired is a historical criticism of the *Ḥadīth* which would be of enormous help to clarify the situation. We shall presently return to the question of the Islami-zation of the society.

One highly welcome change in the Constitution is that it has dropped a paragraph contained in the two earlier Constitutions (1964 *Principles of Policy* 1, *Explanation*): "In the application of this principle [i.e., that no law shall be enacted which is repugnant to the Qur'ān and the Sunnah] to the personal law of any Muslim sect, the expression 'Qur'ān and Sunnah' shall mean the Quran and Sunnah as interpreted by that sect." This principle was obviously in contradiction with that Constitution's expressly limiting the authoritative sources of Islam to the Quran and Sunnah only and would perpetuate the authority of different schools of law of classical Islam. It would thus prevent an achievement of uniformity of the law (and morality) of Islam in Pakistan. This writer had pointed out this ugly contradiction to President Ayūb Khan in a letter in 1964.

In Chapter 2, on the Principles of Policy, Articles 29(1) and 30(1) the present Constitution reaffirms what was said in the earlier Constitution, viz., that it will be the responsibility of each organ or authority of the State to act in accordance with these principles in so far as they relate to that organ or authori-ty or a person officially acting on behalf of such organ or authority, and the reponsibility of deciding whether an act of an organ or authority is or is not in accordance with these principles also resides in such organ or authority or a person acting on behalf of them. This means that in this respect each organ or authority of the State is completely autonomous and will not be open to ques-tion. The new Constitution, however, probably somewhat inconsistently with the foregoing but certainly representing an overall improvement, lays down in Article 29(3) that annual Federal and Provincial reports shall be prepared and each laid before the relevant Assembly "on the observance and implementation of the Principles of Policy, and provision shall be made... for discussion on such report." If a discussion of such report is to be held, it obviously means that some evaluation of the action of each organ or authority will be made and they cannot, therefore, be all that autonomous. As we shall see below, the Islamic

(Advisory) Council is required by the Constitution (as it was by the second Constitution which, for the first time, provided for it) to prepare an annual report for discussion by the National Assembly.

On continuance of the Preamble, the Principles of Policy (Article 31) also state – like the earlier constitutions – that "steps shall be taken to enable the Muslims of Pakistan, individually and collectively, to order their lives in accordance with *the fundamental principles and basic concepts of Islam* and to provide facilities whereby they may be enabled to understand the meaning of life according to the Holy Quran and Sunnah." Finally, this task is entrusted in Part IX (Articles 227–32) to the Islamic (Advisory) Council. Here, the present Constitution differs in certain important respects from the previous constitutions. The 1956 Constitution had envisaged a Law Commission to prepare a report on the Islamization of existing laws and on such principles and concepts of Islam which can be embodied in legal form and a Research Institute which was to undertake research on Islam and diffuse knowledge on Islam generally. According to the second constitution, an Advisory Islamic Council was provided for, charged both with giving advice on the legal side of Islam and with the task of making recommendations to the Central and the Provincial Governments as to how the Muslims of Pakistan may be enabled to order their lives in accordance with the teachings of Islam. Secondly, it also provided for an Islamic Research Institute which both provided necessary research materials to the Islamic Advisory Council and carried on its own research and dissemination of Islamic ideas. However, during this writer's tenure as Director of the Institute (1962–1968) and membership of the Council (1964–1969), in the Institute and Council there was a continuous tension and frequent conflict between the two: While the Institute espoused a definitely Modernist stance, the general climate within the Council was Conservative and often even reactionary. The Institute was also involved in certain public controversies with the very conservative right. Because of this history, the Institute has been dropped entirely from the new Constitution. But the question is: How will this Council discharge itself of these heavy duties of Islamization, particularly when the members of the Council will all be part-timers and will meet only occasionally, since the Constitution does not speak of the Council as though it were an organization requiring full-time work; indeed, it says that its Chairman, who must be a judge, could be a sitting judge of a High Court or of the Supreme Court (Article 228[4]).

Pakistan, indeed, presents a curious case. It is an ideological state, but it has no known ideology. In the case of Communist or Socialist countries, which are the only other ideological states in the world, their ideological blueprints and even their major policies precede the actual establishment of their states, but in the case of Pakistan, which declares itself to be an "Islamic State," Islam is not yet even known and its "fundamental principles and basic concepts" have yet to be formulated. The trouble is that Pakistani masses are emotionally strongly attached to Islam (as are masses so attached to Islam elsewhere), but the developments or distortions through which Islam has passed during the past fourteen centuries are so diverse and are of such sectarian character that the masses blindly follow these forms. The task obviously is to analyze the history of Islamic development, and to come to some point where a genuine enough perception of what the Qurʾān and the Prophet's struggle were all about may be born. But here even the ʿUlamā and the intellectuals in general do not have any adequate idea of what the Qurʾān was saying, why it was saying it, and what it became through the centuries. This whole question once again leads us to a proper organization of Islamic education and, in particular, to its dichotomy. This being the case, one may genuinely ask: How is Pakistan an ideological state?

According to Article 228 (3) (a), the President shall ensure that "So far as practicable various schools of thought are represented on the Council." This is undoubtedly an excellent principle, since the more broad-based the Council will be, the more points of view will be represented, although, of course, this will require some pateince, since it will not be easy to hammer out the differences. It is not clear, however, what is meant by "schools of thought." In the first place, this term must mean the major traditional sects – i.e., the Sunnis and the Shīʿa. But will this include the Ahmadīs? Thorny questions like this are bound to arise. It is to be hoped that the movement of Islamic Modernism, now over a century old, a movement which produced such men as (Sir) Sayyid Ahmad Khan, Sayyid Amīr ʿAlī, Shiblī, and Iqbal (the intellectual parent of Pakistan) will find adequate representation. Most probably, not all members will be appointed to begin with; the Council can start with any number from the minimum eight upward and the remaining (the maximum seats are fifteen) can be appointed later.

The final report of the Council is made due within seven years. Although the Council's role is "advisory," the present Constitution gives it more authority than did the second Constitution. While according to that Constitution, if reference to the Council by the President or a governor or an assembly is likely to cause delay in handling an urgent matter, laws pertaining to that matter may be made, the present Constitution adds, "Provided that, where a law is referred for advice to the Islamic Council and the Council advises that the law [enacted pertaining to an urgent matter] is repugnant to the Injunctions of Islam, the House, ... the President or the Governor shall reconsider the law so made" (Article 230[3]). But on this point there is some disturbing news and Mr. Bhutto seems (characteristically?) to have gone too far. In Article 230 (4), it is laid down that when the Council presents its report – whether interim (i.e., annual) or final – it will be laid before both Houses of the Parliament and all Provincial Assemblies within six months of its receipt, and Parliament and [each] Assembly, after considering the report, shall enact laws *in respect thereof* (note: *not necessarily in conformity therewith*) within a period of two years of the final report.

The language of the article by itself is not necessarily a cause for alarm, since it does not make it mandatory for the Parliament or an Assembly to *accept* in toto what the report has recommended. But the opposition was apparently refusing to sign the Constitutional document unless at least some of their demands were met, one being that the Islamic Council be given veto power over the Houses of Public Representatives. A front-page article in the weekly "Muslim World" of Karachi (a periodical which essentially gives reliable information about the current political, religious, social, and economic issues in various Muslim countries) in its issue of April 21, 1973 has the following: "President [now Prime Minister since the 14th of August, 1973] Bhutto, in his Aide-Memoire to the Opposition leaders, on the eve of the passing of the Constitution, brought to their notice that Article 230 (4) [partly referred to and partly quoted in the preceding paragraph] *obviously* means that the Islamic Council shall exercise a veto on the powers of the National Parliament. The Opposition demand was accepted by the ruling party in the cause of passing the Constitution by consensus of all parties." The Constitution *was* passed by a consensus of the members of the House present: no vote was cast against it, although there were some abstentions. But this has apparently cost the ideological stance of Mr. Bhutto and his party a good deal.

A new Article (No. 2) has been added in the Constitution declaring Islam to be the State Religion of Pakistan. Article 40 stresses the preservation and strengthening of fraternal relations among Muslim countries based on Islamic Unity and goes on to promise support for developing countries and to foster friendly relations with all countries to try to secure settlement of all issues through peaceful means. Here the support for developing countries (of Asia, Africa, and Latin America) is new, while the rest is more or less a carryover from the earlier Constitutions. Among the Fundamental Rights granted to all citizens, the right of freedom of speech, expression, and the freedom of the press is subject to the overall considerations of the "glory of Islam" and the security of the State. The two earlier Constitutions were content to mention the security of the State only, presumably because a threat to Islam would be considered as a threat to the State since Islam is the declared basis of the State. But Mr. Bhutto, with his eyes ever fixed on the emotions of the masses, considered an explicit mention of the "glory of Islam" apparently necessary.

Finally, a novel feature of the present Constitution is the oaths to be administered to the President and the Prime Minister and, to some extent, oaths to be made by other dignitaries as well – the Speaker, the governors, ministers, members of the Assemblies, etc. (Schedule III). The second Constitution (as well as the first) had laid down that the President shall be a Muslim, but the oaths to be administered to all the dignitaries were about the performance of their duties honestly and in accordance with the Constitution and "in the interest of the integrity, solidarity, and well-being and prosperity of Pakistan." Nothing was said explicitly about Islam. In the present Constitution, in view of the great anxiety constantly expressed by the 'Ulamā in general and the Jamā'at-i-Islāmī in particular lest an Ahmadi rise to such high office (in fact, demands have been put forward from time to time to declare Ahmadis a non-Muslim minority!) – an anxiety which has recently been greatly increased by the fact that many Ahmadis now occupy key posts in the Armed Forces – the

Constitution provides oaths for the offices of the President and the Prime Minister which lay out the entire traditional credo of Islam: belief in God, in the Holy Books, of which the last is the Qur'ān (for some reason belief in Angels has been left out), in the Prophets, of whom the final is Muḥammad, and in the Last Day. Other oaths also, while they do not speak of the traditional *credo* of Islam explicitly, certainly ask the entrants upon high office "to strive to preserve the Islamic Ideology which is the basis for the creation of Pakistan." The trouble, of course, is that Aḥmadis do not deny the position of the Qur'ān as the last revelation of God to mankind, nor do they believe that there will be another Prophet after Muḥammad with a new law – in fact, the Aḥmadis are so highly conservative and traditional that they follow the Ḥanafī School of Islamic Law – and, to that extent, they do uphold the finality of Prophethood with Muḥammad. It is doubtful whether an Aḥmadī will have any great qualms in making such an oath. Indeed, if there are groups who are much further removed from the core of Islam, these are certain Shi'ite groups whose content and style of worship and prayer has *nothing* to do with those of Muslims and whom the Shi'ites themselves call "extremists." These are, e.g., Druzes and the Ismā'īlī followers of the Āghā Khān, although it must be admitted that the present Āghā Khān and his grandfather have done much to bridge the gap between their followers and the Muslim community.

Winding up this analysis, we may again point out that this Constitution is progressive in its social and economic parts, although its progressiveness has been much, very much diluted by the anxiety of Mr. Bhutto to get the maximum support – indeed, consensus – of the National (Constituent) Assembly. The Constitution nevertheless has an unsatisfactorily diffuse and desultory character. All through the Constitution, its maker has had his gaze fixed on the emotional attachment of the masses to Islam and has tried to satisfy and exploit it to the full by going out of the way to inject it with heavy doses of emotional Islam.

REFERENCES

Ahmad, Aziz, and G. E. von Grunebaum,
    1970   Muslim Self Statement in India and Pakistan
al-Sibācī, Mustafa,
    1959   Ishtirākīyat'l-Islām, Damascus
Mawhūdī,
    n.d.   The Political Theory of Islam, trans., by M. Siddiqui, Lahore
Pakiston,
    1973   The Constitution of the Islamic Republic of Pakistan, Islamabad
    1972   The Educational Policy, 1972–1980, Islamabad
Rahman, Fazlur,
    1971   The Islamic Experience of Pakistan, Islam and the Modern Age, New Delhi, II, 4.
    1974   Sources and Meaning of Islamic Socialism, in Donald Smith, ed., Religion and Political Modernization, New Haven.
Sumār, A. K.,
    1966   Nusrat, Lahore.

The Emergence of the Federal Pattern in Pakistan

HAFEEZ MALIK

Villanova University, Villanova, U.S.A.

SINCE DECEMBER, 1971 Pakistan's political scene has been dominated by the struggle for power between President Bhutto and the National Awami Party's Chairman, Abdul Wali Khan. This struggle, to an extent, explained the political crisis in Pakistan which followed the seizure of (what the Pakistan Government called), "a veritable arsenal" from the Iraqi Embassy in Islamabad on February 10, 1973, and the dismissal of the NWFP and Baluchistan governors, who belonged to the NAP. Once again a question is being asked: are Baluchistan and the NWFP on the verge of secession in order to create Pakhtunistan? Pakhtunistan could emerge as a separate state if the people in the two provinces are alienated by the Federal Government of Pakistan. However, the odds are that the political elite in the two provinces would not seek confrontation, but exercise all conceivable pressure to gain maximum provincial autonomy in the new Constitution. Behind the facade of the political crisis was a developing constitutional consensus, to which Bhutto and the NAP leaders, including Wali Khan, and his Baluch colleague, Mir Gaus Bakhsh Bizenjo, have made substantial contributions.

The emerging pattern of federalism in Pakistan was reflected in President Bhutto's accord of March 5, 1972 with the National Awami Party (NAP) and Jamiat ulama-i Islam (JUI), and all parties constitutional accord of October, 1972.

Accord of March, 1972

It should, however, be kept in mind that President Bhutto's accord with the NAP and JUI, announced on March 6, 1972 was arrived at after an intense period of crisis which had developed as the result of a contest for power between the PPP and the NAP. This struggle for power was unnecessary, especially at this crucial moment, and it could have been avoided if President Bhutto had not allowed his political lieutenants in the Frontier Province to rupture the PPP-JUI-NAP alliance, which had been brought about since December, 1971.

Why was this alliance ruptured? Basically three issues were responsible for the break down of this alliance:

1) The appointment of governors to the provinces of Baluchistan and the NWFP.

2) The election of female candidates to the provincial legislative assemblies.
3) The introduction of land reforms.

Maintaining their majorities in the NWFP and Baluchistan, the NAP-JUI asserted that the provincial governors should be appointed with their advice and consent. On the other hand, President Bhutto disregarded this demand and appointed members of the PPP as governors. When NAP agitated against governor Raisani in Baluchistan during January, 1971 the agitators were forcefully put down.

In order to undercut the influence and popularity of the NAP in the Frontier Province, the NAP leaders charged that the PPP had organized the Kissan Mazdur Party which was mobilizing the landless tenants against the land owning Khans of the Frontier. Many of these Khans were supporters of the NAP and they felt deeply threatened in their home base, and they blamed the PPP for their rising troubles with the tenants.

The election of female candidates to the provincial legislative assemblies brought the relationship between the two parties to the breaking point. In the Punjab the PPP elected six women to the Legislative Assembly, containing 186 seats; while in Sindh it elected two female members to the Legislative Assembly of 62 members. Simultaneously, however, the PPP nominated female candidates in the Frontier and Baluchistan, and tried to persuade the NAP and JUI members to violate their party discipline and vote for the PPP's nominees. Naturally, these developments created fears in the mind of the NAP leader, Wali Khan, that the PPP was endeavoring to create a dictatorship of Sindh and the Punjab. When Baluchistan and the NWFP legislatures elected the NAP-JUI female candidates, Wali Khan charged that the people have lost confidence in the PPP leadership.

In view of these developments, Wali Khan and his colleagues in Baluchistan, notably Mir Ghaus Bakhsh Bizenjo, developed a program of resistance to President Bhutto's government, in which regionalism was certainly a point of appeal for the Pathans and the Baluchis. They demanded that President Bhutto should lift Martial Law, call the National and Provincial Assemblies in order to restore democratic institutions in Pakistan. Regarding the land reforms, Wali Khan took the position that only the provincial assemblies were competent to adopt them, and if they failed to introduce these reforms then it was none of President Bhutto's business. Despite his lip-service to Socialism, Wali Khan was not anxious to see his supporters' economic base destroyed by the sledge-hammer of Martial Law.

To strengthen their position, the NAP leaders obtained support from the three factions of the Muslim League, retired Air Marshall Asghar Khan's party, and Jamiat-i-Islami. They started agitation in the Frontier, where appeal was also made in the name of Pakhtunistan. Some of the hotheads openly asked for a confrontation with the national government, if President Bhutto failed to accept the NAP's demands. Consequently, during the months of January and February, a heightened sense of crisis developed in Pakistan, leading foreign observers to report that Pakistan was on the verge of break-up.

Had President Bhutto taken the opposition into his confidence regarding the withdrawal of Martial Law this ugly situation might not have developed. On February 18 he gave an interview to London's BBC correspondent, Ian McIntire, suggesting that he would withdraw Martial Law after introducing agrarian reforms in Pakistan, and after the completion of negotiations with Shaikh Mujeeb and Mrs. Indira Gandhi. The vagueness of his commitment on the withdrawal of Martial Law only heightened suspicions regarding his intentions. Although he announced that the elections to the local bodies scheduled to be held on March 15 would be postponed, and that they would be organized by the provincial governments, the NAP leaders' fears were not allayed. While they welcomed the president's decision, they continued to agitate for the withdrawal of Martial Law and for the withdrawal of provincial governors from Baluchistan and NWFP. These governors were accused of having lobbied for the election of the PPP-sponsored female candidates to the legislatures.

NAP's Political Ideology

The NAP leaders, particularly Wali Khan, have a political ideology which is a hodge-podge of regionalism, secularism, socialism and all-Pakistan nationalism. Wali Khan believes that after the establishment of Bangladesh, Pakistan, as it was originally conceived, has ceased to exist. In his eyes, Pakistan as it stands today is a coalition of four nationalities. He perceives nationalities in terms of their mother tongues and asserts that the new Constitution must be the product of a compromise between these four nationalities.[1] In political terms, this strategy amounts to claiming for the NAP a position of parity with the PPP, the former being the majority party in Baluchistan and NWFP and the latter being the dominant representative organization of the Punjab and Sindh. To Wali Khan the new Constitution would be acceptable if it reflects the true distribution of power between these two political parties in Pakistan.

While this is a regional strategy, Wali Khan has recently endeavored to change his image to an all-Pakistan leader by extending the influence of the NAP to the Punjab and Sindh. If, however, the NAP becomes an All-Pakistan party, it may eventually preempt the JUI, the Muslim League and the Jam'at-i-Islami. This probable development could lead to the emergence of a two party system in Pakistan.

To Wali Khan's debit it may be pointed out that the concept of four nationalities negates the concept of a Pakistani nation, and leaves little ideological room for the Muslim Muhajirs (immigrants) who have settled in Pakistan since 1947. After offering many sacrifices for the creation of Pakistan, Muslim Muhajirs came to the promised land to be Pakistanis and not to become Pun-

---

1 For Wali Khan's ideology see two good studies by Anwar Muzdakiy, *Wali Khan Key Siyasat* (Lahore: Tariq Publishers, 1972); pp. 141–4; *Bacha Khan Awr Pakhtunistan* (Lahore: Tariq Publishers, 1972).

jabis, Sindhis, Baluchis or Pathans. Not having any commitment to provincial ethos, they are all-Pakistani nationalists *par excellence*. Wali Khan's ethnic ideology creates a crisis of identity, and is a serious obstacle in the development of a homogeneous Pakistani nationalism. However, his attitude is bound to change if the NAP becomes a truly all-Pakistan party, and thus emancipates itself from the narrow confines of ethnic regionalism.

The Averting of the Crisis

Recognizing the explosive potentiality of the NAP'S agitation, President Bhutto invited Wali Khan and Bizenjo to Islamabad for a round of parleys to resolve their differences. Simultaneously, however, Presidential Advisor for Public Affairs, Mr. Mairaj Muhammad Khan gave a statement in which a crucial concession was made to the NAP leaders. He said on March 4, 1972: "His party had no objection to renaming of the Frontier Province as Pakhtunistan or any other name that is adopted by the [Frontier] provincial assembly, but it must be clear that the province would be within the concept and framework of one Pakistan." Negotiations between President Bhutto, the NAP and JUI leaders lasted for three days (March 2, 3, and 4, 1972) and they laid down the principles of compromise to resolve the crisis as well as some principles to frame the future Constitution of Pakistan. The accord, which was finally declared on March 5, turned out to be a point by point compromise between the three parties. The salient features of the accord are:[1]

The Distribution of Power

The NAP-JUI coalition was recognized as the majority party in the NWFP, while in Baluchistan NAP alone would be the majority party. Consequently in both provinces the NAP-JUI alliance established the provincial governments.

The Withdrawal of Martial Law

The PPP proposed that the National Assembly should convene on April 21, 1972 and after passing a vote of confidence in the Bhutto government should approve and confirm the continuation of Martial Law until August 14, 1972. The NAP-JUI wanted Martial Law to be withdrawn on June 7.

It was agreed that Martial Law would continue until August 14, 1972 and the National Assembly would pass a vote of confidence in the Bhutto government.

The PPP proposed that the National Assembly should appoint a committee

---

1   Dawn (March 5, 1972).

of the House to draft a constitution which would be presented on August 1, 1972. The NAP-JUI suggested that the draft constitution should be presented by July 1, 1972 and the National Assembly should be convened on July, 1972. But the parties agreed that the reports of the committee on the constitution should be submitted by August 1, 1972 and that the National Assembly should reconvene on August 14, 1972.

The PPP proposed that when the National Assembly is reconvened on August 14, 1972, it should act only as a constitution making body to guarantee early drafting of the Constitution. The NAP-JUI proposed that the National Assembly should also act as a representative legislative organ. The compromise stated that the National Assembly would make the Constitution as well as ordinary laws for the country until the final draft of the Constitution was produced.

The Interim Constitution

The PPP proposed that the first session of the National Assembly should start on April 21, 1972 for three days. The NAP-JUI proposed that the National Assembly should meet on March 23. The parties agreed that the National Assembly members would be invited on March 23 for participation, and the National Assembly would actually meet on April 14 for three days. During this brief period, specified topics will be discussed, and the debate would be restricted.

The PPP proposed that the National Assembly should meet in order to endorse an interim constitution on the basis of the Government of India Act of 1935, read together with the Independence Act of 1947, along with subsequent amendmets, or on the basis of 1962 Constitution with subsequent amendments. The NAP-JUI leaders insisted that the interim constitution should be the Government of India Act of 1935 and the Independence Act of 1947 with subsequent amendments, and that the Constitution of 1962 should be kept out of the political picture.

President Bhutto conceded the demand of the NAP and JUI leaders on this point, after obtaining their agreement that the debate in the National Assembly would not exceed three days.

The Provincial Legislative Assemblies

The PPP preferred that the provincial assemblies should meet after the interim constitution was adopted, that is on May 1, 1972. On the other hand the NAP-JUI proposed that the provincial legislative assemblies should be convened on April 10. However, it was agreed that the provincial legislatures will be convened on April 21.

Regarding the provincial governors, after a great deal of discussion, it was

agreed that until the permanent constitution was adopted the federal government would continue to have the right to appoint the governors in the provinces.
As a token of compromise the federal government stated that even during the
interim period, governors would be appointed after consulting the majority
parties in the provinces.

Future Developments

The PPP-JUI agreement resolved the political and constitutional deadlock
in Pakistan, but it also paved the way for the emergence of Pakhtunistan. The
attempt to change the name from NWFP to Pakhtunistan need not be considered a secessionist development. Presently all indications are that Pakhtunistan would not move in the direction of Mujeebism. On the federal nature of
Pakistan's constitution, the NAP's position moved closer to that of the PPP and
other political parties in the country. For example, the NAP leaders indicated
that they would like to transfer matters of defense, foreign affairs, foreign trade,
currency, including central taxation to the central government of Pakistan.
They also indicated their agreement to leave communications, including rail-
road, civil aviation, telegraph and telephones under the care of the federal
government.

Much like President Bhutto, the NAP-JUI leaders recognized that for the
industrial and economic development of Pakistan, private business has a great
contribution to make. Consequently, the NAP leaders invited Pakistan's
financiers and industrialists to invest their capital in the NWFP and Baluchistan, while assuring them that their investments would be safeguarded, and
guaranteed by the NAP-JUI governments in these two provinces.

Highlighting the role of private enterprise in the NWFP, the NAP-Minis-
ter of Finance, Mr. Ghulam Faruq stated in the Budget (1972-73) speech:

> And so of necessity for the major portion of the Province's development programme,
> specially the industrial sector, we must look for a more effective and reliable source from
> a different direction and so out of dire necessity and under compulsion, we have to fall
> back on private enterprise, already dubbed according to common concept, a sinner. The
> House, I hope, will appreciate that in the past it was the ineffectiveness of Government
> operations that paved the way for private enterprise going out of control.
> But the private enterprise wedded to the philosophy of profit will ask for its price in the
> shape of tax holidays, other concessions and a reliable supply of electrical energy and gas.[1]

In the composition of provincial ministries in the NWFP and Baluchistan,
the NAP-JUI leaders also reflected a national trend in their agreement on
March 11, 1972. In the Frontier, the chief minister came from the JUI, while
in Baluchistan the chief minister was provided by the NAP. Wali Khan declared
that he would resign his position from the Frontier provincial assembly and

---

1 Ghulam Faruq, *Finance Minister's Speech: Budget, 1972-73*, Peshawar, Government of
   NWFP, 1972, p. 5.

retain his membership in the National Assembly. The NAP constitution committee included prominent lawyers including former Justice Sheikh Abdul Hameed, Aziz Allah A. Shaikh and S. M. Zafar, the former Law Minister of Ayub's regime. Wali Khan, Bizenjo, and Arbab Sikandar Khan directed the committee on political matters. These trends indicated that the NAP was endeavoring to become a national political organization.

As a regional alliance, however, the NAP-JUI demanded non-interference in their administrations in the Frontier province and Baluchistan. Hardly had this settlement been implemented when the conflicting strategies began to plague the relations between these two provinces and the federal government. Surprisingly the NAP strategy included: 1) "falling back on private enterprise"; 2) scuttling the land reforms to retain the big Khans' political support, and 3) currying favor with the conservative elements by allowing the JUI ministers to make the study of Arabic in the elementary schools compulsory. (This policy also provided jobs to a large number of half-educated *ulama*.) Simultaneously, however, Wali Khan subjected President Bhutto to his unrelenting criticism to erode his popularity in Sindh and particularly the Punjab, the home-base of Bhutto's power. In July, 1972 the language riots in Sindh lowered Bhutto's popularity, and Wali Khan's image appeared as a probable national alternative in the next general elections.

President Bhutto's counter-strategy operated at two levels. In order to create a sense of distributive justice in these two provinces, he increased their developmental allocations – 100% for Baluchistan, and 119% for the NWFP. To undermine the NAP-JUI alliance the Kissan-Mazdur party was encouraged to pit the tenants against the Khans. From Baluchistan, where Baluchi society is largely tribal and divided between Pakistan, Iran and Afghanistan, Governor Bizenjo was sent to Iran to observe the socio-economic power of Iran and Baluchis' situation. However, the Muslim League (Qayyum group) and the PPP concentrated their attacks on the Ata Allah Mengal government. Retaliating, the Mengal tribesmen attacked some Punjabi settlers in the Pat Feeder area, and the Mengal government also decided to return to the federal government all non-Baluchi employees. To subordinate some rival tribes to the Mengals, the Baluchistan government harassed the Bugtis and the Jamote tribes in Lasbela. Consequently the Jam Sahib of Lasbela, and Mir Nabi Bux Zehri (Vice-President of the Muslim League in Baluchistan) were forced to flee the province, and their extradition was denied by the Sindh government. To escape arrest in the Frontier, the Kissan-Mazdur leaders moved out to the Punjab, where their extradition was also refused. Nevertheless, the relations between the federal and provincial governments remained workable.

In September, 1972 occurred the episode of the London Plot, when the government-controlled newspapers, attacked Yusuf Haroon, Mahmud Haroon (both benefactors of Shaikh Mujeeb and the NAP), Ata Allah Mengal and Wali Khan, who were in London for various reasons. The fact that they had visited convalescing Shaikh Mujeeb could not be denied; what made their reunion "conspiratorial" was the newspapers' assertion that they had advised

Shaikh Mujeeb to persuade Mrs. Gandhi to delay the Indian troops' withdrawal from Pakistani occupied areas. Derisively President Bhutto called them
"winter Pakistanis" – who spend summer months in Europe – and denied any
knowledge of the London Plot. Some of the federal ministers, however, continued their bitter personal attacks against the NAP Chief, Wali Khan. Against
this background was the October, 1972 constitutional accord negotiated between all the political parties of Pakistan.

Accord of October, 1972

President Bhutto took the initiative, while Wali Khan was still in London,
to have a broad agreement on federal principles for the new Constitution. By
entering into these constitutional parleys the NAP leaders very substantially
neutralized their own leader, while the "London Plot" had already cast a
shadow over his relatively limited popularity in Pakistan. Unquestionably
President Bhutto made substantial concessions to the oppositions leaders, who
wanted a parliamentary federal system, while he preferred American federalism. On October 20 the accord was signed by Governors Bizenjo of Baluchistan,
and Arbab Sikander Khan of the NWFP (representing the NAP) and Chief
Minister Mufti Mahmud (representing the JUI). Out of the murky skies of
politics emerged a federal parliamentary system with a Prime Minister as the
chief executive responsible only to the National Assembly. A bicameral legislature (the National Assembly and the Senate) was provided, which was
empowered to elect the titular president. For 15 years (or three general elections) the vote of no-confidence could be passed by a two-thirds majority of the
National Assembly, while simultaneously indicating a successor's name. The
power between the Federal Government and the provinces was distributed
according to the interim constitution, with residual powers vested in the
provinces. However, the interim constitution was weighted heavily in the
center's favor.

The 179-page draft of the new Constitution was presented to the National
Assembly on December 31, when Wali Khan had returned to Pakistan. Determined to reassert his leadership over the NAP, Wali Khan virtually repudiated
the October Accord saying that Bizenjo and Arbab Sikander signed it as individuals and that it needed to be ratified by the NAP General Council. Wali
Khan asked to whittle down the Prime Minister's powers, and to have the
Senate share with the National Assembly control over the budget. Again, this
position reflected Wali Khan's regional strategy. The Punjab, he rightly
asserted, having more population (62%) than the other three provinces
combined would have untrammeled control over the national resources, if the
Senate was denied an allocative role. Bhutto compromised once again and
invited the political parties to another round of constitutional parleys to iron
out the differences. Responding enthusiastically on January 20, 1973 Wali
Khan accepted the offer and it seemed that after all the Constitution would

reflect a national consensus. In this hopeful atmosphere exploded the Iraqi Embassy's scandal of February 10, which led to the dismissal of the NAP governors, and chief ministers in Baluchistan and the NWFP.

Emergence of the 1973 Constitution

However, the Government of Pakistan moved rather quickly to normalize relations with Iraq. Iraqi Minister of Education, Dr. Ahmad Abdul Sattar Al-Jawari, visited Pakistan from April 19 to 23, 1973 and had several rounds of discussions with Mr. Bhutto and Minister of State for Defense and Foreign Affairs, Mr. Aziz Ahmad. Both parties frankly discussed Iraqi Embassy's involvement in smuggling of guns to Pakistan. Very shrewdly Iraqis let it be known that the guns were not intended for any political party or a faction in Pakistan, but were meant to be shipped to Baluchis living in Iran.

While this explanation was effectively utilized by the NAP, the Pakistan Government was not pleased with this "diplomatic finesse" of the Iraqis. Finally Pakistan and Iraq resolved to reappoint their Ambassadors, and Iraq reiterated its respect for the sovereignty and territorial integrity of Pakistan. A communique containing this happy understanding was published on April 26, and this unhappy chapter of relations between the two countries was closed.[1]

The NAP-JUI coalition demanded that if the misunderstandings between Iraq and Pakistan had been removed and President Bhutto had accepted Iraq's explanation, there was no reason why their governments could not be reinstated in the NWFP and Baluchistan. Also, the NAP-JUI suggested that if the federal government still suspected their involvement with the Iraqi Embassy, then a high powered judicial inquiry should be held to determine their culpability. Most observers in Pakistan began to suspect that President Bhutto had acted hastily in blaming the NAP and JUI. Practically all the opposition parties came to accept the NAP-JUI's "innocence." Consequently, the opposition political parties coalesced into a United Democratic Front to oppose the PPP's federal government.

President Bhutto now faced the unpalatable choice of either reinstating the NAP-JUI governments in the two provinces, or dissolve the provincial legislatures for fresh elections, or somehow manage to create new coalitions in the two provinces which would form the new governments. President Bhutto adopted the last option, and after considerable juggling created new governments in the NWFP and Baluchistan. Simultaneously, however, he opened negotiations with the opposition parties to achieve a constitutional consensus.

During the first week of April, 1973 the issue of provincial autonomy was resolved and by the time the Constitution was adopted, one could hear no more the outcry of the federal government's dictatorship over the provinces. Some differences remained between the opposition and the PPP in the Nation-

---

1 *The Pakistan Times*, (April 26, 1972).

al Assembly so that the opposition walked out and did not return to the National Assembly until April 11, 1973 when the Constitution was finally adopted.

On April 11 President Bhutto was to wind up the constitutional debate at 11:00 AM in the National Assembly but he did not enter the House until about 1:45 PM. Meanwhile, the Speaker of the House generously invited all back-benchers to make their speeches in order to kill the time. At 12:45 PM an aged leader of the opposition, Mr. Qazi Adil Abbasi, walked into the National Assembly signalling the achievement of a last minute compromise between the opposition and the PPP. Hardly had Qazi Adil Abbasi sat down when the Minister of Law and Parliamentary Affairs, Mr. Hafeez Peerzada, presented a few constitutional amendments for the adoption of the House. A few minutes later some more leaders of the opposition walked into the National Assembly amid loud cheers. Mr. Peerzada introduced some more amendments to the Constitution. Finally at 1:27 PM Mr. Wali Khan and Mr. Bizenjo entered the National Assembly, and were greeted with a thunderous applause. Mr. Peerzada once again introduced some more amendments. When the final vote was counted only three negative votes were cast by one Sindhi and two Punjabi legislators including President Bhutto's former Minister of Law, Mahmud Ali Qasuri.[1] With these three exceptions all members of the National Assembly signed the new Constitution and pledged allegiance to it.

All the amendments were procedural and they hardly touched the distribution of power between the provinces and the federal government, indicating that the issue of autonomy had been settled several weeks ago amicably between the opposition and the PPP. A few minutes before 2:00 PM, President Bhutto entered the National Assembly and made his concluding remarks about the Constitution, reiterating that from now on no polemic would be raised in Pakistan about the federal government's domination over the provinces.

Unlike the Constitutions of 1950 and 1962, the Constitution of 1973 faced the question of provincial autonomy squarely. The NAP and JUI, representing mostly the NWFP and Baluchistan, had expressed their apprehension of the Punjab's and Sindh's economic domination of the two smaller provinces. To allay their fears, a Council of Common Interest (Article 153) was created, consisting of the chief ministers of the four provinces and an equal number of members nominated by the federal government. This Council of Common Interest is to remove economic differences between the federating units and is responsible to the Parliament.

Distribution of water supplies, electricity and natural gas was also constitutionally settled. Any dispute involving these natural resources is subject to the Council of Common Interest's review (Article 155–158). Moreover, the Federal Government assumed the obligation not to deny any provincial government the right to construct and use broadcasting transmitters in the provinces. In any dispute involving this right the issue is to be determined by an arbitrator

---

1 Interestingly enough, as of April 1973, the three dissident legislators were members of the PPP.

appointed by the Chief Justice of Pakistan (Article 159). Parenthetically it may be added that most of these articles had been incorporated in the interim constitution of May, 1972.

The provincial autonomy guaranteed in the Constitution is one thing and autonomy practiced in political terms is entirely different. Maintaining decisive representational majorities in the National Assembly and in the legislatures of the Punjab and Sindh, the PPP can resolve political as well as economic tensions developing in the Punjab and Sindh. However, in the NWFP and Baluchistan, where the NAP-JUI still seem to retain a representational edge in the provincial legislatures over the ruling coalitions, the issue of autonomy assumes not a constitutional aspect, but a practical problem of relationship between the ruling political party and the opposition. To date the PPP and the JUI-NAP have not evolved any workable formula in the exercise of power. Until they do, the debate over autonomy would continue to be a divisive issue in Pakistan.

Bhutto's Foreign Policy, 1972-73

LAWRENCE ZIRING

Western Michigan University, Kalamazoo, U.S.A.

ZULFIKAR ALI BHUTTO's primary interest before becoming President of Pakistan on December 20, 1971 lay in the realm of foreign affairs. Nothing has happened since that dramatic date to indicate he is now less concerned with his country's external relations. While clearly preoccupied with domestic problems, President Bhutto continues to demonstrate an unusual appreciation for the international linkages that influence his programs and generally shape his national objectives. This brief essay aims at examining the key features of President Bhutto's current foreign policy, particularly those which suggest a style or nuance different from that displayed by his predecessors. After mentioning the latter, however, it is important to cite two facts. First, during his tenure as Pakistan's foreign minister in the Ayub Khan administration, Bhutto enjoyed wide latitude in establishing the framework for Pakistan's contemporary foreign policy. And second, Pakistan's foreign policy reflects a continuity with the past that is almost remarkable for its consistency. Hence it is to nuance that we look for a hint of change. It is this and the style of the principal decision-maker that may make Pakistan's foreign policy different from that of his predecessors, a change noticeable more in form than substance. Even a cursory reading of the main parameters of Pakistan's foreign policy assists in illuminating us on this point.

From that day in August, 1947, which marked Pakistan's emergence as a sovereign, independent state, to the time of this writing, Pakistani officialdom has been especially aware of the posturing, declarations, policies and actions of the Indian leaders. The contention always has been strongly held that India seeks to undermine, weaken and eventually destroy the Muslim state (Choudhury 1968; and Burke 1973). It is this conviction that has often kept opposed political groups from intensifying their disputes, and indeed, which provides post-1971 Pakistan with a tenuous equilibrium. Despite bitter political factionalism, strong efforts are underway to prevent a recurrence of the Bangladesh tragedy. As Anwar Syed (1972:27) has written: India "can subvert Pakistan only if Pakistanis, in large enough numbers, are dissatisfied with the prevailing political order. The East Pakistani secession has shown that Pakistan cannot be defended unless the people of her various regions are determined to remain together as one independent nation." While it cannot be ascertained whether provincial loyalties can be transcended, let alone how long inter-province rivalries can be contained, it is clear that Zulfikar Ali Bhutto's performance is predicated on maximizing fear of India in order to keep his detractors from further fractioning the state. At the same time, it is obvious that Bhutto cannot begin to control Pakistani regionalism if he is not prepared to yield to those pressures that it invariably produces (Malik, 1972; 1973).

Zulfikar Ali Bhutto: A Policy Overview

Of Bhutto's several publications, most important is his *The Myth of Independence* (1969). In it he traces Pakistan's external relations, particularly those relating to the major powers, and, with exceptional interest, relations with the United States. This treatise is the clearest delineation of Bhutto's philosophy, perceptions and attitude toward international affairs. Early in his career as a public official, Bhutto voiced disenchantment with Pakistan's almost total reliance on the United States. He was the first member of his generation to rise to a station of political significance, and it was from the platform made possible by these public offices that he publicized a view which veered away from the orthodoxy of the middle and late 1950's. That orthodoxy characterized Pakistan as the *sole* Asian country which the United States could truly depend upon, given the latter's interest in the containment of international communism.

From 1954 until the Sino-India border conflict in 1962, Pakistan's foreign policy began and terminated with the United States, and this proved to be more and more unpalatable to the seemingly more radical, younger generation. Thus as early as the Ayub coup in October 1958, this generation adopted Bhutto as their spokesman and go-between with higher authority. Bhutto's sudden rise to national notoriety was in part a consequence of the several ministerial portfolios he held in the Ayub administration. But a major factor in his skyrocketing popularity was his repeated attacks on the country's "unbalanced" foreign policy. Pakistan, he would argue, should cease posing threats to China and the Soviet Union. By supporting American fears of international communism Pakistan was adding to its list of immediate enemies without strengthening its defenses against India. Moreover, so long as Pakistan was wedded to the United States, it was handicapped in its relations with other Muslim states. Because of these widely broadcast beliefs, Bhutto assembled a large following. He attracted the educated young people, members of the professional intelligentsia, conservative and orthodox Muslims, and politicos with leftist tendencies. Furthermore, when the United States rushed military aid to India after its border skirmish with China in 1962, Bhutto's criticism of the United States was transformed into holy writ. And in the following year when Bhutto succeeded to the Foreign Minister's post, he insisted that the country must modify its long-standing foreign policy if it was to maintain its self respect while protecting itself from the machinations of Indian leaders, who, he declared, were emboldened by the receipt of military hardware from the United States.

Bhutto is credited with Pakistan's warm embrace of China although it is obvious that others before him had laid the foundation for the amicable relations that were to follow. Pakistan recognized the People's Republic in 1950, and Prime Minister H. S. Suhrawardy visited China after a similar visit to Pakistan by Chou En-lai in 1956–57. Foreign Ministers Manzoor Qadir and Mohammad Ali Bogra worked arduously with Bhutto to open commercial and cultural programs with China as well as the Soviet Union in 1960, and discussions on legalizing the border between Pakistan and China were initiated by these same individuals between 1961–62. Still, it was Zulfikar Ali Bhutto who received national acclaim for establishing Pakistan's independent foreign policy.

Bhutto was more vocal on the subject, he also had the foreign minister's portfolio passed to him at a fortuitous moment. Mohammad Ali Bogra's sudden death vaulted Bhutto into the Foreign Office somewhat prematurely. The transfer of American arms to India occurred over the opposition of the Ayub administration, and within months of Mahammad Ali's death. Pakistani anti-Americanism therefore was on the ascendant and Ayub Khan found it necessary to placate public opinion without rupturing Pakistan's relations with the United States. Bhutto was in the best position to satisfy popular sentiment, and in so doing, to help stabilize Ayub's administration.

Given these circumstances, it comes as no surprise that the Ayub-Bhutto relationship should shatter on the issue of foreign policy. Bhutto accompanied Ayub to Tashkent following the 1965 Indo-Pakistan War but the foreign minister disagreed with the terms of the declaration signed in that Soviet city. Although he told Ayub he wanted to leave the government, his resignation was held up for several months thereafter. Nonetheless, once free of governmental responsibilities, he joined other members of the opposition who were seeking to use the Tashkent issue, not only to discredit, but ultimately to bring Ayub Khan down. The failure of the United States to assist Pakistan in its trial with India in 1965 was grist for the mill of the opposition, and Bhutto's ambition was clearly expanded in the heat of the anti-Ayub campaign that followed. The fact that Zulfikar Ali Bhutto set about to organize his own Pakistan People's Party (PPP) rather than join a standing opposition party also illustrates his desire to draw his following into a political arrangement unencumbered by traditional, older political personalities. Over the years all other movements, parties and politicians had been stigmatized in one way or another, and Bhutto sensed that this was his opportunity to begin afresh and from the top.

Even Bhutto, however, could not have anticipated in the winter of 1969 when Ayub Khan's system crumbled, the circumstances whereby he would eventually succeed his erstwhile leader. The Yahya Khan interregnum, the election results of December 1970, and the tragedy of East Pakistan followed by the crucial encounter with India in December 1971, occured with such velocity that it is doubtful anyone on the scene at the time fully grasped the consequences of each daily event. Nevertheless, Bhutto's success at the polls in the December 1970 general election made him the dominant figure in what was then West Pakistan. Hence, when Yahya Khan accepted the India surrender terms, the only civilian with a "national" reputation as well as with the proper leadership credentials was Zulfikar Ali Bhutto. Moreover, the army had had its fill of frontline political leadership. Badly humiliated by Indian arms, it now sought to retire from the scene where it could lick its wounds and attempt the restoration of its once vaunted image. As President Bhutto now had the opportunity to shape Pakistan's foreign policy in his own likeness, this among other pressing affairs of state received his immediate attention.

Bhutto is a firm believer in the theory of interdependence. "World developments have now become so complex and interconnected that no important decision tolls the bell for one people alone." Pakistan, argues Bhutto, is caught up in a web of global proportions and its problems cannot be isolated from those of other nations, nor can these nations ignore what transpires within and against Pakistan. It is Bhutto's opinion that Pakistan's foreign relations can be divided into two segments; the pragmatic where the country is compelled to react to changing world currents, and the sentimental which ties it to a peculiar value system and hence fixed perceptions and preferences. These two segments interact with each other. One may dominate the other at any particular time, but nothing permanent should be concluded from this process. Thus Pakistan must practice, as Bhutto insists today, a "bilateral foreign policy" (Bhutto 1973a). Such an approach permits the country to relate equally to the United States, the Soviet Union, and the People's Republic of China. Bhutto prides himself on having promoted this policy before it was considered fashionable or feasible, and there is no gainsaying the fact that he feels vindicated given the intimate relations developed between the United States, the Soviet Union and China in the last eighteen months. Perhaps secretly, Bhutto senses that Henry Kissinger has stolen a page from his book. In an article in *Foreign Affairs* Bhutto writes:

> By maintaining friendly relations with all the great powers on the basis of principles and not expediency, Pakistan hopes to avoid involvement in disputes and struggles between them. It is part of our new policy that one should refrain from participating in multilateral pacts directed by one bloc of powers against another. Thus we have recently withdrawn from SEATO, in which Pakistan had in any case little part over the past few years. Bilateralism with the greater flexibility it implies will characterize our relations in the future (1973b: 552).

Bhutto cannot fail to recognize the role played by the Nixon administration during the 1971 hostilities with India. Nor can he fail to take advantage of the material assistance the United States is likely to make available to Pakistan in return for its friendship. Hence Bhutto's change of pace and termination of criticism toward the United States. Moreover, the United States is no longer judged an impediment to Pakistan's relations with the communist countries.

President Bhutto also stresses Pakistan's new geopolitical orientation at every opportunity. His country is clearly more intimately linked with South-western Asia. By contrast, Southeast Asia is only remotely identified with Pakistan's destiny. It is this Southwest Asian orientation that gives Pakistan a semblance of balance vis-a-vis the dominance of India in the subcontinent. Therefore, Pakistan looks even more fervently than before to Iran, Turkey and other Muslim states. Bhutto has declared that Pakistan is strategically situated at the head of the Arabian Sea and flanks the entrance to the oil-rich Persian Gulf. This means that Pakistan is important to Iran's security and possibly the security of the sheikhdoms along the Persian Gulf. Hence Iran can incrementally add to Pakistani strength vis-a-vis India, while a reasonably sound Pakistan is a significant asset to Iran. The reported plan of the Shah of Iran to purchase approximately two billion dollars in the latest military equipment from the United States, i.e., helicopter gunships, F-5E supersonic interceptors and F-4 fighter bombers, – and, possibly later, F-15 interceptors, would permit the Shah to transfer older weapons, including aircraft to Pakistan. There is also no reason to believe that the United States government would not encourage such a program given the Nixon Doctrine's emphasis of regional self-defense.

As much as Bhutto may wish to publicize the independence of Pakistan's foreign policy, therefore, sincerity notwithstanding, no degree of rhetoric can disentangle the country from a web of global plays and counterplays. South Asia, like other regions of the world, has been made the interest of the major powers and neither Pakistan nor its large and menacing neighbor can ignore or avoid this reality. The Indo-Pakistan War of 1971 clearly placed the United States and the Soviet Union on opposite sides and neither the subsequent visitations by President Nixon and Secretary Brezhnev or the large emphasis placed upon *detente* between their two countries will alter the pattern of rivalry and confrontation in the vicinity of the Indian Ocean and the Persian Gulf. The Soviet Union has historic interests in the area, and it can only pursue them at the present time by undermining the United States twenty-five year association with India. This is not to suggest that the United States has not supplied the Soviet Union with an opportunity to maximize its friendship with India. The United States decision to support Pakistan at the expense of India in the Bangladesh affair was made demonstrably clear when the aircraft carrier U.S.S. Enterprise sailed into the Bay of Bengal. Moreover, the secret documents passed and later published by the columnist Jack Anderson only tended to dramatize in a personal way what was already clear in general terms.

Before the winter of 1971 the United States had managed a delicate equilibrium between the principal antagonists in the region, allying with one side while simultaneously assisting the other. The tragedy that erupted in Bengal shattered this gymnastic diplomatic act, however, and the consequences were not only detrimental to the United States promoted status quo, they also had direct bearing on the degree of latitude open to the indigenous policymakers. In Pakistan's case, Zulfikar Ali Bhutto may be more, not less, susceptible to major power maneuver; even though he might prove to be less constrained by formal international arrangements.

On January 28, 1972, approximately five weeks after assuming office,

Bhutto addressed his nation on the occasion of the Muslim festival day of Id-ul-Azha. The President was determined not to share in the traditional happiness that marked the day. His words were solemn and remindful of what had befallen the country in the previous month. "We have lost our honor and we have suffered national humiliation," was his theme (Bhutto 1972). Bhutto had just returned from a whirlwind tour to eight Middle East and North African countries. His itinerary included Iran, Turkey, Morocco, Algeria, Tunisia, Libya, Egypt and Syria.[1] On the one hand, such visits aimed at reassuring Pakistan's close and marginal friends that the country was repairing the damage done by the war, and under new leadership was dedicated to playing a significant role in world politics. On the other hand, the country needed a boost in its confidence and the new government sensed that such travels would assist in this effort. On January 30 President Bhutto carried this latter point a step further. Dramatizing his administration's "new" foreign policy, Bhutto revealed he was taking Pakistan out of the Commonwealth. The President's action was prompted by the decision of Great Britain, Australia and New Zealand to recognize the Bangladesh government. In fact, Bhutto called his action "an appropriate countermeasure" (*New York Times*, January 13, 1972). At the same time he revealed that normal bilateral relations would continue between Pakistan and the countries involved. After adding that relations with Britain remained cordial, Bhutto commented that "national honor is more important than pounds, shillings and pence" (*Ibid*). Thus, struggling to restore a sense of well-being to a demoralized population, Bhutto, through his actions and foreign tours, linked Pakistanis with their Muslim brethren in other lands. By breaking with the Commonwealth, he seemed to be cutting Pakistan free of its colonial past. In the latter, Pakistan was thought to be giving up little material advantage. Britain's entry into the Common Market transformed the Commonwealth into little more than an historic relic and the economic value of the organization was judged to be minimal. Taken together, the Middle East tour and the severance of Commonwealth ties aimed at giving the Pakistani people pride in themselves and their new government.

Bhutto's next foreign journey was arranged to reinforce this initial effort. Bhutto visited the People's Republic of China on February 1 and 2, 1972, and on the former date he had a publicized audience with Chairman Mao Tsetung. Bhutto's visit to China had more than ceremonial significance, however. The President was seeking military stores needed to replenish the Pakistan armed forces, and Premier Chou En-lai's statement that the Chinese were not "ammunition merchants" but would meet Pakistan's defense needs on a gratis basis was considered a very friendly gesture. More important at the moment

---

1 In May, Bhutto would make an even more extensive journey visiting fourteen countries in the Middle East and Africa. They were: Kuwait, The Union of Arab Emirates, Iraq, Lebanon, Jordan, Saudi Arabia, Somalia, Ethiopia, Sudan, Nigeria, Guinea, Mauritania, Turkey and Iran. Bhutto did not visit Afghanistan, Pakistan's northwestern Muslim neighbor, in either journey. A discussion of Pakistan-Afghanistan relations will be found below.

though was China's decision to cancel a $ 110,000,000 debt growing out of the 1965 Indo-Pakistan War while deferring for twenty years the repayment of a $ 200,000,000 loan made in 1970. China also put India on notice that there would be no peace in the subcontinent until all Pakistani territories were evacuated. Nonetheless, there was only the hint that China was going to forward new military supplies to Pakistan, but an understanding to this effect is found in the communique following the visit. Moreover, the Chinese were less fulsome in their condemnation of India as well as their warnings to that country. It need only be recalled that Chi Peng-fei, the Chinese Foreign Minister assured the Pakistani nation in November, 1971, only weeks before the Indian attack, that his government would "resolutely support them in their just struggle to defend their State sovereignty and national independence" (*Pakistan News Digest*, November 15, 1971). Chinese declarations, however, are not always measured by subsequent actions.

President Bhutto's visit to the Soviet Union followed in mid-March, 1972, despite the role played by that communist state in the events of 1971. Bhutto made the trip in order to demonstrate his neutrality vis-a-vis the great powers. Although little of substance emanated from his talks with Soviet leadership, it was agreed in principle to restore economic relations damaged by the war. Another aspect of the visit, however, was Bhutto's projected summit meeting with the Indian Prime Minister, Madame Gandhi. Bhutto wanted to lay Pakistan's case before the Soviet leaders prior to meeting with Madame Gandhi. By so doing it was hoped the Soviet Union would use its influence to resolve some of the larger issues, such as the return of the 93,000 prisoners captured in East Pakistan by the Indian army.

Although Bhutto did not visit the United States during his first year in office, relations with the United States were warm and constructive. On March 30, 1972 an agreement was signed in Islamabad which pledged the United States to continue funding the development of the Indus Basin Hydro-Electric Project. The project underway since 1961 at a cost of two and a half billion dollars is scheduled for completion in 1976, with the United States providing approximately 40 percent of the total financing. The American Charge d'Affairs noted the project helped strengthen the bonds existing between the two countries.[1]

While Pakistan's external fences were being mended and reinforced, the domestic scene was also receiving considerable attention. Of crucial importance in this period was the presidential order lifting martial law and the call to the National Assembly to adopt an Interim Constitution. Both were accomplished between April 17 and 21. The National Assembly also proceeded with the establishment of a committee to draft the new permanent constitution and the date of August 14, 1973 was targeted for its promulgation. President Bhutto also used the occasion to sum up his administration's work in both the domestic

---

1 The United States did not appoint an ambassador to Pakistan until December 1973.

and foreign fields. After noting that the country was stable and beginning to raise itself out of the rubble of the 1971 war, he turned to the subject of foreign policy.

In this section of his speech President Bhutto alluded to his upcoming talks with Madame Gandhi and reiterated a stand he had taken long before his assumption of the President's office. He cited many outstanding differences with India and that Pakistan sought the return of its territory as well as those captured in the war. But he insisted there would be no yielding to a "dictated, imposed peace." He also singled out the Muslim bloc of nations, China and the United States as having demonstrated the greatest friendship toward Pakistan. And so as to give more meaning to this remark, President Bhutto placed Pakistan's policy in its new geopolitical setting:

> The severance of our eastern limb by force has significantly altered our geographic focus. This will naturally affect our geopolitical perspective. The geographical distance between us and the nations of South East Asia has grown. This does not mean that we have lost interest in the welfare of these peoples. Nevertheless, at the moment, as we stand, it is within the ambit of South and Western Asia. It is here that our primary concern must henceforth lie.

> There is the whole uninterrupted belt of Muslim nations . . . Clearly we have to make a major effort in building upon the fraternal ties that already bind us to the Muslim world (*Pakistan Affairs*, May 16, 1972).

Pakistan has always looked to the Muslim states for support and encouragement but it is only with Iran and Turkey that it has managed to develop full-blown relationships. First, through the Central Treaty Organization, and, since 1964, with the help of the Regional Cooperation for Development (RCD) – Turkey, Iran and Pakistan, it has engaged in a variety of economic, cultural and military ventures. There is no avoiding the importance of Pakistan to Iran and vice versa and the turbulence on their shared border in Baluchistan is of great concern to both countries. There is also no ignoring the Shah of Iran's alleged fears that the next breakaway nationalist movement may be found in Baluchistan. Despite an outward appearance of friendship toward the Soviet Union, there is the strong belief that the Soviet Union seeks the "liberation" of Baluchistan from both Pakistani and Iranian rule. The Shah is reported in the *Christian Science Monitor* of February 2, 1973, as having "told visitors that Iran would react energetically if Pakistan were threatened with internal breakdown," particularly in proximity to its own frontiers. The seriousness with which the two leaders view the situation can be gauged by the numerous visits that they make between each other's capitals.[1] The joint communique issued on May 14, 1973, for instance, declares that both President Bhutto and the Shah of

---

1 According to the *Christian Science Monitor* "Members of the Shah's government. . . use the Baluchi argument as one justification for the huge buildup of Iranian military and naval forces in the Persian Gulf and the establishment of two naval bases at Chah Bahar and Jask, on the Indian Ocean." February 2, 1973.

Iran would resolutely stand by each other in all matters bearing on their national independence and territorial integrity."

The troubles in Baluchistan and on Pakistan's frontiers in general were heightened when the Bhutto government revealed that Soviet arms had been smuggled into the country and secreted in the Iraqi Embassy at Islamabad. It was further reported that security agents had discovered copies of a map showing a liberated Baluchi state that stretched from the Soviet border in Iran's northeast province of Khorassan to the Persian Gulf. India has also been implicated in this plot but has denied such allegations (*India News*, July 6, 1973 and July 13, 1973). Baluchi nationalism has its roots in the 1950's but remained inchoate until 1971. The use of Pakistani troops against tribal factions in this vast, desert-like region also has a long history, but the fact that the Army is being utilized at this time must be considered significant. A World Baluchi Organization organized by Mahmoud Hisham Sindjari, and the Baluch Warna, a more radical group under the leadership of Akbar Khan Bugti, were both formed in 1972. Each organization insists on creating a unified, independent and sovereign Baluchi nation, and both appear to have ties to the Baluchistan Liberation Front which operates clandestinely in Iran.

As noted in the beginning of this essay, Pakistan's future may well rest on its ability to cope with dissident provincialists. Military force is not the sole answer, both Iran and Pakistan understand this simple fact. Joint economic projects in the vicinity of the Pakistan-Iranian frontier can be anticipated in a concerted effort to come to grips with the problem. Still, it is not extraordinary that the Pakistan government should announce a large defense budget for the fiscal year 1972–73. The report stressed that approximately 60 percent of all government revenues would be used for refurbishing the armed forces. Of a total budget of 7.43 billion rupees, military spending was anticipated to be in excess of 4.46 billion (*New York Times*, June 18, 1972). With such an outlay for defense it was more than obvious that Pakistan would have to look to its more affluent friends and allies in order to fund its development programs. In this context the United Sates, China, and Iran were envisaged as playing important roles.[1]

The Afghanistan Dilemma

Pakistan and Afghanistan have never been especially friendly. The history of their antagonism is traced from the independence of Pakistan in 1947. Afghanistan did not accept the Durand Line (1893) which established the frontier between the two states and has promoted the creation of a separate

---

1 The Pakistan government labeled all reports that their defense budget was the largest ever as "tendentious." It went on to cite the following: "During the last fiscal year Pakistan earmarked $ 714 million for defense at the devaluation rate as compared to a defense provision in the new budget of $ 402 million. As for allocations in the developmental sector, the budget makes plain that the exceptional circumstances of the past

Pathan state in the region of Pakistan's North West Frontier Province since that date. The would-be state that the Afghans call "Pakhtunistan," and the movement organized in its behalf has caused the two countries to clash militarily. Border skirmishes have been numerous, with the last serious altercations occurring in the early 1960's. Unlike India and Pakistan, however, Pakistan and Afghanistan have avoided major engagements. Relations between the two countries, therefore, have run between poor and lukewarm. And the neighboring states continue to eye one another suspiciously.

It must be emphasized that Pakistan, more so than Afghanistan, has sought to improve relations. Afghanistan has ignored all Pakistani overtures, turning them aside on the theory that Pakistan is not a free agent and seeks to embroil the land-locked state in a struggle with tne great powers. It is for this reason that Afghanistan not only refused to join the Baghdad Pact (CENTO) in 1955, but was among the first to condemn it. Even the Regional Cooperation for Development (RCD) was judged an instrument of the United States, and Afghanistan has never shown the slightest inclination in joining that organization. It may also be recalled that Afghanistan cast the only vote against Pakistan's admission to the United Nations in 1950. It is against this background that Pakistani-Afghan relations must be evaluated, and the recent developments in Afghanistan which witnessed the overthrow of King Zahir Shah and the return to power of his cousin, Sardar Daoud, point to intensified and not diminishing tension.

If the difficulties in Pakistan's Baluchistan province and Iranian Baluchistan are in any way related to the policy of the Soviet Union, then the re-establishment of Sardar Daoud's power in Afghanistan must be considered ominous. Daoud was the power behind the throne between 1953 and 1963 and perhaps the most vocal proponent of "Pakhtunistan." In 1954, through Daoud's efforts, Afghanistan became the first Muslim country to receive Soviet military

---

year notwithstanding, Pakistan is determined to press ahead with its program of economic development."

Revenue Expenditure

	1971–72 Budget	1971–72 Budget Revised	1972–73 Rs. in crores Budget
Rev. Collecting Depts.	7.72	5.77	5.30
Debt Service	128.96	156.78	193.56
Civil Admin.	80.56	78.29	90.35
Defense	340.00	426.00	423.00
Grants to Provinces	18.48	25.20	3.98
Others	29.96	25.86	28.85
Total	605.23	717.90	743.44

Source: *Interim Report Series* Pakistan's Fourth Five Year Plan, 1970–75, Vo., 14, No. 9, July-August 1972.

assistance. (Egypt was to receive its first arms shipments in 1955). In 1955 the Soviet leaders visited Kabul and extended long-range economic aid and renewed a treaty of nonaggression. Afghanistan also received military and economic development aid from the United States, and the latter is still continued. In 1956 Daoud signed still another agreement which brought Afghanistan jet aircraft as well as heavy armor and artillery. As a result, both United States and Turkish military assistance was phased out. Soviet advisors replaced both and the Afghan army almost doubled its size, approaching approximately 100,000. Senior Army officers and rank-and-file elements were recruited from the tribal population, namely the Hazaras, Pathans, Uzbeks and Tajiks. Daoud's influence among the undisciplined tribal people was unquestioned. And as he modernized the Afghan army with Soviet assistance, these same tribes became less troublesome for the ruling elite in Kabul. Relative peace among the tribes provided the more sophisticated urban population with new political opportunities.

Although small in size, Afghanistan's intelligentsia in the capital began to assert itself in the early 1960s and their insistence on political reform apparently convinced King Zahir Shah that the medieval political family system was no longer fashionable. The same reform gave the King a chance to rid himself of Daoud's shadow. Hence, Daoud was dismissed from his post and a commoner made Prime Minister. A new constitution was put into force in 1964–65, and Article 24 clearly specified that no member of the royal family could participate in political parties, hold ministerial offices or obtain seats in the parliament or supreme court (Weinbaum, 1972). Daoud did not fight the King's action and accepted the new constitutional order despite his continuing control over the tribal people and Army.

Daoud looked on as Afghanistan fumbled with its new parliamentary experiment. The King still refused to yield his personal power and governments rose and fell with frequent abandon. Riots involving the intelligentsia, particularly the student population of Kabul, were common and by 1969 conservative elements gained control of the parliament. Governmental corruption and inefficiency became especially pronounced when the country was seized by drought and famine conditions took a heavy toll of life. Moreover, the King had promised to establish a political party system but kept postponing the implementation of the proposal. Thus when Zahir Shah departed the country for medical treatment, public discontent was rampant and the scene was set for a dramatic change.

On July 17, 1973, King Zahir Shah was deposed, the monarchy was abolished and Prince Daoud proclaimed the country a republic.[1] It is note-

---

1   ["The King of Afghanistan, Mohammad Zahir Shah, announced his abdication in a statement issued by the Afghan Embassy in Rome. The King was deposed last month while he was visiting Italy.

"In the statement, the 59-year-old former monarch said he would 'abide by the wishes of the people' of his country who had 'welcomed the establishment of a republican regime as their future form of government.' In addition, he said he was placing himself 'as an Afghan citizen under the banner of Afghanistan.' " He did not indicate whether he would live in exile or go home (*New York Times*, August 25, 1973). Ed.]

Table 1

Horizontal Social Groups in Afghanistan

Horizontal Group	Number	Identity	Vertical Element Included in Horizontal Group
1. Elite	2–3 thousand	Royal family Top government officials Wealthy merchants Large landowners Tribal chiefs	Pathans-Sunnis
2. Intelligentsia	8–10 thousand	High government employees Professional men Teachers, students Literati Top religious leaders Army officers	Pathans, Tajik-Sunni but, some Shia Qizilbash
3. Urban Middle Class	800,000 to 1,000,000	Lower civil servants Shopkeepers Scribes Accountants Artisans Literate religious leaders, etc.	Tajiks, Uzbeks, Pathans, some Turkomen and Hazaras
4. Lower Classes a. Urban	8 million		
1. Proletariat	20,000	Factory and semi-skilled workers	Tajiks, Hazaras, Pathans
2. Military, Police, etc.	40,000	Enlisted men in Armed Forces, Police, gendar-merie	Tajiks, Hazaras, Uzbeks, Turkomen
b. Rural			
1. Cultivators	7 million	Small landowners, peasants and semi-nomads	Pathans, Tajiks, Uzbeks, Hazaras
2. Nomads	200,000	Pure nomads, nonculti-vators	Pathans, Turkomen

Note: Population figures are estimates.
Source: "Afghanistan" *An Asia Society Paper,* January, 1963, P. 5.

worthy that Daoud put aside his royal title and assumed the leadership of the country as a Lieutenant General in the Afghan army. Daoud felt compelled to issue a statement on July 25 that the Soviet Union had nothing to do with the coup d'etat. Rumors were already circulating that the Soviet Union had engineered the plot against the King and that Daoud would not hesitate to heat up the "Pakhtunistan" issue with Pakistan. In this context, it is interesting to note that the Soviet Union and India recognized the new Republic on July 19th. Pakistan followed on July 22nd.

Pakistan's early recognition of the Daoud government did not transform Afghanistan into an instant friend. Pakistan's immediate domestic political problems lay along her western frontier. President Bhutto has virtually no power in this heavily tribal belt and he defers to local leadership that does not reflect his Pakistan People's Party interest. Thus when General Daoud announced on July 29th that Afghanistan's "political dispute" with Pakistan is "unresolved," Bhutto could not remain silent or pretend friendship. He is quoted as saying: "The claim for a new state is not new. We have lived with it in the past. But if, God forbid, certain developments should put a strain on our relations, we are quite capable of looking after our national interests" (*New York Times*, August 2, 1973).

Barring Soviet intervention Pakistan should be able to cope with a possible threat from Afghanistan. But the picture is made complicated by the role that India might choose to play, and above all, by the uncertain loyalties of the tribal population, and especially its leadership in the North West Frontier Province. Should the latter decide to join Daoud in a joint endeavor against Bhutto, and should the Baluchistan situation worsen at the same time, Pakistan's future, to say nothing about Bhutto's would be in grave jeopardy. Iran, as already noted, could play a role in such a scenario. A conflict would also indirectly involve the United States. The situation at this writing therefore must be considered fluid. If Daoud is bent on pressing his claim to "Pakhtunistan" Bhutto's new Pakistan could face its most severe test.

India and the Simla Conference

The summit meeting between President Bhutto and Prime Minister Gandhi was slated for June 28, 1972. It was the first face-to-face meeting between the leaders of India and Pakistan since the Tashkent Conference and which Bhutto had attended in his capacity as foreign minister in the Ayub Khan government. Tashkent became a symbol of Ayub's weakness and was ironically exploited by Bhutto in his rise to political power. Now, however, it was Bhutto's turn to meet with Indian leadership, and he was careful to protect himself from his indigenous adversaries who might seek to use the earlier precedent for their own advantage. Granted, Bhutto's situation was not the same as Ayub Khan's when he had met with Indian Prime Minister, Lal Bahadur Shastri. Ayub had led Pakistan into the war with India and it was also he who had decided to lead the country out of it. Bhutto, on the other hand, came to power after a decisive military defeat, and he was not associated with that decision-making process. Bhutto, therefore, could negotiate from a base of political support which Auyb did not enjoy. All the same, Bhutto did not take any chances. Addressing the nation on the eve of his departure, he reiterated the need and his desire for peace but he steadfastly adhered to specific principles. Pakistan, he declared, wants the prisoners returned, its territory restored in the Sind and Punjab, and a solution to the Kashmir problem.

Before this speech the prisoner issue had been among the less prominent concerns expressed by the Pakistan government. But as the months dragged on and the Indians refused to release the POW's, and indeed when it appeared that a number of them would be placed on trial for war crimes in Bangladesh, the Pakistan government could no longer pretend that they were a lesser matter. Time apparently was not on Pakistan's side in this dispute. And despite the material cost, not to ignore the cost in prestige, the Indians were determined to use the prisoners as a major chip in their negotiations. Nevertheless, it seems reasonable to assume that Bhutto felt this was an issue that could be resolved at the summit.

At Simla, President Bhutto was disturbed to find the Indians determined to secure a "No-War" pledge and a formal treaty of "non-aggression" before agreeing to any Pakistani demands. He was sensitive to the interpretation that his opposition could give to such a pact, but perhaps more important, he could not afford to antagonize the armed forces against whom such a treaty would be directed. A treaty of nonaggression might well include articles calling for a mutual reduction in forces which the Pakistan military would not accept. In the opinion of high army officials such an agreement would also mean Pakistan must disengage itself from Kashmir, an unthinkable thought even in the country's current state. Hence Bhutto was compelled to reject even a simple declaration to the affect that Pakistan would resolve never to go to war with India again. It might be noted that the last "No-War" pact between the two countries was signed in 1950. It has been alleged that as a consequence of that act the then Prime Minister, Liaquat Ali Khan, faced a challenge from his military hierarchy, the affair being known as the Rawalpindi Conspiracy. Bhutto had no intention of testing his popularity by accepting such terms from Indira Gandhi.

The Simla talks lasted five days and an accord was signed and publicized, but neither side viewed it with much enthusiasm. In the concrete areas of the accord the following are noted:

Steps shall be taken to resume communications, postal, telegraphic, sea, land, including border posts, and air links, including overflights.

Appropriate steps shall be taken to promote travel facilities for the nationals of the other country.

Trade and cooperation in economic and other agreed fields will be resumed as far as possible.

Exchange in the fields of science and culture will be promoted. In this connection delegations from the two countries will meet from time to time to work out the necessary details.

Indian and Pakistani forces shall be withdrawn to their side of the international border.

In Jammu and Kashmir, the line of control resulting from the cease-fire of December 17

1971, shall be respected by both sides without prejudice to the recognized position of either side. Neither side shall seek to alter it unilaterally, irrespective of mutual differences and legal interpretations. Both sides further undertake to refrain from the threat or the use of force in violation of this line (*New York Times*, July 3, 1972).

The withdrawal of forces noted in the accords was to take place within thirty days following ratification by the appropriate national organs. The question of ratification pointed to President Bhutto's pledge upon entering the talks that he would not impose a settlement on his country. Hence the Pakistan National Assembly met on July 15, ratified the agreement, and legitimated the actions of their President.

The Simla accord did not satisfy India's desire for a "No-War" agreement. Nor did Bhutto agree to recognize Bangladesh. On the Indian side, there was no urgency to release the Pakistani prisoners or to prevent the Bangladesh government from putting a significant number on trial. Moreover, the Kashmir clause did not satisfy Bhutto's continued call that "self-determination" be granted the people of the mountain state.[1] But even the one significant agreement, namely, the withdrawal of forces could not be satisfied according to the agreed schedule. It was not until December that this latter issue was finally resolved. The inordinate delay created new tensions between the two antagonists and whatever goodwill may have been created by the Simla talks was quickly dissipated. Thus the second summit which would have brought Madame Gandhi to Pakistan was put off indefinitely, and the prisoner issue was permitted to fester.

Bilateral and Multilateral Relations

As noted above Bhutto has had to work with a legacy that is not easily transformed. Among other things, he inherited a variety of associations and alliances which in his judgment required a more systematic appraisal of their value and continuing utility. If Bhutto was going to assure China and the Soviet Union that Pakistan did not represent a threat to them while at the same time remaining in the good graces of the United States, it was certainly necessary to steer a middle course between them. Hence the only alliance which Pakistan publicizes is the one which does not involve any of the great powers. This grouping, known as the Regional Cooperation for Development (RCD), was formed in the summer of 1964 between Pakistan, Iran and Turkey. Zulfikar Ali Bhutto was foreign minister at the time and in a speech at the Fifteenth Ministerial Council Meeting of RCD in Izmir, Turkey, on April 7,

---

1 The settlement finally thrashed out on December 7, 1972, made the existent "line of control" in Kashmir a firm boundary for the indefinite future. It is ironic that the very arrangement which Ayub Khan agreed to at Tashkent in January, 1966, and which Bhutto disputed so vehemently, was now an accepted fact. See the author's *The Ayub Khan Era: Politics in Pakistan, 1958-1969*, Syracuse: Syracuse University Press, 1971, pp. 50-113.

1972, Mahmud Ali Kasuri, the then Pakistan Law Minister, identified the President as one of the principal architects of the alliance.

RCD does not address itself to political union. Nor is military affairs a focal point of RCD's deliberations. Rather, RCD continues to represent a group of nation-states having geographical contiguity, harmonious political relations and the mutual desire to improve their economic performance. RCD is an alliance without anger; it is directed at no particular state or states and is relatively free of military encumbrances. RCD focuses specific and exclusive attention upon the positive goals of furthering understanding and generating material progress within the region. Its existence helps to stabilize and ensure the friendly relations now obtaining between the three countries. It is also a further reminder that economic development can be accelerated if nations can find a way to cooperate rather than antagonize one another.

RCD can best be described as an Asian mini-Common Market (Bhutto, 1973). The organization has a complex structure and various components meet on a continuing basis for economic, cultural and informational purposes. It was only in September, 1972, however, that the three countries seriously considered an agreement aiming at the liberalization of trade through the removal of all national barriers.

Bilateral economic and cultural activities with other countries have reinforced this RCD initiative. On October 18, 1972, Pakistan and the United States entered into an agreement extending the work of the United States Education Foundation in Pakistan (USEF/P). A similar cultural and scientific pact was signed with Rumania. In the economic area agreements were completed with Japan, Yugoslavia, Great Britain, France, Italy, the Netherlands, Norway and the Federal Republic of Germany. All were concerned with the rescheduling of debts, or the acquisition of new loans to ease Pakistan over 1972–73.

On November 8, 1972, the Bhutto government took a more celebrated step when it formally announced its decision to withdraw from the South East Asia Treaty Organization (SEATO). The very next day the Pakistan foreign office declared it would recognize the Democratic Republic of Vietnam, and, two days later, the Democratic People's Republic of Korea. Later in the year, East Germany was also recognized. These announcements, taken together, were described by the Pakistan government as a watershed in the country's foreign relations. Although nothing sinister lay behind the decisions, they are of special importance and deserve limited analysis.

President Bhutto was on record since 1962 as having less than genuine interest in Pakistan's western alliances (Bhutto, 1964; 1966; 1969). CENTO in addition to SEATO has been linked with the foreign policy position of the United States, and member states such as Iran and Turkey were pressured by President Johnson to refrain from aiding Pakistan in its war with India in 1965. On numerous occasions, and prior to his becoming President, Bhutto called upon the Pakistan government to withdraw from the alliances. That SEATO, therefore, was considered ripe for cutting is not surprising in the circumstances.

President Bhutto is said to have informed the United States that his country would leave SEATO at an appropriate moment. When that moment did come Pakistan acted within the limits specified under Article 10 of the Treaty and hence did not move rashly. It was also obvious that SEATO ceased to encompass Pakistan after the severing of its eastern wing, and the emergence of the new state of Bangladesh. Pakistan was now geographically removed from Southeast Asia and Bhutto earlier in the year had taken pains to explain that Pakistan's concern would be with South and South West Asia. Moreover, SEATO was organized in 1954 at the urging of the Eisenhower-Dulles administration following the Geneva Accords which ended the French struggle in Indochina. It was intended to put the Chinese on notice that their attempts at penetration of Southeast Asia would be met by the combined forces of the nations of the area, but essentially by the United States.

The alliance, however, was a constant embarrassment to Pakistani leadership which sought to normalize relations with China. Nevertheless, all thought about taking Pakistan out of the alliance had to be weighed against the cost in relations with the United States. Neither Ayub Khan nor Yahya Khan felt they had the clear opportunity to make such a break and yet Zulfikar Ali Bhutto could proceed without fear of serious repercussions. With the United States involvement in Indochina winding down, with Washington-Peking relations established and being nourished, and with Pakistan no longer identified with Southeast Asia, such a decision proved not only painless but perfectly reasonable. Thus when the United States, the Philippines and Thailand all recognized Bangladesh there was no longer a need to sustain the relationship. Furthermore, SEATO countries failed to aid Pakistan either in the 1965 or the more recent 1971 war with India. The utility of the organization to Pakistan had proven to be non-existent.

With this action Pakistan also put all the major powers on notice that it would no longer consider new military alliances as relevant for its requirements. Hence the Soviet Union's pressing of an Asian security pact was taken note of but was to be carefully avoided by the Pakistan government. Pakistan's ties to CENTO are still heavily military but the country is linked with that organization because its principal neighbors, Iran and Turkey, have shown no indication of quitting. The three countries, and particularly Iran and Pakistan as we have seen, are dependent on one another for defensive purposes and in the present unpredictable situation neither country is prepared to take unilateral action simply out of principle. In other works, judged on the basis of cost-benefit analysis, Pakistan needs CENTO and Bhutto is not about to follow the SEATO decision with a like determination. The Middle East, and, in particular, the Persian Gulf, is the most strategic region in terms of great power rivalry in the world today. Moreover, United States national security policy stresses open sea lanes and resource access, and Pakistan is viewed as playing an essential role in this regard. If Pakistan can expect to receive military assistance from the United States it will be with this understanding. At the same time, Pakistan insists on maintaining friendly relations with the Soviet Union. The latter, however, will also be on notice that its intimacy with India is a prime consideration in their future relationships.

On balance, then, Pakistan's foreign relations will be pursued on a country-by-country basis with the possible exception of the RCD arrangement. The United States and China will be treated somewhat equally and efforts will be made to satisfy the Soviet Union that Pakistan poses no threat to it. But the relationship with the Soviet Union must be on a different level from that of the other major powers given that state's support of India. This also means that Pakistan's principal source of aid in both military and economic spheres will have to come from the United States, with China supplementing what it can. Unfortunately, however, Bhutto's reasonably good relations with the Nixon administration may not be sufficient to satisfy his government's requirements for assistance, given the low esteem in which Pakistan is held in the United States Congress. Cuts in Nixon's foreign aid program for 1973–74 do not augur well for Pakistan. Sufficient residual ill-will exists in the Congress toward Pakistan to make the likelihood of large-scale assistance most unpromising.

Nor can Bhutto threaten to move closer to China, or indeed to become more familiar with the Soviet Union. It is difficult to envisage Pakistan being any closer to China than it is at present. China is not about to take up the Pakistan cause with India in any fashion different from that followed in the last eight years. And relations with the Soviet Union are regulated by perceptions of India. Certainly the Soviet Union has more to gain by maximizing its advantages in India than in Pakistan. And again, Pakistan is linked ever more closely with Iran and that middle eastern country is not about to alter its relations with the United States so long as the Shah remains the master of the political situation.[1]

Pakistan and Bangladesh

Pakistan's relations with Bangladesh remain strained and somewhat obscure. President Bhutto's release of and assistance in returning Sheikh Mujibur Rahman to Dacca has not been reciprocated by the Bangladeshi authorities. On the contrary, Bhutto has been charged with sheltering ulterior motives. It is alleged that he seeks a working confederation with Bangladesh, prior to re-absorbing the east wing into the Pakistan union. The Bangladeshis have therefore turned aside all such suggestions as unrealistic and tantamount to sub-

---

1 Hartirath Singh, editor of the Foreign Trade Review, an Indian publication, is quoted as having said: "The meteoric increase in the Iranian armaments has caused tremors of anxiety in India. The hazy picture that seems to be emerging—perhaps in the not-too-distant future—is one of China-United States-Pakistan-Iran axis." Such rumors as well as one in Pakistan insists the Indians and Iraqis are conspiring against both Pakistan and Iran by provoking the Baluchi independence movement (*The New York Times*, July 5, 1973).

verting the nation's independence. It is also important to note that Pakistan continues to direct broadcasts to Bangladesh as well as report the plight of that society since the Indian invasion. Moreover, Pakistan has issued no definitive statement sanctioning or recognizing the separation of a sovereign, independent Bangladesh. Pakistan, with China's help, has also blocked Bangladesh's admission into the United Nations.

The justification for preventing the Bangladesh government from taking its seat in the United Nations remains the prisoner of war issue and the threats to their well-being. So long as Bangladesh insists on retaining and putting on trial some POW's as war criminals, the Bhutto administration refuses to accept the existence of Bangladesh, let alone permit it a seat in the UN. To illustrate this problem there is the statement by Bhutto during a press conference on December 20, 1972. The President explained that many Pakistanis oppose recognition and given the alleged severe treatment of the POW's they were calling upon him "to beat the life out of the Bengalis" living in Pakistan. "Yet they [the Pakistanis] say they can't abandon their brothers. If they're your brothers why the hell are you badgering me to knock the hell out of them here?" When a query followed about the 300,000 Bengalis living in Pakistan being returned to Bangladesh, Bhutto is reported to have replied: "The point is, I don't want to use them as a lever, but if they [Bangladesh] are going to keep our people – 90,000 – and give all sorts of unreasonable and unethical arguments for it, I can't just keep on unilaterally making one gesture after another" (*Pakistan Affairs*, January 1, 1973). In a later interview Bhutto voiced the fear that if trials of Pakistanis are held in Bangladesh, his army would demand that trials be held in Pakistan of Bengalis who are accused of conspiring against the government and nation.

The difficulties in overcoming this impasse are obvious. Neither the Bangladesh or Pakistan governments are strong enough to act independently of their constituents. Mujib was released as Bhutto himself has remarked, while his country was in a "stupor." Had he delayed taking this action it would have been impossible in the circumstances that followed – or so it would seem. Bhutto has since offered to send more than 300,000 tons of rice to the food-short state but Bangladesh has refused to accept this largesse. Suggestions that the Bengali population in Pakistan be exchanged for the POW's have likewise been rejected. In fact, Bangladesh, according to Pakistani authorities, has not indicated they are prepared to negotiate with Pakistan on any terms suggesting mutual compromise. Hence, if a breakthrough is to be achieved, it is India that will have to lead the way. Thus far, however, India is reluctant to force Mujib's hand, possibly fearing that by so doing the Bangladesh leader would lose the much needed support of his followers. The consequences of Mujib's fall could force the Indians either to take more forceful action in Bangladesh or allow for the emergence of a government which might not be in India's best interest. It is not to be concluded that a new Bangladesh government would be any more friendly toward Bhutto's Pakistan. Rather, such a chain of developments could lead to the further radicalization of Bangladesh. Such a development might have direct bearing on the Congress Party's control over the Indian Union and it is bound to have repercussions in Pakistan as well.

Arms and Pakistan's National Security

Pakistan's dependence on outside sources for military hardware is critical. Pakistan has never been able to develop even a minimum defense industry, and its leaders are in a constant quandry on how to obtain the necessary arms to maintain a modern military establishment. Up to the 1965 Indo-Pakistan War the United States was Pakistan's chief supplier, providing an estimated $ 800 million of military goods (Barnds, 1972: 323). Since 1965, however, the United States has kept arms shipments comparatively small. The Johnson administration never could resume the flow in the aftermath of the Indo-Pakistan War and the simultaneous escalation of the American effort in Indo-china. Moreover, the Nixon administration was too consumed with the Vietnamization program, and Pakistan had become too much of a critic of United States policies for it to receive large shipments of armaments. Changes apparently were in the offing, given Yahya Khan's assistance in laying the groundwork for Henry Kissinger's and later the President's visit to Peking. But before the Pakistan government could capitalize on these developments, the tragedy in East Pakistan nullified whatever efforts were underway.

The Nixon administration sought to bolster Pakistan vis-a-vis the threat from India. Relatively small transfers of military equipment were made possible through Jordan, Turkey and Iran but by and large any significant supply of American arms was out of the question. The U.S. Congress was determined to prevent Pakistan from receiving new, large stores of weapons, and the revelations concerning the administrations's "tilt" in favor of Pakistan and away from India only reinforced this determination. It was not until March 14, 1973, that the United States government decided to resume some military shipments.

Up to this date the total embargo on military weapons to Pakistan had been very effective. The Nixon administration, however, decided that some 300 armored personnel carriers, other spare parts and "non-lethal" military equipment could now be passed to Pakistani authorities. The United States government justified its action by noting that: a) Pakistan is in a defensive position since its military defeat in December, 1971; b) in no way can these shipments alter the balance of power which is so preponderantly in favor of India; c) that for political and psychological reasons the shipment is absolutely essential not only to United States-Pakistan relations but also for stabilizing the Bhutto government domestically, and d) it was the United States government's hope that such shipments would make it more possible for Pakistan to reach a political settlement with India.

With the United States announcement, Pakistan was in a position to receive $ 1.2 million in spare parts, parachutes, and reconditioned aircraft engines ordered before the embargo was imposed in December, 1971. The 300 personnel carriers were valued at $ 13 million and this was supposedly contracted for in 1970 and a downpayment made sometime thereafter. An American State Department official noted that this would "wipe the slate clean." Although this may be the case, it was only a token of what Pakistan was seeking and there is the suggestion that more will be forthcoming if the Congress grants the Nixon administration its foreign aid requests. In the meantime the United States signaled its desire to step up assistance to Pakistan when the Agency for International Development made public two loans of $ 60 million to permit the importation of iron, steel, non-ferrous metals, fertilizer and tallow. This followed several other loans dealing with foodstuffs, general commodities, and the continued financing of the Tarbela Hydroelectric Project. The sum total of this economic assistance from March 1972 to March 1973 totaled approximately $ 280 million. In sum: the Bhutto government was no less dependent on the United States than its predecessors.

The Most Recent Phase

Pakistan's foreign policy for the remainder of 1973, and possibly beyond, appeared to focus on President Bhutto's six-day state visit to the United States in July. The sudden illness of President Nixon, however, forced cancellation of the tour but it was rescheduled for September. The consequences at this writing are far from clear. Events move with such rapidity that it is virtually impossible to predict even the most immediate developments with any accuracy. There are, nonetheless, patterns, and these can be traced and evaluated – and from this analysis conclusions can be drawn.

Bhutto is far from secure in his own homeland. The opposition is both vocal and powerful and all Bhutto's gifts of persuasion are required to maintain even a surface equilibrium. The POW and recognition of Bangladesh issues have overshadowed the production of a new constitution and the reinstatement of the parliamentary system. Moreover, solid gains in the economic sector have been generally disregarded, as have a whole series of agrarian, education and social reforms. As in the past, the key issues consuming the highest levels of government are in the sentimental and emotional realms.

It is fair to assert that Bhutto wished to clear away the debris left by the 1971 war with India before the new constitution went into force on August 14, 1973. This meant obtaining the release of the POW's and the simultaneous recognition of Bangladesh. The Joint Statement from India and Bangladesh of April 17, 1973, declared the former's willingness to continue negotiations with Pakistan if the Bhutto government recognized Bangladesh, permitted the 260,000 Biharis living in Bangladesh to leave for Pakistan, and accepted the fact that 195 POW's would be retained for trials as war criminals. The Bhutto government was incensed by the "take-it-or-leave-it" nature of the offer, but agreed to study its contents. Several weeks later it was judged to be entirely unacceptable and Pakistan announced that it was requesting the International Court of Justice to consider the problem under the 1948 Convention of the Prevention and Punishment of the Crime of Genocide. Pakistan argued that under the 1948 Convention only it had the right to exercise jurisdiction over the accused. India, it noted, had no legal justification for transfering the accused POW's to Bangladesh. Pakistan also insisted that the remaining POW's could not be detained while the question of the 195 alleged war criminals was being deliberated. In the case of the 93,000 POW's the Geneva Convention of 1949 concerning the treatment of prisoners of war, of which India is a signatory, was considered binding. According to Pakistan, the Joint Statement of April 17 was in complete contravention of this Convention, and the prisoners should have been returned following the formal surrender.

Despite the bitterness expressed between India and Pakistan, efforts at bringing the antagonists together were made at various levels. The new United States Ambassador to India, Daniel Moynihan, pressed the matter with the Indian authorities while the Nixon administration sought to move President Bhutto closer to a compromise situation. Of special importance was President Bhutto's scheduled trip to the United States. It is not surprising therefore that Bhutto should press his National Assembly for a vote on the issue of Bangladesh. On July 9, 1973, the Pakistan National Assembly in fact did authorize the President to recognize Bangladesh, but it was not a unanimous response. The opposition members in the Assembly walked out of the session and Bhutto accused them of aiding India, who he said no longer wanted Pakistan to recognize Bangladesh. "If we are foolish we will make Moslem Bengal into Hindu Bengal and that is why I want to recognize Moslem Bengal (*New York Times*, July 10, 1973).

Bhutto's continuance in office is seemingly dependent on how he weathers these next several months. The opposition in the Assembly was only symbolic of the real opposition that is to be found among members of the armed forces, the student community and conservative Muslim leaders – all of whom see Bhutto as selling out to the Hindus on the one hand, and possibly the United States on the other. Shades of Ayub Khan! This is why the talks with President Nixon were so vital. The United States had been increasing its economic and technical aid, but what Bhutto was desperately in need of was heightened military assistance. Only such shipments could temper the sentiment in the military and provide Bhutto with the leverage required to resolve, even minimally, the Indian and Bangladesh dilemmas.

It was anticipated that talks with India would commence immediately following the President's return from the United States.[1] Such talks are still

---

1 The new Pakistan-India talks were scheduled for July 24, 1973, and it was anticipated that a second summit would emerge from these meetings. In an obvious gesture of some goodwill India returned 438 sick and wounded POWs on July 11. This brought the total released to 2,264 which includes all the troops taken on the western front in the 1971 war. The Pakistanis months earlier returned all the Indian POWs in their possession (*The New York Times*, July 12, 1973).

planned for a date in August but can the Pakistan leader afford to meet with Indira Gandhi before he has certain assurances from the United States? At the present writing, President Bhutto will not meet with President Nixon before September and much history can be written between now and then.

Postscript

On August 29, 1973, P. N. Haksar, Mrs. Gandhi's special representative and Aziz Ahmed, Pakistan's Minister of State for Defense and Foreign Affairs signed an agreement in New Delhi which held out the possibility of repatriating the prisoners of war and exchanging those populations which found their lot in Bangladesh and Pakistan intolerable. The agreement read as follows:

1. The immediate implementation of the solution of those humanitarian problems is without prejudice to the respective positions of the parties concerned relating to the case of 195 prisoners of war referred to in clauses 6 and 7 of this paragraph;

2. Subject to clause (1), repatriation of all Pakistani prisoners of war and civilian internees will commence with utmost dispatch as soon as logistic arrangements are completed and from a date to be settled by mutual agreement;

3. Simultaneously repatriation of all Bengalees in Pakistan, and all Pakistanis in Bangladesh referred to in clause (5) below, to their respective countries will commence.

4. In the matter of repatriation of all categories of persons *the principle of simultaneity* will be observed throughout as far as possible.

5. Without prejudice to the respective positions of Bangladesh and Pakistan on the question of non-Bengalees who are stated to have "opted for repatriation in Pakistan," the Government of Pakistan, guided by considerations of humanity, agrees, initially, to receive a substantial number of such non-Bengalees from Bangladesh. It is further agreed that the Prime Ministers of Bangladesh and Pakistan or their designated representatives will thereafter meet to decide what additional number of persons who may wish to migrate to Pakistan may be permitted to do so. Bangladesh has made it clear that it will participate in such a meeting only *on the basis of sovereign equality.*

6. Bangladesh agreed that no trials of 195 prisoners of war shall take place during the entire period of repatriation and that pending a settlement envisaged in clause (7) below, *these prisoners of war shall remain in India.*

7. On completion of repatriation of Pakistani prisoners of war and civilian internees in India, Bengalees in Pakistan and Pakistanis in Bangladesh referred to in clause (5) above, or earlier if they so agree, Bangladesh, India and Pakistan will discuss and settle the question of 195 prisoners of war. Bangladesh has made it clear that it can participate in such a meeting *only on the basis of sovereign equality.*
   The special representatives are confident that the completion of repatriation provided for in this agreement would make a signal contribution to the promotion of reconciliation in the sub-continent and create an atmosphere favourable to a constructive outcome of the meeting of the three countries.

8. The time schedule for completion of repatriation of Pakistani prisoners of war and civilian internees from India, Bengalees from Pakistan, and Pakistanis referred to in clause (5) above from Bangladesh, will be worked out by India in consultation with Bangladesh and Pakistan, as the case may be. The Government of India will make logistic arrangements for Pakistani prisoners of war and civilian internees who are to be repatriated to Pakistan. The Government of Pakistan will make

logistic arrangements within its territory up to the agreed points of exit for repatriation of Bangladesh nationals to Bangladesh. The Government of Bangladesh will
make necessary arrangements for transport of these persons from such agreed points
of exit to Bangladesh. The Government of Bangladesh will make logistic arrangements within its territory up to the agreed points of exit for the movement of Pakistanis referred to in clause (5) above who will go to Pakistan. The Government of
Pakistan will make necessary arrangements for transport of these persons from such
agreed points of exit to Pakistan. In making logistic arrangements the Governments
concerned may seek the assistance of international humanitarian organizations and
others.

9. For the repatriation provided for in this agreement, representatives of the Swiss
    Federal Government and any international humanitarian organization entrusted
    with this task shall have unrestricted access at all time to Bengalees in Pakistan and
    to Pakistanis in Bangladesh referred to in clause (5) above. The Government of
    Bangladesh and the Government of Pakistan will provide all assistance and facilities
    to such representatives in this regard including facilities for adequate publicity for
    the benefit of persons entitled to repatriation under this agreement.

10. All persons to be repatriated in accordance with this agreement will be treated with
    humanity and consideration. The Government of India and the Government of
    Pakistan have concurred in this agreement. The special representative of the Prime
    Minister of India, having consulted the Government of Bangladesh, has also con-
    veyed the concurrence of the Bangladesh Government in this agreement.[1]

The above mentioned agreement is a step in the direction of resolving the
human dilemma but is does not answer the vital questions concerning the
trial of alleged war criminals or the recognition of Bangladesh by Pakistan. It is
this observer's opinion that much hard bargaining still lies ahead, and, given
the emphasis on the principle of *simultaneity* it could be many months and
possibly years before this particular chapter is closed.

BIBLIOGRAPHY

Barnds, William J.
   1972   India, Pakistan, and the Great Powers, New York: Praeger.
Bhutto, Zulfikar Ali
   1964   Foreign Policy of Pakistan, A Compendium of Speeches Made in the National
           Assembly of Pakistan, Karachi, Pakistan Institute of International Affairs.
   1966   The Quest For Peace, Karachi, Pakistan Institute of International Affairs.
   1969   The Myth of Independence, London: Oxford University Press.
   1972   Radio Address to the Nation, January 28, Islamabad.
   1973a Address to the Sixteenth Ministerial Council Meeting of the Regional Cooperation
           for Development, January 11, Islamabad.
   1973b Address before the National Assembly of Pakistan, April 14, Islamabad.
   1973c "Pakistan Builds Anew," Foreign Affairs, 51:3, April.
Burke, S. M.
   1973   Pakistan's Foreign Policy: An Historical Analysis, London: Oxford University
           Press.
Choudhury, G. W.
   1968   Pakistan's Relations with India, 1947–1966, New York: Praeger.
India News, New Delhi.

---

1 The text of this accord will be found in *India News*, September, 7, 1973. Italics have been
   added.

Jahan, Rounaq
    1972   Pakistan: Failure in National Integration, New York: Columbia University Press.
Malik, Hafeez
    1972   "Problems of Regionalism in Pakistan," presented at the American History Association, New Orleans, December.
    1974   "Emergence of the Federal Pattern in Pakistan: PPP-NAP Settlement," In, J. Henry Korson, ed., Contemporary Pakistan—Problems and Prospects, Leiden: E. J. Brill Co.
The New York Times, New York.
Pakistan Affairs, Washington, D.C.
Pakistan News Digest, Islamabad
Syed, Anwar
    1973   "Pakistan's Security Problem: A Bill of Constraints," Orbis, 16, 4, Winter.
United States
    1973a U.S. Foreign Policy, 1972: A Report of the Secretary of State Washington, D.C.
    1973b Foreign Policy for the 1970's: A Report to the Congress by Richard M. Nixon, President of the United States, May 3, 1973, Washington, D.C.
Weinbaum, Marvin G.
    1972   "Afghanistan: Non-Party Parliamentary Democracy," The Journal of Developing Areas, 7, October, 57–74.
Ziring, Lawrence
    1971   The Ayub Khan Era: Politics in Pakistan, 1958–69, Syracuse, Syracuse University Press.

Economic Reforms under the Bhutto Regime*

W. ERIC GUSTAFSON

University of California, Davis, U.S.A.

THERE IS AN Urdu couplet which, in free translation, runs, "The elephant has two sets of teeth, one for eating and one for show." Ripping this couplet rudely out of context – if it had one – I would like to pose the question of the extent to which the economic reforms of the Bhutto regime are for show, and the extent to which they get down to real business. It seems to me that there are some of each, but there is also the melancholy prospect that none of them will work, and we will be left only with the show. Cynicism about Pakistan has become one of Pakistan's most prominent exports, and I hope that I will not add unduly to the supply.

I

In the first burst of reform moves, clearly the "show" motivation was dominant. After an election campaign which made much of the evildoing of Pakistan's twenty-two families, it was only natural that on his second day in office, Bhutto should attack. He seized the passports belonging to the twenty-two richest families and their relatives and dependents, and sealed the borders of the country to all but religious pilgrims to prevent the flight of capital from Pakistan. This act was showing the tusks; it seems hard to imagine that the Government thought it could in fact accomplish much in the way of stemming the flight of capital by prohibiting exit. But the move did provide action, and action which was easy to take.[1]

In January the tempo accelerated. On the second of January it was announced that Ahmad Dawood and Fakhruddin Valika, two prominent industrialists, were under house arrest in Karachi (*Pakistan Times*, 1/2/72, 1:2), and this news was followed in the papers the next day by the announcement of the nationalization under the Economic Reforms Order (1972) of twenty firms, most of which were owned by members of the twenty-two families, with the

* This paper covers the reform efforts through early September 1973. I am grateful to a number of Pakistani friends for comment. They prefer to remain nameless.

1 New York *Times*, 22 December 1971, 1:6. The passports were later returned at a meeting in Karachi at which Bhutto adopted a somewhat conciliatory tone towards the businessmen. *Pakistan Times* (Lahore), 3/6/72. The President told them that "all restrictions on their travel abroad had been withdrawn to enable them to increase exports."

headline STATE CONTROL OVER TEN INDUSTRIES, and a subsidiary headline
FOREIGN INVESTMENT NOT AFFECTED. These twenty firms were supposed to be in
ten industries which sounded like what Nehru used to call the "commanding
heights" of the economy: iron and steel, basic metal industries, heavy engineering, heavy electrical machinery, assembly and manufacture of motor vehicles,
tractor plants, heavy and basic chemicals, petro-chemical industries, cement,
and public utilities. The experienced observer of Pakistan's economy would be
less bowled over by the list than the innocent reader of the *New York Times*,
since he would recognize that Pakistan's capacity in almost all of these areas
was slim indeed, and not very much at all was being nationalized (*PT*, 1/3/72,
7:8). Further, Bhutto promised, "It is not the intention of the Government to
extend control over other categories of industry" (7:8). No compensation was
to be paid to dismissed directors or managing agents, although they – along with
other shareholders – were permitted to retain their shares (1:4). The Government was to appoint new managing directors.[1]

The next salvo was fired on 16 January. Under the "Managing Agency
and Election of Directors Order, 1972," Dr. Mubashir Hasan, the Finance
Minister, announced the abolition of the managing agency system, terminating
the agents' agreements and contracts without compensation. (The order
simultaneously abolished sole selling agencies.) Control of companies previously
wielded by the managing agencies was transferred to the directors of the
companies.[2] In strong language Hasan said, according to the *Pakistan Times*,

---

1   Allegations have flown about that the choice of industries to nationalize depended on
whether they were run by Bhutto's enemies or not. The San Francisco *Examiner and
Chronicle* reported on 16 January 1972, under a picture of Yusef Haroon in a Fifth Avenue
apartment decorated with fresh flowers, that he said he "qualifies as a refugee 'because
the government has nationalized all my properties, my industries,' an action he claims
was taken 'because of my political differences' with Bhutto" (2A:1). As an aside, the
same article gives a clue as to the level of foreign reporting about Pakistan; the article
asserts that the 22 families "have surnames like Saigol, Valika, Fancy, Ghandara [*sic*]
and Habib." Gandhara Industries (one of those nationalized) was of course named after
the ancient Gandhara culture of the North-West Frontier Province, and was the creation
of Captain Gohar Ayub Khan, the son of the deposed President, and of his father-in-law,
General Habibullah. Political motivation might be looked for here as well, but Gohar
Ayub had apparently managed to sell all his shares in Gandhara Industries to the National
Investment Trust and the Investment Corporation of Pakistan in August 1969, after his
father's fall, curiously enough (Feldman 1972: Appendix B). In any case, a move which
appeared to strike at Gohar Ayub's interests would have evoked intense pleasure in many
people, even if by that time the gesture might have been a bit too late to have real meaning.
Local observers say that the real exercise of political vengeance came with the cancellation
(in the closing days of martial law) of the Government's sale of the Bannu Sugar Mills
and the Sutlej Textile Mills to General Habibullah. I have been unable to find the text
of the Economic Reforms Order. It is doubtless in the *Gazette of Pakistan*, to which I have
no access.

2   *PT*, 1/17/72, 1:1. Another eleven industrial units were also taken over the same day,
falling in the ten industrial categories previously announced. "According to APP, the
Minister said that the Government had taken over all the units it wanted under the

that "managing agencies were one of the worst institutions of loot and plunder through which the 'cream of profit was skimmed by a handful of people who were able to control capital worth about Rs. 50 to 60 crores with an investment of Rs. 50,000 or so.' They had a complete stranglehold over the industry" (*PT*, 1/17/72, 1:2).

The managing agency system was born in India in the nineteenth century. It exists mainly in India and Pakistan, and has long been a focus of criticism. Under this sytem, the management of a company is given over by its directors to a managing agent, a separate corporate entity, which then has a relatively free hand in running things. The opportunities for siphoning off profits and putting them where the shareholders of the actual operating company have no control over them are obviously considerable. Sole selling agents have the same convenient property; goods produced can be sold to the sole selling agent at artificially low prices, thus allowing the profit to appear on the books of the selling agent and under its control rather than under that of the operating company. Under Ayub, the Company Law Commission of 1961 had recommended the "progressive elimination of the managing agency system." The report, although printed in 1963 in an edition of 3,000 copies, was not released to the public. It apparently has been made public under the Bhutto regime,[1] perhaps to place a prop of legitimacy under the actions of 16 January – if they needed one; my impression is that hostility to the managing agency system was widespread. The *Pakistan Times* headed its 18 January editorial "Good Riddance" (4:1). The editorial gives a few snatches of the history of trying to control the managing agency system: the Company Law Commission recommendation; the attempt in 1963 to increase the tax liability of private limited companies; an ordinance of 1968 "empowering the Government to inquire into the affairs of a public limited company and to remove its managing agent if necessary and appoint an administrator. Nor has one heard of any action under that ordinance." Within a few days, the *Times* published "random data collected by some economists since the information gathered by the Central Cartel Law Group set up in 1966 was kept secret," indicating that at least 78 managing agencies, controlling 106 companies, had been abolished (*PT*, 1/20/72, 1:1).

All-in-all, the actions taken represented a mild spurt of nationalization, not affecting foreign enterprises at all (there are few in Pakistan, compared with

---

categories announced earlier. The rest could now start their work in right earnest" (1:3). The *Pakistan Times* on 11 January (3:1), had pointed out that "the 20 units taken over do not include all the major establishments falling in the ten categories selected for immediate state control by the President." See Patel and Memon (1972) for the orders on managing agencies and election of directors.

1 The quotation in the text is from (Pakistan 1963: 126). Security was obviously lacking; I got a copy under the counter from a bookdealer in 1964. Its current public distribution I deduce from its appearance in *Accessions List—Pakistan* 11: 56 (July 1972), published by the Library of Congress PL 480 Project for acquisition of Pakistani books. The chairman of the Commission was Syed Sharifuddin Pirzada, later Attorney General under Ayub. Perhaps significantly, the majority of the Commission were Bengali.

many underdeveloped countries), leaving the financial interest of shareholders intact, and nationalizing industries which, whatever their ultimate importance might be, could hardly be characterized as the industrial powerhouse of Pakistan's economic growth.

The whole nationalization episode appears to have been marked by a good deal of caution. This impression is confirmed by discussions with highly-placed Pakistanis, who claim that the Bhutto regime was unsure of the ability (or the goodwill) of the bureaucracy in running the nationalized industries. According to some, this lack of confidence accounts for the absence of compensation to directors and managing agents. Bhutto is reported to have said, "If we can't make the nationalization work, we'll just hand it back to them." The administration's caution seems entirely well-placed, given the record of the bureaucracy in efficient management (both in Pakistan and in India), but some powerful officials in the administration wanted to go much farther on the route to nationalization.

The President continued to assure the country that "the Government has no intention to take over any more industries" (PT, 4/2/73, 3:3), and attached no conditions, at least in the instance just quoted (an address to the Lahore Chamber of Commerce and Industry). The *Pakistan Times* account of the address reported Bhutto as saying that the Government had no intention of taking over any more industries "till new elections were held" (1:1), although the printed text of his speech did not include the remark. In June 1973 the Government took over purchase from the growers of the cotton crop and also the rice export trade, "to ensure the best possible return to the growers," the Finance Minister said (PT, 6/21/73, 1:5). Perhaps these forms of economic activity did not count as "industries," but early in September the Government nationalized the 26 mills in the *vanaspati ghee* (cooking oil) industry. *Ghee* is an important consumption item, and nationalization came "because of persistent refusal of industrialists to increase production in spite of their solemn promises to the country and in spite of the incentive of a raised price," as Bhutto put it in an address to a group of industrialists (PT, 9/10/73, 1:1). Pervez Tahir's account in the *Pakistan Times* (9/8/73, 4:4–5) gives a list of the malpractices of the *ghee* manufacturers which, if true, goes a considerable distance towards justifying the naionalization (though not of course towards making it work).

Bhutto continued to promise that the Government would nationalize no more units, but added that this was so only if industrialists co-operated by increasing production and "directing their efforts in the best interest of the country," as the *Times* reported the speech. It is not surprising that the nervousness of the private sector continues, despite Bhutto's assurances that "we believe in the concept of a mixed economy in which both private and public sectors play their due share... We, however, do not believe in absolute state power manifesting itself in a totally nationalised, centralised and directed economy" (PT, 4/2/73, 1:4). The question is whether the discouraging effect on private investment of the continuing nationalization will be outweighed by its effect in discouraging monopolistic and exploitative practices on the part of the private sector. There is certainly plenty of room for hope.

The final step in nationalization at this writing is the Government's move to purchase the proprietary interest in companies whose management it took over in January 1972. Under the Economic Reforms (Amendment) Ordinance of 1973, the Government suspended trading in the stocks of 18 of the firms, and may purchase the whole or a portion of the shares (or of the proprietary interest) of any of the firms taken over. Compensation may be paid in cash or in bonds redeemable at the option of the Federal Government and bearing interest of one per cent above the bank rate. The Ordinance states the terms for compensation in technical accountant's jargon, but to the bystander innocent of accounting it sounds as though the expropriators will be expropriated in grand style. Compensation will depend on stock market valuations, and according to Pervez Tahir,

> These owners so manipulated the stock exchange quotations that the enhanced operational efficiency of the taken-over units never got reflected correctly. However, the market would certainly have been up if the Government had not suspended dealings. In this way the capitalists have fallen in the trap laid by themselves (Tahir 1973: 4).

A clause enables the Government to exempt shareholdings up to a declared maximum, to protect the small shareholder. The *Pakistan Times* (9/2/73, 7: 1–7) gives the complete text of the Ordinance, which also empowers the Government to reorganize any firm taken over.

II

Next followed a group of labor reforms, within seven weeks of Bhutto's assumption of office, as he pointed out. The full meaning and effect of a number of these would not be clear except to the specialist, which excludes the present writer. Some which look minor may be of major import. I shall nevertheless attempt comment. A number could be lumped under the general heading of fairness to the workers: "a new labour policy which will guarantee to workers their fundamental rights consistent with the requirements of industrial development of the State." A compulsory system of shop stewards was set up, with a grievance procedure to go along with it, with appeal to a Labour Court. Workers will have the option to refer disputes to the Works Council, composed jointly of management and workers. Workers will further have the right to take matters to the Labour Court on their own initiative; this move had previously required the consent of management. "Thus, the workers, while retaining their right to strike, will have the option to get immediate adjudication by the Court." Reasons for firing would now have to be given in writing. The application of the Payment of Wages Act (1936) and the Industrial Employment (Standing Orders) Ordinance (1968) were extended to labor contractors; obviously employers had evaded these enactments by dealing with contractors rather than directly with labor.

A second set of provisions sweetened the pot for labor a bit: payment of

bonus was made compulsory; profit-sharing was upped from two to four percent; the payment by the worker of two percent of wages for medical facilities
was abolished; provision for old-age pensions was announced; and employers
were required to provide education up to matric for one child of each worker.
But Bhutto – most wisely, in my view – stopped short of a minimum wage:
"an increase in money wages will further aggravate the inflationary situation."
Bhutto declared the intention of linking wages to the price level "as is the practice in Scandinavian and some other advanced countries," after inflation had
been brought under control.

But then in the last five paragraphs of his speech, after presenting these
concessions, Bhutto demanded his *quid pro quo*:

> Since the 20th of December, Martial Law notwithstanding, "gheraos and jalaos" seems
> to have become the order of the day. This unruly and rowdy practice, negative in its pur-
> pose, anarchist in its approach, nihilistic in its results has been endured regrettably by
> the Government and the people for over seven weeks ... It is a self-destructive procedure.
> The majority of the people have shown their disgust over these demonstrations of hooliga-
> nism... National leaders have spoken against it... Taking all these factors into account
> now I want to make it clear that the strength of the street will be met with the strength of
> the State.. [This] intolerable form of threat and thunder ... must stop.[1]

Bhutto's problem here was that he clearly had a tiger by the tail. Much of
his urban support came from labor, and the stance of the Pakistan People's
Party on labor issues – and against the 22 families – had emboldened labor
considerably from its old passive attitude. Faiz Ahmed Faiz had predicted at
least thirty years earlier that this would happen, in his poem "Dogs," about the
oppressed of the subcontinent:

> Ye chahen to dunya ko apna bana-len,
> Ye aqa'on ki haddiyan tak chaba-len—
> Koi inko ihsas-e-zillat dila-de,
> Koi inki soi hui dum hila-de.

> Once roused, they'll make the earth their own,
> And gnaw their betters to the bone—
> If someone made their misery itch,
> Just gave their sluggish tails a twitch.
> (Faiz 1971: 85)

Labor's new hyperactivity had reached the point where the regime could no
longer control it. Bhutto's response was to make substantial improvements in
procedural matters, increase the real income of workers by a conceivably large
amount, but to brandish the Big Stick – a policy whose success was not noticeable in the next few months.

---

1 All quotations in the above paragraphs are from President Bhutto's address to the nation
over Radio Pakistan, reported *verbatim* in the *Pakistan Times* (2/11/72, 7:1–3). Complete
texts of the relevant ordinances are found in Chaudhary (1972a and 1972b). Also worthy
of note is Haidari (1972).

III

The next major area for reform was land. March 3 was declared a national holiday to celebrate the land reforms, accomplished by a Martial Law Regulation. Briefly, the land reforms cut the limit on holdings per individual (*not* per family) from 500 to 150 irrigated acres and from 1,000 to 300 unirrigated acres. Lands above the ceiling were taken without compensation, and it was announced that they would be given free to the peasants. Installments due from farmers on account of the 1959 reforms were cancelled, and arbitrary ejection of tenants from the land was no longer permitted; they could be ejected only for non-payment of *batai* (the landlord's share of the crop). A number of special features attracted attention, given the background of cynicism about the land reforms carried out under Ayub. (1) No concession or exemption granted under the 1959 reforms was to be retained. Apparently in some cases these were quite substantial. Feldman (1972: 6) reports (with documentation) that the Nawab of Kalabagh and his sons were allowed to retain 18,619 acres on lease. The Nawab was the Governor of West Pakistan under Ayub. (2) Transactions in land in excess of the new ceilings after 20 December 1971 (the date of Bhutto's take-over) were void; apparently there had been many fictitious transfers on the land books in anticipation of reforms, since the new administration had started announcing its intentions in January, and of course the People's Party election manifesto had promised them as well. Also invalidated were land transfers which brought land back into the family through a third party; a clever touch. (3) Civilian officials were required to surrender all lands in excess of 100 acres acquired during their tenure of service or in course of retirement. This provision was of course a response to the widespread view among the public that there had been considerable hanky-panky in land sales to favored officials. President Bhutto noted that "vast barrage lands acquired by the official class both in Punjab and in Sind through disgraceful abuse of power, formed the most sordid and shameful chapter in the story of land-grabbing in Pakistan" (*PT*, 3/2/72, 1:3), (4) Land on the Pat Feeder Canal in Baluchistan, the source of much bloodshed because of its apparent distribution to Government favourites, involving inter-tribal struggles, was to be resumed in its entirety without compensation and distributed to poor farmers.[1]

The tribal areas were exempted from the order – I suppose because of inability to make it stick there, and perhaps because it was unnecessary as well.[2] One concession was worthy of note: if a farmer had installed a tubewell or bought a tractor on or before 20 December 1971, the limit was raised for him by twenty per cent. This gesture to the *kulak* class seems a bit peculiar, but perhaps helpful in somewhat reducing the sting of the reforms to a rather

---

1 Feldman (1972: 202–208) gives some background on the Pat Feeder incidents. Documentation is sparse, and I do not pretend to understand the situation fully.

2 A friend from the tribal areas tells me that only the first reason given in the text holds. He continues, "My grandfather owns miles and miles of land [in the tribal areas] and I am quite sure that he could do with a lot less."

numerous class, without conceding anything of substance to the really big landlords.[1]

The absence of compensation clearly raised some eyebrows. Rightist parties in Pakistan had been forced into a position of advocating some land redistribution, and as Mohammad Jafar (1972) commented, "though the Rightists never said this in so many words, yet it was common knowledge that their insistence that the 1956 Constitution be re-enforced was motivated only by the circumstance that that Constitution had effectively protected the capitalistic interests both of the feudal landlords and the industrialists," and in particular provided for compensation, which a court judgment had interpreted to mean compensation at market value. According to Jafar, the theoretical bases for the lack of compensation were two: (1) "...the better and preponderant view is that private ownership of land, in its absolute concept, is not permitted in Muslim Law." (2) "...contrary to general thinking on this subject, even under the British rule in the subcontinent, the State did not recognize an absolute private right of ownership of land."[2]

Pakistani government publicity pulled out all the stops on the land reforms. A pamphlet of the Department of Films and Publications pointed out that the limits set were a quarter of what was allowed in Iraq and less than a sixth of what was allowed in Iran, but there has been no mention that I can detect in the Pakistani press that the Congress Party in India has introduced guidelines for ceilings much lower, 18 acres of irrigated double-cropped land or 54 acres of dry land.[3]

Government land in the future is to be disposed of to the landless, not at auction (which allegedly benefit absentee landlords); the significant exception here is that Government land will continue to be available to the defense services, an exception which may have been politically necessary, but as the *Pakistan Times* commented the next day, "while nobody will grudge the defense personnel some reward for their services and sacrifices, grant of this reward in the form of land is not easily justifiable" (3/3/72, 6:1).

---

1 The announcement of the reforms is in *PT*, 3/2/72. The Land Reforms Regulation, 1972 (Martial Law Regulation No. 115) was published complete in *PT*, 3/12/73, 1:4 ff. It is also available in Sarwar (1972). Some changes were made later: the ceilings were reduced by 20 percent (*PT*, 4/24/72, 1:7; editorial, 4/25/72, 3:1). The limitations were from the beginning stated in terms of produce-index units if computations on that basis yielded a larger holding. I have ignored these complications, but one effect is that larger holdings are permitted in Sind than in Punjab, because of poorer soil fertility.

2 Why general thinking should have been misled is unclear: the British were always explicit that the State was the ultimate landlord. See also Rafi Ullah (1972) and Zeno (1973), which concerns Guraya (1971), a book advocating limitations on the right to property. It was banned under the Yahya regime, on which see Khalid (1972). On right-wing theorizing on the land question, the views of Maudoodi (1950), the head of the Jamaat-i-Islami, might be interesting, but I have been unable to locate a copy.

3 (Pakistan 1972: 12). In India, actual implementation depends on the States, of course, and is apparently moving at a glacial pace. See Ladejinsky (1972) for a most interesting analysis—skeptical of the virtue of ceilings taken by themselves—by one of the oldest hands in the land reform field.

The amount of land involved appeared considerable: in initial euphoria, the *Pakistan Times* reported an area of three million acres (3/3/72, 1:1). It later reported four million acres (12/18/72, 8:6), and said that three-quarters of that had already been distributed (1/7/73, 6: 1–2). The Government's most recent claim is only that 724,000 acres have been resumed (Pakistan 1973: 11). Large or small, the area will make only a minor dent in rural poverty, given that nearly two million peasants were reported to have no land at all.

IV

On 11 May came what may be the biggest reform of all – although to a large extent it was only the culmination of a gradual process of piecemeal reform. In what was described as a long-awaited move, Bhutto announced the devaluation of the rupee from its old (and largely fictitious) parity of Rs 4.76 to the dollar to a new official rate of Rs 11 to the dollar. The Finance Minister gave a bit of the history of the move towards devaluation in his announcement speech, which took up nearly an entire page of the *Pakistan Times* (5/13/72, 5: 1–7):

> The proposal for exchange reform is not new. It was first mooted as far back as 1963. No positive decision was taken at that time. It was taken up again in 1966. The decision was again postponed. At the end of 1967, the question was raised once again but the decision was postponed once again. Finally, in June 1970, the decision was taken by Yahya Khan in principle and it was decided to [devalue] the currency in October of that year. In February 1971, a written commitment was made by Yahya Khan in a letter to the International Monetary Fund notwithstanding [which] his request for standby credit was turned down. Yahya Khan tried once again to obtain a standby credit and simultaneously gave an undertaking to devalue Pakistan rupee to a dual exchange; one fixed at a rate of Rs 9.50 and the other Rs 11 (excluding one rupee tax) as a floating rate. By then Pakistan's internal situation had become so alarming that the world of finance decided to keep all financial decisions in abeyance until the situation crystalized one way or the other (5:4–5).

The Finance Minister's speech was extraordinarily frank: he refers to "the conspiracy to maintain the existing rate of exchange" (5:2).[1]

The move was much less radical than it sounded in one sense, since in point of fact the bulk of imports had been entering at rates a good bit higher than Rs 4.76, and exports as well were subject to higher rates. Indeed, Pakistan had

---

1 Proposals for exchange reform go back a good bit further than the Finance Minister indicated. See Emile Despres' memorandum to the Planning Board of 1956, proposing an import surcharge for many of the same reasons the Finance Minister mentioned as motivating the devaluation (Despres 1973). The whole area of foreign exchange is absolutely essential to an understanding of the Pakistan economy over the last twenty years, and is much too technical to enter into here in detail, except to state my assessment of the results of the devaluation. Those in need of more technical exposition would do well to turn to a pair of articles by two of my colleagues: Glassburner (1968) and Child (1968).

been running a multiple-exchange-rate system with seven rates, but, as the Finance Minister noted in his speech to the nation, "The most favourable ones are meant for those who are the most favourably placed. The most unfavourable ones are for the least fortunate ones" (*PT*, 5/13/72, 5:2). The picture he painted is a bit overdrawn, but as a two-sentence description, it would be hard to improve.

The major reason for the maintenance of the artifical Rs 4.76 to the dollar, in my interpretation, was the existence of East Pakistan. The East Wing's major export was jute, whose supply and (especially) demand were both thought inelastic. If that were the case, then an across-the-board devaluation would have led to *decreased* export earnings from jute, the country's major foreign exchange earner. A reinforcing factor was that the Central Government controlled the foreign exchange earned by jute; the East Wing got the Rs 4.76, and the Central Government got the foreign exchange, worth far more. Devaluation coupled with an export tax to avoid a decrease in earnings from jute would have been a possibility, but then the taxation of the East Wing would have been rather more explicit than anyone (in power) wanted it to be.

Second, the East Wing offered a protected market for much of West Pakistan's industry. This market had now vanished, and aggressive competitiveness in world markets was called for – and the excess capacity was now there to back it up. The bonus-voucher system had, to be sure, already devalued the rupee for exporters by differing amounts. The effective exchange rates were Rs 5.60 for primary products, Rs 7.81 for semi-manufactures, and Rs 8.61 for manufactures. The difference in rates itself was not readily defensible, and now, with devaluation to Rs 11, all Pakistan exports were at one stroke made more competitive in world markets, although export duties cancelled out a portion of this advantage for primary products thought to be in inelastic demand.[1]

Export figures now argue for considerable success, both in diverting products formerly sent to East Pakistan and in taking advantage of the devaluation. Pakistan is at the crest of an export boom as I write in August 1973, partly the result of high world demand and prices for Pakistani primary products, but significant contributions have been made by cotton piece goods, and lesser contributions by products of small industry: sporting goods, carpets, leather and leather goods. These latter are encouraging portents for the future.

---

1   The export rate calculations are taken from *Outlook* (1972a). The calculations are based on the then prevailing bonus premium of 180 percent. Note the date of the article: discussion of the need for devaluation had been taking place in public. (The reappearance of *Outlook*, banned in effect by the Ayub administration in 1964, is one of the cheering results of the new dispensation of press freedom.) The article cited is quite explicit about the role of the loss of East Pakistan: "As in other aspects of our national life, East-West rivalry had distorted our vision in respect of exchange parity as well" (10). Another article in *Outlook* (1972b) makes much the same points under the title "Three Cheers for Devaluation." (The article is apparently by a different hand.) An added note on the bureaucracy's view of devaluation: the Finance Ministry was apparently leary of the increased budgetary cost (in rupees) of debt service. It was ultimately convinced that increased revenue from export duties would make up for this paper loss.

I take the rapid expansion in these sectors to be largely the result of devaluation, and to presage further improvement. The boom is due for interruption, of course, because of the disastrous floods of summer 1973. (See Pakistan 1973: Ch. VIII and Appendix Table 37, as well as the writings of Burki cited at the end of this article.)

So on the export side there was apparently a considerable boost to the competitiveness of Pakistani exports. On the import side, foreign products have of course become more expensive for many categories of purchasers – and uniformly expensive for all. Several effects seem important here:

(1) The price of industrial imports (both capital and raw materials) will now (hopefully) fully reflect their scarcity value to the economy. Previously the Government had handed imports of industrial goods a gift of the difference between the value of inputs valued at the official rate and the scarcity value in the local economy of these imported goods, realizable either directly (although illegally) or through their embodiment in products to be sold at protected prices on the local market. As the Finance Minister put it, "under the present system of exchange rates [the capitalist] already doubles the value of his money the moment he gets a permit to establish a plant and the loan is approved with nothing whatsoever on the ground" (5:2). East Pakistan enters here in another way. Latterly East Pakistani economists had advanced the argument in high circles in the early 1970's that a devaluation would inhibit the development of East Bengali entrepreneurship, just as it appeared ready to start rolling. These spokesmen wanted Bengali entrepreneurs to enjoy the same advantages which their West Pakistani counterparts had had: possession of an import license at the artificially low official rate was an automatic guarantee of bank credit: banks knew a good thing when they saw one. The argument seems a bit perverse, since in general the old exchange rate system subsidized industry at the expense of agriculture, and East Pakistan was the most heavily agricultural wing. (For a clever argument to this effect see Soligo (1971), who does not draw the moral that since the East Wing was agricultural and the West Wing industrial, interprovincial transfers were involved.)

(2) Luxury consumer goods had previously been imported at the bonus voucher rate (the highest, roughly Rs 13 or 14 to $ 1). This arrangement had what would appear to be the desirable effect of making these luxuries expensive; but these high import prices gave a much higher degree of protection from the world market than was given to capital goods or raw materials, and thus incentive for local production, to a group of goods which had been placed "on bonus because of the lowest priority having been assigned to them in the national objectives," as a Karachi commentator pointed out (*Outlook:* 1972a). Making all imports available at the same high rate will have the effect of raising the incentives for local manufacture of capital and intermediate goods relative to luxury consumer goods.

(3) Since under the new import policy licenses are to be freely available, and all commodity imports – except those completely banned – will be "freely importable," much of the cumbersome machinery for the administration of the

baroque import-control apparatus may no longer be necessary, a considerable saving in national time, energy, and tempers. One might also note that the possibilities for official corruption will be much reduced (as indeed will those of the private sector, since over- and under-invoicing will now be markedly less attractive).

(4) The effect on small-scale industry is worthy of separate note. In all the Byzantine intrigue of the license system, it was the small entrepreneur who found his way most effectively blocked. The Finance Minister was quite explicit here as well:

> At last the small manufacturer will be able to compete with the big producer and will no longer depend on buying raw materials from him in the black market. The big producer will have to work hard to compete with the small man to sell his goods (5:6).

Already the free availability of art silk yarn has led to the mushrooming of small establishments with only a few looms each.

Under the new import policy, industrial plants costing less than Rs 200,000 will be freely importable against cash. This step, if effectively carried out, will mean a tremendous relative boost for the small-scale sector, which has suffered from twenty-five years of neglect. A later announcement made it seem as though hurdles were once more being put in the way of the small manufacturer. The Ministry of Commerce announced that "persons intending to import industrial plants costing Rs 2 lakh against cash and up to Rs 5 lakh against barter/credit, should obtain sanctions of the respective Provincial Governments for the setting up of the new units or expansion of the existing units before applying for the import licenses" (*PT*, 6/7/72, 1:7). A sophisticated local observer points out to me, however, that because provincial governments are unabashedly promotional, and now in competition with other provinces, they will be – *Inshallah* – considerably less likely to place roadblocks in the way of small industry (or large, for that matter) than the "mandarins" (his word) of the central government.[1]

V

The final set of reforms involved the financial sector. The life insurance companies (largely in the hands of the 22 families) had already been nationalized on 19 March – a tempting target. The Government set up a State Life Insurance Corporation of Pakistan on 1 November, with three competing divisions into which the 43 old companies were merged. The action put their Rs 130 crore of assets in the hands of the Government. The assets of the firms were not apparently the prime factor, however. In fact, some of the life insurance sector was near bankruptcy. Eastern Federal, the largest insurer, report-

---

1 When the dollar was devalued in terms of gold by ten percent in February, 1973, Pakistan maintained its gold parity, thus reducing the official rate to Rs 9.90. This enhancement in terms of the dollar was partly cancelled out on the import side by the imposition of additional import duties on consumer goods in the June 1973 budget (*PT*, 6/10/73).

edly had the majority of its liabilities in West Pakistan, but the majority of its assets in East Pakistan, largely in real estate. A dramatic failure in the life insurance sector would clearly have been most unsettling at an inopportune time.

This left banking as the remaining target, also largely in the control of the 22 families. On 19 May the Finance Minister announced a set of procedural reforms, to be embodied in legislation. The banks had long been criticized because they were the private preserve of a small number of the ruling families. The complete text of Dr. Mubashir Hasan's address (*PT*, 5/21/72, 5:3–6) provides a fairly complete catalogue of the alleged misdeeds of the banking sector – some of them of considerable interest, displays of indigenous ingenuity. The reforms sought to curtail the banks' power sharply, but stopped well short of outright nationalization – a step which India had taken in 1969. The reforms in many cases are technical, and I will not describe them in detail, but the basic drift was to introduce a much greater measure of supervision of the operation of private banks by the State Bank of Pakistan, which was now empowered, for instance, to appoint a director of its own for each bank, the director to have no connection with banking. (The motivation of this provision is clear, but it would also seem to limit the potential effectiveness of the State director.) Unsecured loans to directors and their families, firms, and companies, were outlawed, nor could banks any longer make loans to directors and their families against the security of shares. Banks were now constrained in their choice of auditors. A number of similar procedural reforms in sum seemed to promise much less of the sort of overly cozy arrangements under which the banks had been run.

The regime aimed additional reforms at the mal-distribution of credit. Commercial banks will be forced into more participation in agricultural credit, but also in credit to other neglected sectors, in particular local production of machinery, the small-scale sector, and refinancing for non-traditional exports. A National Credit Consultative Council will supervise this end of things. One clever twist is that the Government is to amend the Public Demand Recovery Act to allow banks the power to have their agricultural loans recovered as arrears of land revenue. Although this sounds like grinding the faces of the poor, in fact it is likely to lead to a greater amount of rural credit by providing effective security for loans, which banks now lack (*PT*, 5/21/72, 5:6).

Bhutto clearly put the banking system on notice; to prevent their missing the point, the *Pakistan Times* commented:

> The reform is realistic and well intended, but if it does not work as well as it is hoped, then the Government may have no choice but to nationalise the banks (*PT*, 5/21/72, 6:2).

Bankers would remember that land had been nationalized without compensation.

VI

Where are we left, then? What in these reforms is showing the tusks, and what use of the teeth for constructive reform?

The nationalization seems to be tusk-showing; I expect no great results from it, and the portion of Pakistani industry involved is not large.[1] Performance under nationalization, however, has apparently been surprisingly good; a report to the National Assembly in June, 1973 was most encouraging. (See *PT*, 6/20/73, 6: 1–2, "A Myth Exploded.") Watchful waiting is of course still called for. The abolition of the managing agency system is probably all to the good; it will promote a tendency for greater accountability in corporate affairs, and a better break for the stockholders of the corporations, through easing to some extent the stranglehold of the twenty-two families on industrial affairs. (Representation of minority shareholders has, in particular, been assured through cumulative voting and proportionate representation.)

The procedural labor reforms deserve applause to the extent that they make labourers better able to secure just treatment – even at some cost. But the economic reforms apparently will make employing labor in the large-scale sector considerably more expensive. There is question as to whether this is really a good idea. It is of course soul-satisfying to most of us to see the rich get soaked; but if the soaking largely tends to produce a more pampered class of urban labor at the expense of the rest of the country, and in particular at the expense of those priced out of the employment market by the rise in the costs of employing workers, it is not clear that society at large will have a gain to record. Some action was certainly necessary, and the Bhutto administration seems to have been careful to avoid wild gestures in this area, perhaps to its own initial detriment, since peace on the labor scene was a long time coming, if indeed it has arrived, which seems possible. The *Economic Survey* (Pakistan 1973: 13) reports man-days lost due to strikes, lockouts, and plant closures down in February 1973 to about one-eighth of the half-million lost in July 1972 in the disturbances which continued after the labor reforms. And as far as the effects of the rise in the cost of labor are concerned, the system is apparently proving elastic. It seems likely that capital will be driven to some extent out of the large-scale sector, where labor is organized, and into the small-scale sector, by definition difficult either for labor to organize or the Government to police. Observers tell me that the better-than-doubling of carpet exports in a single year (Pakistan 1973: Appendix Table 37) represents the effects of large-scale capital pumped through a modern putting-out system into the small-scale sector, where wages are much lower.

The land reforms are both tusk and teeth: tusk in that they deliver less than they sound as though they do. The property limitations after all are not on a

---

1 Salamat Ali (1972) says that 82 percent of industry remains privately owned. The figure actually is larger, since small-scale industry is not included in his calculations (or those of anyone else), because there are no decent figures covering the sector.

family basis, but on an individual basis, so that holdings of very considerable size (on a Pakistani scale) are still possible. One is eager for more detail about the actual land distribution; my earlier comments indicate that the amount of land involved has apparently been less than hoped early on. If the provisions on ejection of tenants – or rather on the non-ejection of tenants – can be made to stick, this also can be counted as a substantial achievement: teeth, not tusk. Informed Pakistani friends suggest that they may be *made* to stick in parts of Sind and the N.W.F.P. where the landlords are especially non-supportive of the Pakistan People's Party.

Banking reform sounds like it means business, but *quis custodiet custodes ipsos?* The experience with regulated industries elsewhere in the world suggests that the regulated end up regulating the regulators; one would scarcely be willing to wager large amounts of money that this process would not happen in Pakistan. Reports indicate that life insurance was nationalized (rather than propped up financially and regulated) for exactly this reason: the Controller of Life Insurance was a relatively low-ranking official, and much more subject to manipulation than the Governor of the State Bank of Pakistan, who regulated the banks and was normally an ex-Finance Minister and consequently of considerably higher rank in the Government. The mere existence of the laws (and of the focus of public attention on the banking sector) may make it much more difficult for the industrial families to play footsie with their captive banks and may open up sources of capital to more people in the society. The nationalization of life insurance may have the same effect, if the assets of the new life insurance corporation are not just poured down Governmental rat-holes. Tusk certainly; teeth maybe.

The centerpiece of the reforms seems to me to be the devaluation. It is hard to convey to anyone who has not worked through the economics of an over-valued currency rationed by licensing how pervasive and pernicious its effects were, reaching into every corner of the economic life of the country, corrupting everyone it touched, either in the narrow sense of the word "corrupting," or "corrupting" in the sense that it presented a perverse set of economic incentives: encouraging imports, discouraging exports; encouraging foreign-made capital goods, discouraging domestic; encouraging luxury-goods production, discouraging capital-goods production; encouraging the flight of capital, restricting personal freedom. The devaluation can hardly fail to do something simultaneously about all those evils. An important clue to the way the administration regards the matter seems to me is found in the forceful language and great length of Dr. Mubashir Hasan's speech – which he wrote himself – announcing the devaluation. He condemned nearly every evil in the Pakistani economy in the most vivid language and laid the evils at the door of the exchange rate. The tone of the announcement is in great contrast to that accompanying the other reforms: passionate, moving, and intense. And at least eighty percent of what Mubashir Hasan had to say is quite correct, in spite of his vigorous hyperbole: the overvalued currency had encouraged a bizarre variety of cancers in the Pakistani economy and polity, to the point where a Pakistani economist once said to me, "Ah, the glory that was Greece, the grandeur that was Rome, and the racket that is Pakistan!" In the long pull, I think it is the devaluation which will be regarded as Bhutto's greatest single contribution on the economic side of the ledger.

Postscript

After this article had been completed, Bhutto, acting as Prime Minister (having assumed that office on the 14th August) announced a new reform which may ultimately have significant economic impact in a number of ways. On 21 August he announced the abolition of all special services (cadres) in government employment, including of course the elite Civil Service of Pakistan, the focus of much resentment in Pakistan (*PT*, 8/21/73,1; text of statement on 4).

Bhutto had stated earlier that

> in a democratic state where the government is popularly elected, with its main aim the improvement of the condition of the common man, the question of exploitation by the State does not arise (*PT*, 4/2/73, 3:3).

But clearly it does arise, as the Prime Minister noted in his announcement speech:

> It is often averred that the bureaucratic apparatus is a neutral instrument which can be bent to any kind of policy. But this neutrality is mythical. The bureaucracy itself is a powerful vested interest, concerned more with its own good than with the good of the public (*PT*, 8/21/73, 4:4).

Civil service reform had clearly been on Bhutto's agenda; the manifesto of the Pakistan People's Party had noted that a "Socialist regime will need a different structure of administration." The Prime Minister presented the main thrust of his remarks forcefully:

> No institution in the country has so lowered the quality of our national life as what is called "Naukarshahi." It has done so by imposing a caste system on our society. It has created a class of Brahmins or mandarins, unrivalled in its snobbery and arrogance, insulated from the life of the people and incapable of identifying itself with them (4:3).

Although Bhutto did not mention the C.S.P. anywhere in his statement, no one familiar with Pakistan would need special instruction to know what this paragraph was about.

The new system, resulting from the deliberations of the Administrative Reforms Commission, abolishes all the special services and of course the reservation of high policy-making posts for members of these elite services. "Classes" of government servants (I to IV) will no longer exist, and the Prime Minister explicitly stated that, "The road to the top will be opened to all on merit" (4:6).

Bhutto's statement emphasized the role of specialists:

Above all [my italics], the new service structure will enable the Government to gain the full contribution [of] scientists, engineers, doctors, economists, accountants, statisticians and other professionals and specialists, in policy-making, management and administration (4:5).

A "people's government," said Bhutto, "cannot condone a system which elevates the generalist above the scientist, the technician, the professional expert, the artist or the teacher" (4:3–4).

As I noted above in the body of the paper, one of the Bhutto Government's anxieties about its program of nationalization was the fear that the bureaucracy was not up to the task of managing industrial enterprises. Bhutto noted that:

New demands have been placed on the administrative machinery by the various reforms introduced by the Government. Competent persons with experience of running industries are required to take charge of various industries and institutions, financial and otherwise, brought under public control (4:6).

He made special mention that there would be encouragement to lateral entry into the Government service for talented individuals from banking, insurance, industry, and trade.

These reforms promise much new blood and new spirit to make the reforms of the regime work for the good of the people.

REFERENCES

Ali, Salamat
 1972 "The Crisis Continues," Far Eastern Economic Review, 2 December, p. 45.
Burki, Shahid Javed
 1972a "Our Economic Future," Pakistan Times, 13 May, p. 4.
 1972b "Export Oriented Growth," Pakistan Times, 28 May, p. 4.
 1972c "Pakistan's Export Boom," Pakistan Times, 4 and 11 December.
Chaudhary, Muhammad Anwar
 1972a Latest and Most Uptodate Commentary on the Industrial Relations Ordinance, 1969. Lahore: Lahore Law Times Publications.
 1972b New Labour Laws and Policy, 1972. Lahore: Lahore Law Times Publications.
Child, Frank C.
 1968 "Reform of a Trade and Payments System: the Case of Pakistan," Economic Development and Cultural Change 16 (July): 539–558.
Despres, Emile
 1973 "Price Distortions and Development Planning: Pakistan," pp. 133–145 in International Economic Reform: Collected Papers of Emile Despres. New York: Oxford University Press.
Faiz, Faiz Ahmed
 1971 Poems by Faiz, trans. V. G. Kiernan. London: George Allen & Unwin.
Feldman, Herbert
 1972 From Crisis to Crisis: Pakistan 1962–1969. London: Oxford. Appendix B: "Wealth Acquired by Captain Gohar Ayub Khan."
Glassburner, Bruce
 1968 "Aspects of the Problem of Pricing Foreign Exchange in Pakistan," Economic Development and Cultural Change 16 (July): 517–538.

Guraya, Muhammad Yusuf
    1972   Nizam-i-Zakat aur Jadid Ma'ashi Masa'il. Islamabad: Idara-i-Tahqiqat-i-Islami.
Haidari, Iqbal
    1972   The New Labour Policy: Impact and Implications. Karachi: Economic & Indu-
            strial Publications.
Jafar, Malik Mohammad
    1972   "Resumption of Land and Compensation," Pakistan Times, 14 March, p. 3.
Khalid, Detlev H.
    1972   "A Book that was Banned," Outlook n.s. 1 (12 August): 12–14.
Ladejinsky, Wolf
    1972   "Land Ceilings and Land Reform," Economic and Political Weekly (Bombay) 7
            (Annual Number, February): 401–408.
Maudoodi, Syed Abul 'Ala
    1950   Mas'alat-i-Milkiyat-i-Zamin. Lahore.
Outlook (Karachi)
    1972a "High Time for Devaluation," Outlook n.s. 1 (22 April): 11.
    1972b "Three Cheers for Devaluation," Outlook n.s. 1. (20 May): 9.
Pakistan
    1963   Company Law Commission of Pakistan. Report, 1961. Karachi: Manager of
            Publications.
    1972   Department of Films and Publications. A New Beginning: Reforms Introduced
            by the People's Government in Pakistan, December 20, 1971–April 20, 1972.
            Islamabad.
    1973   Office of the Economic Adviser. Pakistan Economic Survey, 1972–73. Islamabad.
            (Ch. II, "Socio-Economic Reforms.")
Patel, M. Adam, and A. Ghafoor Memon
    1972   The Law of Managing Agency and Election of Directors. Karachi: August Publi-
            cations.
Rafi Ullah, M.
    1972   "No Compensation in Islamic Law for Land," Pakistan Times, 23 April, p. 7.
Sarwar, Malik Ghulam
    1972   The Land Reforms Regulation, 1972 (M.L.R. 115), with Land Reforms Address.
            Lahore: Lahore Law Times Publications.
Soligo, Ronald
    1971   "Real and Illusory Aspects of an Overvalued Exchange Rate: the Pakistan Case,"
            Oxford Economic Papers n.s. 23 (March): 90–109.
Tahir, Pervez
    1973   "Changing Mix in Mixed Economy," Pakistan Times, 8 September, p. 4.
Zeno
    1973   "Cultural Notes: Islam and the Right to Property," Pakistan Times, 3 January,
            p. 4.

Pakistan's Population in the 1970's: Problems and Prospects

LEE L. BEAN
University of Utah, Salt Lake City, U.S.A.

A. D. BHATTI
Population Council, New York, U.S.A.

For advocates of family planning and fertility control, Pakistan, circa 1968, was a nation of hope and promise. Social and cultural conditions in Pakistan were assumed to run counter to those typically associated with rapid fertility declines (see Section II). One could thus argue that if family planning were to be a success in Pakistan, family planning as a voluntaristic approach to fertility limitation had a good chance of success in many of the developing countries where demographic problems seemed most severe.

There were many positive features of the Pakistan family planning program in 1968. Pakistan had adopted a population policy based upon ambitious demographic targets calling for a reduction in estimated birth rates of 20 percent in five years. Starting in selected districts in 1965, by 1968 a nation-wide program was in operation. Available statistics suggested that Pakistan had stimulated a remarkable degree of successful adoption of family planning, often using a wide range of innovative activities.

By 1970 a degree of disenchantment had arisen with respect to Pakistan's family planning program. Leadership of the program had changed with the removal of President Ayub Khan and the dismissal of large numbers of senior civil servants including the head of the family planning program. Statistics related to the family planning program from 1965 through 1968 were viewed with increasing skepticism and entirely new organizational forms were introduced to "make up for the false starts" introduced earlier (see Section III).

The events of 1970 *et passim* have overshadowed the normal operation of social service programs such as family planning in Pakistan and have introduced new demographic dimensions into the development and administration of population policies in the country. Without representative elections, the relative voting strength of distinctive "ethnic" or linguistic groups was unimportant. The 1970 election and the "block" support provided to Sheikh Mujibar Rahman in East Pakistan introduced a new element in the consideration of population policies in Pakistan, even after the break-up of the country into Pakistan and Bangladesh.

While this paper is concerned only with the country of Pakistan as con-stituted in 1973, the issue of relative population size among various ethnic or linguistic groups cannot be ignored. That issue now focuses on the strength of the four major provinces in Pakistan – Punjab, Sind, Northwest Frontier, and Baluchistan – and the relative strength of the four dominant ethnic groups – Punjabis, Sindis, Baluchis, and Pathans. To what extent these differences will influence the operation of population programs will be explored in Section IV. In Section II, however, we will note that issues of relative population strength have already influenced the collection of population statistics in Pakistan.

Although a new population policy issue has emerged in Pakistan, the social and economic problems underlying the earlier adoption of a strong population policy in Pakistan remain. In this paper, we shall argue that it is the social and economic factors associated with population change which will be most important in the management of population programs in Pakistan, or even in the four autonomous provinces, during the 1970s.

The Population of Pakistan

The Difficulty of Knowing. For the scholar interested in the population of Pakistan, it is important to recognize the degree to which analytical work is restricted by the availability of population statistics and by the quality of those statistics which are available. To utilize a now hackneyed expression, popula-tion statistics in Pakistan must be treated with *caution*. Problems associated with population statistics in Pakistan arise from a number of sources: organizational problems, lack of continuity in statistical systems, and the inherent difficulty of collecting demographic data in a country such as Pakistan.

In spite of the existence of the Central Statistical Office, the collection of and analysis of population statistics has been widely diffused in Pakistan since independence. Each of the three censuses carried out since independence has been the responsibility of a special, temporary census office set up within the Ministry of Home and Kashmir Affairs.

The Ministry of Health has been responsible for the collation and analysis of vital events, but this system which eventually depends upon reports by the village chowkidar (village watchman) has never produced adequate reports. To provide current estimates of fertility and mortality, the Central Statistical Office in 1962–65 in conjunction with the Pakistan Institute of Development Economics undertook the Population Growth Estimation (PGE) Survey (Farooqui and Farooq, 1971). In 1968 the PGE was replaced by a different form of survey, the Population Growth Survey-I (PGS-I). Where the PGE study utilized two independent data collection systems to provide pooled estimates of fertility and mortality (continuous registration and quarterly retrospective surveys), the PGS-I utilized monthly retrospective surveys. The monthly system proved unworkable, and in 1969 it was replaced with PGS-II which employed quarterly retrospective surveys. Data from PGS-II have yet to be analyzed and, since the two surveys depend upon quite different methodologies, the PGS will not provide an accurate time series in conjunction with the PGE surveys.

The discontinuity in statistical series is also seen in the three censuses of Pakistan. The 1951 and 1961 censuses included a "complete" enumeration of the population including questions on social and economic characteristics of the population. The 1971 census as planned was to be undertaken in three phases. First, there was to be a total count (the "Big Count") of the population with few items of information being collected: head of the household, relationship to the head of the household, age, sex, and marital status of the members of the household. A second phase was to provide a postenumeration check to validate the accuracy of the "Big Count." From the census lists developed in these first two phases, a sample was to be selected randomly, and details on the socio-economic characteristics of the population collected in what was entitled the HED – Housing, Economic, Demographic Survey. Because of the war, the 1971 "Big Count" was postponed until September 1972, thus coinciding with the language riots in the Sind. This, along with vying for political representation among the four provinces, appears to have resulted in erroneous recording of the population (see below) and delayed further work. The post-enumeration check had not been completed by the spring of 1973, and the HED Survey was postponed until fall 1973.

Aside from the censuses and vital statistics surveys, there are a few other important sources of population statistics. Many of these are associated with the operation of the family planning program. In 1968 a national sample survey of fertility and attitudes toward the practice of family planning was developed under the general auspices of the Family Planning Division. This project, entitled the IMPACT Survey, was under the combined supervision of personnel, national and expatriate, from several agencies: WEPREC (West Pakistan Research and Evaluation Center), the West Pakistan Family Planning Evaluation Center, and NRIFP (National Research Institute for Family Planning), now NRIFC (National Research Institute for Fertility Control).[1] While the field work for that study was completed in 1969, the director of the Family Planning Program in Pakistan refused permission to release the preliminary report. Data from the IMPACT Survey are now being analyzed at Johns Hopkins University and a major publication from that study is anticipated late in 1973 or early in 1974.

Thus at the time of the writing of this paper, the major sources of demographic data for Pakistan remain the 1951 and 1961 censuses. Only the preliminary total counts from the 1972 census were available in mid–1973 (Pa-

---

1   We have cited only those agencies in then West Pakistan involved in this major survey. Representatives from various agencies in then East Pakistan participated in the planning and design of the survey, and assumed major responsibility for the execution of the survey in East Pakistan. The study was designed to provide independent estimates for each Wing separately.

kistan 1973). Estimates of fertility and mortality can be taken only from the 1962–65 PGE Survey.

Population Impediments to Social and Economic Development: Economic-demographic studies carried out in the late 1950's and early 1970's have often been cited as evidence that the developing countries of Asia, Africa, and Latin America cannot expect to achieve high levels of economic growth without the control of population growth. Perhaps the most important of these studies is Coale and Hoover's *Population Growth and Economic Development in Low-Income Countries* (1958) which focused primarily on India as a case study. Thus the conclusions which indicated the importance of controlling population growth in the context of an economic development plan were easily transferable to and acceptable in Pakistan.

Increasingly over the past five years, such economic–demographic studies have been criticized as oversimplified on the one hand and as political "tracts" representing capitalistic-imperialistic studies of a Malthusian nature on the other hand (Amin 1972). Rejection of such studies on the grounds of unwarranted determinism or on the basis of a particular political ideology is illusory. Whether economic growth can take place in a planned economy in the face of rapid population growth is not the issue. The basic issue is the degree to which population growth slows or impedes social and economic development through the increasing demand for goods and services due to population growth alone, thereby restricting the flexibility of a government in the allocation of funds and resources to economic development and social welfare programs.

This portion of the paper deals with some of the problems being generated in Pakistan by high rates of population growth, following a brief description of the estimates of levels of population growth. While raw numbers reflecting population growth are intuitively uninteresting, it is worth noting that in Pakistan population growth rates have, in some cases, been deliberately falsified and passionately defended as accurate even in the face of overwhelming evidence of inaccuracies. For example, the Third Five Year Plan accepted a population growth rate of 2.7 percent as a basis for planning while studies available to the Planning Commission at that time indicated a population growth rate in excess of 3.0. The then chairman of the Planning Commission, Mr. Said Hasan, has publicly acknowledged that this lower figure was accepted to avoid pessimism[1]. In addition, officers associated with the 1961 census have consistently argued that the figures collected in the 1961 census were accurate while much evidence exists to indicate an undercount of approximately 9 percent.[2] Thus one must recognize that any figure cited below for population represents only one estimate.

---

1 The statement by Mr. Hasan was made at the Seminar on Population Problems in the Economic Development of Pakistan where he chaired the opening session of June 2, 1967 (Pakistan, 1967).

2 Among the numerous population projections prepared for Pakistan, those produced by the Census Organization of the Ministry of Home and Kashmir Affairs utilize the 1961 census figures as a base population without adjustment (Government of Pakistan, Ministry of Home and Kashmir Affairs, Census Bulletin 7, May 1968).

Population growth in Pakistan has experienced a rapid acceleration in the past quarter of a century. Between 1901 and 1951, the population approximately doubled, increasing from 17.82 million to 33.82 million.[1] Growth during this period was much influenced by epidemics, particularly the influenza pandemic which, along with other disease entities, resulted in a growth rate of .08 percent between 1911 and 1921, whereas the growth rate was 1.31 percent in the preceding decade and 1.03 percent in the succeeding decade.

It required slightly more than half a century for the population of Pakistan to double after the turn of the century, but the doubling time for the population was reduced to less than a quarter of a century after 1951. If the population figures for 1972 are accepted as accurate, the population of Pakistan increased by 92 percent in a period of 21 years.

It is the opinion of the authors, however, that the population figures provided for Pakistan based upon the 1972 census represent over-counts of the population in contrast to under-counts in the 1961 census. The evidence, however, is sketchy because at the time of this writing only a brief report on the census has been released. Consider, however, the figures by provinces for the period 1951–72.

Table 1
Pakistan Population By Province 1951, 1961, 1972

Area	Millions			Rate of Growth	
	1951	*1961*[1]	*1972*[2]	*1951–1961*	*1961–1972*
Pakistan	33.74	42.88	64.89	2.40	3.45
North West Frontier	4.55	5.73	8.40	2.30	3.19
Centrally Administered T.A.	1.33	1.85	2.51	3.30	2.54
Federal Capital Territory Islamabad	n.a.	0.09	0.24	—	8.17
Panjab	20.64	25.49	37.37	2.11	3.19
Sind	6.13	8.37	13.97	3.11	4.27
Baluchistan	1.09	1.35	2.41	2.14	4.83

1 Pakistan, Ministry of Home and Kashmir Affairs, *Census of Pakistan, Population, West Pakistan Tables* and *Report*, Vol. 3, Table 1, (Karachi: Manager of Publications) 11–58 to 11–77.
2 Pakistan, Census Organization, Interior Division, Islamabad Population Census of Pakistan 1972, *Census Bulletin* 1, *Provisional Tables*, Tables 1 and 2: 1–3.
Note: 1951 population figures are adjusted for the new administrative units of the former West Pakistan.

---

1 The figures cited here are based upon the study by the staff of the Demographic Unit of the Pakistan Institute of Development Economics, *District Boundary Changes and Population Growth for Pakistan, 1881–1961* (East Pakistan Geographical Society, Table XVII, p. 65). The adjusted figures for each census between 1901 and 1961 are as follows: 17.82, 20.31, 31.92, 24.30, 28.69, 33.82, and 42.98 million.

Based upon the reported population figures for 1972 (64.89 million), the reported inter-censal growth rate of 3.45 percent, and the political conditions under which the census was taken, it may be argued that the 1972 census represented an overcount. The census count took place in September 1972, coinciding with the language riots in Karachi and elsewhere in the Sind. At that time, Baluchistan and the Northwest Frontier areas were under the control of the Pakistan People's Party which was vying for political power based upon population representation in the promised new elections.

Differences in growth rates between the two census intervals and among the four major provinces theoretically may be due to variations in migration – interwing migration over the census periods and inter-province migration with respect to province differences in growth – or due to variations in fertility and mortality. None of these factors would seem to account for the high growth figures between 1961 and 1972 or for the intra-province variations in growth.

While there was some net migration from East Pakistan to West Pakistan during the period 1961–1972, the total is probably negligible. However, since details on whether Bengalis were counted in 1972 were not available at the time this paper was prepared, it is not possible to determind whether this figure entered into the 1972 count or not. Assuming that inter-wing migration in no way accounted for the higher rate of population growth between 1961 and 1972, what about the influence of fertility and mortality?

Population projections prepared by Bean, Khan, and Razzaque in 1968 (1968:88) provided a high population estimate for West Pakistan, now Pakistan, for 1970 (July 1, 1970) of 61,579,000 if there was no drop in fertility and a moderate decline in mortality. Using the same projection estimate and linearly projecting the 1970 figure to the period of the 1972 census, one would estimate the population at 64,490,000, or 400,000 less than was reported in the 1972 census.

Consider the underlying assumptions of what appears to be an amazingly accurate population projection. The high population projection developed by Bean, et al. assumes no change in fertility between 1960 and 1970, thus suggesting that the family planning program had no influence on fertility levels. It was further assumed that the crude death rate fell from 17.8 per thousand in 1960 to 12.3 per thousand in 1970.[1] Given the dislocations associated with political disturbances, two wars over the period, and the failure of each development plan to meet health targets, such a reduction in mortality in retrospect appears to be unreasonable. Assuming that death rates declined, however, to about 15 per thousand, this would imply a comparable increase in the crude birth rate of 3 per thousand, suggesting a negative influence of the family planning program. Given the implausibility of these various assumptions, we are led to reject the idea that the reported population figures for Pakistan in 1972 are accurate and that the reported growth rate of 3.45 is without error.

---

1 PGS 1968 published the crude birth rate of 36 per thousand and the crude death rate of 12 per thousand.

Our conclusion is further supported by examining the relative growth by province. (See Table 1.) Over the reported period, two provinces could have been expected to grow disproportionately because of in-migration due to relatively higher employment opportunities associated with differential investments in industry and agriculture – the Punjab and the Sind. Yet the Northwest Frontier province is reported to have grown as rapidly as the Punjab, and Baluchistan is reported to have grown more rapidly than the Sind.

The population of the Sind is dominated by Karachi, and Karachi has clearly continued to grow rapidly over the last decade. However, the growth of Karachi is questionably high, 81.3 percent (increasing from 1.9 million to 3.5 million) during the last census period, and Karachi's growth accounts for only one quarter of the growth of the population of the Sind. Thus it would appear that it is implausible to assume that differences in internal migration can fully account for the variations in provincial growth rates. And at this time, there is no evidence to suggest differential patterns of fertility and mortality of such magnitude as to account for the variations in provincial growth.

Although more direct evaluation of the 1972 census must await the release of more detailed data, the evidence is strongly suggestive that the 1972 census is defective, representing an over-count of the population in contrast to the experience of under-counting the population in the previous census. The only conclusion that one might reach at this time, then, is that the population of Pakistan is growing rapidly, probably in excess of 3 percent per year and current growth rates may be as high as 3.5 percent per year.[1]

The consequences of these high growth rates for social and economic development in Pakistan may be seen in the context of selected population related problems: employment generation, education of the population, and food supplies.

Employment Generation: In "Demographic Aspects of Potential Labor Force Growth in Pakistan," Bean introduced his 1967 study as follows:

Within the framework of Pakistan's current 20 year Perspective Plan, the Planning Commission has set five explicit development goals; of these, the target of full employment ranks as a monumental task. Its achievement will be strongly influenced by the rate of growth of the population and effective manpower planning. Not only must work be provided for those entering the labor force between 1965 and 1985, but additional employment opportunities must be provided if the level of unemployment and underemployment is to be reduced. This is a major task in its own right since the Planning Commission, combining the concepts of "under-employment" and "unemployment" under the single term "unemployment" estimates its level at 20 percent of the labor force in 1965." (1967:87)

---

1   It is not inconsistent to argue that growth rates may be as high as 3.5 percent a year while arguing that the intercensal growth rate reported at 3.45 percent is too high, since the former refers to current levels while the latter refers to an average figure over twelve years which would perforce require a much higher growth rate currently.

As noted above, the Third Five Year Plan was based upon assumptions of population growth which were not consistent with available data, and failed to take into account under-enumeration in the 1961 census and age reporting errors. Applying constant 1961 labor force participation rates and utilizing the population projections prepared by the Pakistan Institute of Development Economics, Bean concluded that through 1985, the end of the prospective plan period, the Planning Commission had underestimated the labor force by 8 to 12 million persons or 13 to 19 percent, under varying conditions of population growth.

The task of providing full, productive employment for the labor force of Pakistan is unquestionably an important yet sensitive issue.[1] Certainly the measurement of the labor force in Pakistan is difficult (see for example Islam 1964). Unemployment is clearly underestimated, with a reported level of unemployment which is much lower than one would expect due to frictional unemployment in a free market system.

There are several reasons why the issue of full employment for the labor force in Pakistan is sensitive. First, full employment in Pakistan is endangered by the same forces which will lead to successful growth in the agricultural sector. For example, the quantum increase in wheat production in Pakistan during the 1960s occurred with the introduction of the high yield wheat varieties (Mexi-Pak). Between 1966–67 and 1967–68, the index of wheat production (Base: 1959–60 = 100) increased from 112 to 164 and continued to increase through 1970–71 (Pakistan 1972b:85). This type of seed requires relatively high inputs of fertilizer and water, factors consistent with more mechanized forms of agriculture. Unless cooperative farming arrangements are organized with the financial inputs necessary to supply such resources, mechanization of large-scale landholding offers the most productive possibilities. Consequently, small landowners and tenant farmers may be replaced by mechanical equipment. The development of a more extensive system of agriculture thus may restrict employment opportunities in the agricultural sector, even though in Pakistan the net sown area of agricultural land has increased (see below).

Secondly, it has been assumed that surplus labor is generally to be found in agricultural areas, even though urban unemployment is undoubtedly relatively high. Under this assumption, absorption of increasing supplies of labor is

---

1   The sensitivity of the employment issue is reflected in the manner in which population employment statistics are published by the Government of Pakistan. For example, in *25 Years of Pakistan in Statistics, 1947–1972*, none of the 1961 census data on the labor force is published in numerical terms. In the section on "Population," 1951 census data only for the labor force are presented while the 1961 and 1951 census data on literacy, marital status, age and sex distribution, and urban populations are republished. Only urban labor force data for both 1951 and 1961 are presented. In the "Labour" section of the volume, 1961 census data are utilized as a base line for subsequent survey data, but only in percentage terms. One is therefore forced to refer to original sources to determine 1961 census labor force information and to find the basic numerical data from which the percentage distributions are derived for various labor surveys, and the Pakistan Economic Survey of 1971–72 provides no information on the labor force (Pakistan, 1972a).

largely dependent upon industrial growth. Selected industries, such as cotton manufacturing, were heavily dependent upon the East Pakistan market. While much of the export trade has been reoriented – with some positive economic benefits – since the breakup of Pakistan, industrial growth in recent years has been hampered. Because of the political and social problems associated with the changes in government, the war, and civil/labor unrest, the gross domestic product from manufacturing decreased by 3.8 percent between 1970–71 and 1971–2 (Pakistan 1972a:3). Thus to date, the growth of the non-agricultural sector has not, in general, been able to provide employment markets for surplus labor.

Thirdly, female employment in Pakistan is low (Bean 1968) and because of the religious barriers surrounding the appearance and work of women outside of the immediate household, opportunities for female employment may be expected to remain low. At the same time, the greater educational opportunities for females will create a demand for employment which will be difficult to restrict. Thus any form of social change which leads to improved status of women will increase the pressures on the labor market.

Fourthly, Pakistan is systematically pursuing a policy which leads to an unbalanced growth of the labor force. Because of the foreign exchange earnings which accrue through the migration of middle and high level occupational groups, such migration is encouraged. Indeed, during the first part of 1973, contracts were arranged for 300 physicians in Iran while Pakistan is suffering from a lack of physicians, particularly physicians in the public/rural sector.[1] Such a policy which is dependent only upon the short term gains of foreign exchange, can only lead to a labor force stripped of skills, entrepreneurship, and professional abilities.

Thus, while continuing high rates of population growth are creating increasing demands for employment, the policies of Pakistan are more likely to led to unfulfilled expectations for full employment.

Education for All: A policy designed to provide full and universal education for the population has been an essential part of the planned program of social development in Pakistan for years, and with the emphasis on social welfare espoused by President Zulfikar Ali Bhutto, this policy has been reaffirmed. The current education policy of Pakistan announced on March 8, 1972 contained the following elements (Pakistan 1972a: 17):

    (a) education to be made universal and free up to class ten throughout the country in two phases, i.e., up to class 8 by October, 1972 and matriculation by 1974;
    (b) privately-managed schools and colleges to be nationalized without compensation;
    (c) salaries and service conditions for teachers in all privately-managed schools to be brought to par with those of Government schools;
    (d) five new Boards of Intermediate and Secondary Education to be set up at Saidu Sharif, Rawalpindi, Gujranwala, Bahawalpur, and Khaipur;
    (e) three new Universities to be opened at Saidu Sharif, Multan and Sukkur;

---

1   Contained in an internal office report of the Population Council Iran office (March–May, 1973, p. 1).

(f) the number of universities to be doubled by 1980;
(g) the N.E.D. Engineering College, Karachi and the Sind University Engineering College, Jamshoro to be raised to university status;
(h) a national foundation for book production to be set up.

Certain aspects of this policy such as nationalization, salaries, and boards (b, c, d) are dependent upon administrative/political actions only. Expansion of the university programs and raising of colleges to university status are dependent upon the availability of professional manpower to staff these programs, and retaining highly qualified university personnel is becoming increasingly difficult in Pakistan. The even more difficult part of the policy to implement effectively is the primary target of universal education, and the difficulty to a large degree stems from the demographic conditions extant in Pakistan.

On the one hand, the continuing high rates of population growth mean increasingly larger cohorts of young children requiring education. Consider the number of children between the ages of 5–9 in Pakistan. Bean, et al. estimated that the number of children (male and female) in West Pakistan in this age group was 6.6 million. Under the high population projection, which is roughly consistent with the 1972 census count, there were approximately 9.7 million children in 1970 and there would be 10.9 million in 1975. Thus merely to maintain adequate education facilities in the primary schools, physical facilities and teachers would be required for an additional 1.2 million children between 1970 and 1972 – or essentially creating an education system capable of handling the total primary enrollments of the New York City area. While creating additional facilities is difficult, catching up on educational facilities for the vast number of children currently not receiving education is a monumental task in itself.

In a study entitled "A Demographic Approach to Educational Planning in Pakistan" (1967: 199), Khan noted that early in the last decade, West Pakistan enrollment ratios (the proportion of children in school of a given age cohort) were among the lowest in Asia. Based upon educational statistics for 1962, approximately 44 percent of males between the ages of 5–9 were in school and only 27 percent of males between the ages of 10–14. The picture was even worse for females, 13 percent and 6 percent respectively.

In the light of these low enrollment levels and the increasingly large number of children entering the school ages, Khan concluded: "The educational objectives of the Pakistan long-term perspective plan (then universal education by 1985) are thus not only highly optimistic, they are rather unrealistic, and especially so under sustained high fertility..." (1967: 198). Given the unrealistic nature of the educational target espoused in 1965 – universal education by 1985 – the educational target announced in 1972 must be regarded as statement of political promise rather than a statement of planning commitment. With the existing low levels of education in Pakistan, and the continuing high rates of population growth, universal education cannot be achieved in the forseeable future.

Feeding the Multides. During the 1960s the improvements in agricultural production in Pakistan appeared to assure that Pakistan would soon be self-sufficient in food production. Agricultural outputs increased due to a series of factors. Expansion of irrigation programs, desalinization projects, and land reclamation programs resulted in increased land available for agriculture. In 1960–61, 32,110,000 acres of land were sown, and by 1967–68, this had increased to 35,779,000 (Pakistan 1972b: 82). In addition, Pakistan shared heavily with other countries in the "Green Revolution." With the adoption of the new seed varieties, which for Pakistan with its heavy wheat consumption the Mexi-Pak wheat was most important, production increased dramatically. Between 1955–56 and 1958–59, the average annual wheat production was 3,562,000 tons, and the yield per acre averaged 691 pounds. By 1970–71, the average annual yield was 6,596,000 tons with a yield of 971 pounds per acre, or a yield per acre increase of 40 percent. Thus in terms of cereal grains, Pakistan was not only able to provide for its growing population but was also able to provide for increased consumption. For example, the *Pakistan Economic Survey* for 1971–72 notes that "The consumption of food grains has shown a rising tendency in recent years. After fluctuating in the range of 270–285 lbs. per year per capita, there was a distinct rise to 318 lbs. in 1968–69 and to 350 lbs. in 1970–71" (Pakistan 1972a: 21).

Because of recent drought conditions, however, and in part because of dislocations associated with the war, production decreased in 1970–71 and 1971–72. Thus Pakistan which had become a net exporter in the last years of the 1960s became again a net importer. "In 1971–72, however, it became necessary to arrange for imports of food-grains of 7.5 lakh tons in order to control price levels and to maintain daily per capita consumption at 9.6 oz. per day (as compared with 11.05 oz. in 1970–71)" (Pakistan 1972a: 21).

The agricultural achievements in Pakistan during the last decade were indeed remarkable, and were in no small measure due to the "Green Revolution." Certainly there remains capacity to extend the type of agriculture associated with the "Green Revolution" to additional areas in Pakistan through the distribution of the new seed varieties, making available more fertilizers and pesticides. There is a limit, however, to the amount of land which can be included under such agricultural practices, and there are the imponderables – the availability of water. Continued success in agricultural production however is needed, because one certainty Pakistan faces is continued population growth and growing numbers of citizens to be fed: somewhere between 11.7 million and 8.2 million more individuals to be fed between 1970 and 1975.[1]

Conditions Supporting Continued High Population Growth. Pakistan's social and economic development plans for this decade must consider not only the elimination of social inequality, but must also consider taking care of, or providing

---

1 Under the lowest population growth estimate, to maintain the per capita availability of food grains achieved in 1968–69 of 318 pounds, the high output of wheat in 1970–71 of 6,596 thousand tons (or 350 pounds per capita) would have to be increased by 20 percent, assuming all additional food grains derive from wheat.

for a growing population. Employment opportunities are required for an increasing potential labor force, and the new entrants to the labor force for this decade are here now, having been born roughly 10–15 years ago. Educational opportunities must be provided at the primary school level for children born between 1965–70 in the first half of this decade, and for children born in the first half of this decade, facilities must be provided in the last half of the decade· To achieve self-sufficiency in food supplies and to increase nutritional levels, increasing agricultural production is required for the *increasing numbers* of children being born. (Because of the increasing numbers of couples entering the childbearing years of life, even with a rapidly declining fertility rate – see Bean et al. (1968: 91), fertility assumption III – there will be approximately 500,000 more children in the age groups 0–4 in 1975 than in 1970.)

A rapid fertility decline appears less and less likely to take place in Pakistan in the short run. It is important to note that the social and cultural factors in Pakistan do and will continue to support high fertility values. First, women enter marital unions at an early age and marriage is nearly universal. For example, using the Hajnal method which enables one to estimate mean age at marriage from census distributions of the proportion married at given ages, Sadiq reported the mean age of Pakistan women in 1961 at 17.6 (Sadiq 1965: 242). By the end of the childbearing years of life, age 50–54, according to the 1961 census, only 8,894 women in Pakistan had never married. Although widowhood is quite high in Pakistan, it generally does not become significant until after the peak childbearing years. Thus for the group between the ages of 20 and 29, the percentage of currently married women in 1961 was 89.2 percent.

Secondly, within marriages, the social-cultural structure of Pakistan tends to support moderately high fertility values. Many of the variables associated with declining marital fertility simply are not present in Pakistan. Coale, for example, in 1965 summarized the factors associated with the decline in marital fertility (1965: 208):

(1) The decline in mortality. With more children surviving, fewer births are needed to achieve a given family size.
(2) The rising cost and diminished economic advantages of children in urbanized industrial societies. In a rural family children assist in production at an early age and are a source of support for parents in their old age...
(3) Higher status of women. The extension of education to women, women's suffrage, and the employment of women in occupations formerly reserved for males are objective indications of wider opportunity and higher status for women... these changes in opportunity and status promote the spread of birth control.
(4) Religious changes and differences.
(5) The development of a secular, rational attitude.

While Coale notes that there are counter examples to each of these variables, the evidence would seem to suggest that none of these changes which may be associated with declining marital fertility exist in Pakistan at the beginning of this decade.

Infant mortality during the first half of the last decade remained high. A minimum estimate for the period 1963–65 in Pakistan indicated that at least one of each eight children born alive would die before reaching the age of one. Approximately one of each six live births could be expected to die before the age of 14. The uncertainty of knowing that children born would reach adulthood – and therefore would be available to support the parents in their old age – tends to reinforce high fertility.

The status of women remains low in Pakistan. Few are educated (see above) and few are employed – only 6.14 percent of the women age 10 and over in 1961 (Pakistan 1964a).

The population is largely rural and illiterate. In 1961 only 22.5 percent of the population lived in urban areas and only 16.3 percent of the population above the age of 5 was reported as literate (Pakistan 1964b). The Muslim religion tends to reinforce high levels of fertility according to studies by Kirk (1966), and this certainly tends to be borne out in Pakistan.

In summary, all of the factors which would tend to support high fertility levels appear to be present in Pakistan. Furthermore, it is unlikely that one can predict any significant changes taking place in this decade that would substantially influence fertility levels based solely on social and economic changes.

Given these conditions, what might the Government do? The rate of growth of per capita income slowed from the beginning of the last decade to the end of the decade and with the war, per capita income actually decreased by 5.1 percent in 1970–71. Agricultural productivity has slowed in part because of the negative climatic conditions of the past three years. Industrialization has been retarded by labor problems and nationalization programs, and so on. In the face of these negative conditions, therefore, what can one expect from a government policy and program to limit fertility?

Population Policy Implementation in Pakistan

The Government of Pakistan has supported population programs since approximately 1952 and the nature of the policies and programs through 1968 have been summarized in a variety of publications. Because of the complexity of these changes and programs, it is difficult to encapsulate them in a paper of this scope. For a more detailed history of population program activities to 1968, see Bean and Bhatti (1969).

In 1968, Pakistan was operating under a population policy which broadly supported specific demographic goals for fertility reduction to be achieved through a national family planning program. Organizationally, the program operated as a sub-division or division of the Ministry of Health, Labor, and Social Welfare. Between 1968 and 1972 there have been several changes in leadership and levels of governmental authority, but the mandate of the program remained relatively constant. Following a full-scale government review of the program in 1972, it was recommended that family planning be given a broader responsibility and be renamed and upgraded to the Division of Population Planning within the Ministry of Health, Social Welfare, and Population Planning (labor having been taken out of the Ministry). Nevertheless, at the time of this writing, the only significant operational change introduced by these administrative shifts occurred in 1968 with the appointment of a new joint secretary for family planning.

Operationally, family planning in Pakistan from 1965 onward has been a separate group, operating independently of the health program with which it has been allied ministerially. The program stressed the utilization of intrauterine devices and the distribution of conventional contraceptives – condoms and foams, primarily. Sterilizations – primarily vasectomies – were reported to be widely popular in East Pakistan, and some administrative pressures were exerted to increase the rate of vasectomies in West Pakistan without a great deal of success.

Heavy utilization of incentive payments to family planning acceptors was made with respect to IUDs and sterilizations, and incentive fees were also made to "finders" (largely village *dais*) and to the medical personnel responsible for the insertion of IUDs and the performance of sterilizing operations. Conventional contraceptives were sold under a government subsidy.

Stress was placed on having family planning personnel achieve specific targets for IUD insertions, conventional contraceptives distributed, and sterilizations performed. These program statistics were converted into estimates of periods of protection against the risk of pregnancy under a set of simple and questionable statistical assumptions and the protection period (couple years protection) converted by a simple ratio estimate into births averted. Working from the opposite direction, given the demographic target of reducing the estimated crude birth rate from 50 to 40 between 1965 and 1970, the births which must be averted to achieve this goal could in turn be translated into couple years of protection to be achieved, and thence into family planning targets such as IUDs inserted, etc. (Bean, Seltzer 1968).

The combination of large sums of money available for incentive payments and the stress on achieving performance targets clearly established a framework within which misreporting and corruption could take place. Yet the accuracy of the figures and the success of the program were never questioned until late in 1968.

Dissatisfaction with the family planning program in 1968 appeared to derive from two factors. First, the field organization was largely based on the utilization of part time village *dais* (illiterate midwives) to recruit clients for family planning programs. Even if the reported numbers of family planning acceptors were accurate, the productivity of these women in 1968 was very low since on the average a *dai* was recruiting only 1.3 IUD acceptors per month. Secondly, emphasis had been placed on acceptors of family planning methods with little emphasis on developing continuous users of contraceptives(Ahmad 1971).

Thus in 1970 the family planning program introduced a new organizational structure in the Sialkot Division, a structure which, because of its initial testing point, has become known as the Sialkot Project or Program. Under this new program, full-time male and female workers – motivators – were to be utilized to maintain records on a fixed population in order to identify couples in the childbearing years of life, i.e., target couples. The motivator couple concept was based upon the assumption that the success of the family planning program in Pakistan depended on activities which would reach the dominant figures, the males, in the households. Through personal contacts with target couples supported with mass education programs, the motivators were expected to recruit acceptors for the family planning program and to maintain contact over time with the couples. Incentive payments were to be made under this program to the motivators not at the time of acceptance, but at the end of a twelve month period with the payment calculated on the basis of the number of couples recruited and continuing to use contraceptives so that the wife remained non-pregnant for a continuous twelve month period. Longer periods in a non-pregnant state resulted in higher incentive payments. Although there have been no detailed evaluations of this new program, it has been adopted as the model to be expanded throughout Pakistan, and by 1973, it had been introduced into nine districts.

The Record to Date. The performance of the Pakistan family planning program during the period 1965–68 has been summarized in Bean and Bhatti (1968). The performance since mid–1968 may be summarized very briefly (see Table 2). In the first six months of fiscal 1969, family planning outputs continued to rise over all previous periods with outputs by reported IUDs inserted conventional contraceptives distributed, and vasectomies or tubaligations performed. Since that period, family planning performance statistics have continued to decline. Although the records from July 1970 onward are discontinuous, clearly the record for the last six months in 1972 is dismal. Extrapolated to a twelve month period, the data would suggest that the recent performance is worse than the performance during the first year of the developing program introduced with the third Five Year Plan (1965–66).

Table 2
Pakistan Family Planning Performance Statistics 1965–72

Year	IUDs Insertions	Conventional Contraceptives Sold(000)	Sterilizations Vasectomies/ Tubligations
July 1965–June 1966	155,829	23,819	1,365
1966–67	337,880	62,903	1,826
1967–68	425,955	97,167	14,558
1968–69	438,348	102,431	58,435
1969–70	342,952	102,715	10,297
July 1970–Oct. 1970	100,739	31,239	2,187
Jan. 1971–April 1971	72,525	19,352	1,382
July 1972–Dec. 1972	51,595	1,175	1,582

Source: Pakistan Family Planning Council Monthly Reports 1965–72.

The low level of performance of the family planning program late in 1972 as reflected in the available statistics may be due to three factors, singly or collectively. First, the reported statistics may reflect more valid reports of actual performance. Second, certainly the problems associated with the recent war and breakup of the country have made it difficult to maintain and operate social welfare programs such as family planning. Third, the political disputes among the now four provinces in Pakistan have had deleterious organizational consequences and probably operational consequences. For example, under the East-West Pakistan arrangements, family planning was a provincial activity, conjoint with the central government. With the dominance of the Punjabis and refugees in then West Pakistan, a disproportionate number of the senior trained personnel were Punjabi. With the development of the four provinces in Pakistan today, family planning became a provincial activity, conjoint with the new central government. Thus in the Northwest, Baluchistan, and the Sind, many of the Punjabis were replaced with local people, often lacking in both training and experience. Further, provincial governments have not been able to maintain the provincial financial contribution under the economic crisis which has affected the entire country, in spite of the fact that central government funding appears to be ample, largely because of foreign aid provided for family planning from the United Nations Fund for Population Activities and the United States Agency for International Development. Thus, as we shall note in the concluding section of this paper, the politics of population in a fragile state may become more significant in the balance of this decade than ever before in the history of Pakistan.

Population Prospects to 1980

From the point of view of the authors of this paper, there will be several significant population issues in Pakistan at least through 1980. The relative importance of these issues varies, as we shall note below, and all of the issues may become trivial in the face of continuing and mounting political instability now furthered with the change in government in Afganistan and the re-emergence of the Pukhtoonistan issue.

Population Statistics: Continuing Uncertainty. As noted above, recent demographic statistics, particularly the 1972 census, are of questionable validity and no sound basis currently exists for anticipating improved estimates of vital rates or estimates of family planning program activities. However, some recent governmental changes have been made which would appear to strengthen the capacity to generate effective population statistics.

The Census Office has been made a permanent organization, thus establishing the potential for effective long-term planning for the next census. The Census Office has been officially removed from the Ministry of Home and Kashmir Affairs, and is to be combined with the Central Statistical Office in a new Division of Statistics within the Ministry of Planning and Statistics. The integration of census and statistics has not yet been accomplished, and as of mid–1973, the CSO remained in Karachi and the Census Office in Islamabad. Offsetting the benefits which might be derived from an organizationally coherent statistics structure, new duties and responsibilities have been assigned to the Division of Statistics. The President of Pakistan mandated the registration of all adults for the purpose of establishing valid voter registration rolls. Faced with the completion of the census post-enumeration check, the HED Survey and the analysis and publication of the census data, the enormity of the registration program may eliminate any effective planning and development of an improved statistical system for some years to come.

Therefore, given the current state of statistical programs in Pakistan, it is unlikely that adequate population statistics will become available before 1980.

Family Planning in Pakistan. The prospects for a nationally supported family planning program in Pakistan during the balance of this decade hinge upon three questions. Is family planning socially and culturally feasible in Pakistan at the present time? Is the Pakistan government really serious about supporting an effective family planning program? Finally, can fertility control succeed in the face of ethnic and provincial competition for political – representational power?

Is a government-sponsored fertility control program feasible? In Section II of this paper, we outlined a series of conditions which have traditionally been associated with spontaneous declines in fertility in a variety of countries. That is, fertility has declined without the intervention of a government to foster fertility limitation.

There is strong evidence to suggest that some governmentally sponsored fertility limitation programs have influenced the birth rate, and most of the examples are located in Asia; Taiwan, Korea, Hong Kong, and Singapore are good examples. But each of these good examples represents a society culturally and economically distinct from Pakistan: more urbanized, higher levels of education, more industrialization, higher status of women, and so on.

There does not appear to be a country with a level of social and economic development as in Pakistan that has clearly demonstrated that a governmentally sponsored family planning program can induce a *long-term secular decline* in fertility, and there is now little reason to expect that Pakistan will be the first example.

One would expect that family planning would have some effect on fertility, since it would appear that there is some demand for family planning in Pakistan, but there is at the same time no evidence to indicate that the Pakistan family planning program has substantially increased the demand for family planning services.

The demand for family planning services appears to be somewhat limited in Pakistan, and one must question the efficacy of a national family planning program alone to stimulate demand in Pakistan. Nevertheless one must recognize that other government investments in industrialization, educational programs, and other social welfare programs may encourage the adoption and spread of a small family set of norms. But these changes will occur slowly and gradually in the face of a rapidly growing population.

Is Pakistan really serious about limiting the rate of population growth? On the surface, Pakistan had mounted one of the most serious efforts in the world to limit fertility through a family planning program. In the face of left wing opposition to family planning, a high-level government commission reviewed the issues in 1972 and supported continued government activities in population. From this commission arose the recomendation to upgrade and expand the family planning program through the creation of the Population Planning Division.

Nevertheless the Government of Pakistan undermines its family planning efforts through several direct and indirect actions. Family planning remains a conjoint activity of the central government and the four provinces. While under the concept of conjoint activities as defined by the Central Law Minister the central government could assume larger responsibility for family planning, the provinces have been allowed to founder because of inadequate provincial budgets and the assignment of locally acceptable but poorly trained personnel to the family planning program.

In addition, within the central family planning organization, support has not been provided for sufficiently high salaries and for job security to insure stability of the family planning personnel. Related to that issue is the fact that the government is apparently now pursuing a policy indirectly related to the family planning program which limits the possibility of securing the type of high level personnel essential to operate a family planning program. That policy seems to encourage the emigration of skilled manpower as a means of securing foreign exchange. For example, Pakistani physicians, statisticians, and demographers are employed widely in the Gulf States, and the majority of all Pakistani social scientists with Ph.D. degrees with training in population are employed outside Pakistan. Thus it would appear that while Pakistan has mounted a major family planning effort, the government has maintained policies which impede the development of an effective organizational machinery.

Can fertility control programs succeed in the face of ethnic and provincial competition for political representation? The lesson learned through the block voting of an absolute majority of the population of Pakistan which led to the emergence of Bangladesh is not likely to be soon forgotten. Yet in a political/ demographic sense, the idea that fertility control programs can mitigate the development of a more evenly balanced population distribution by province or ethnic group is patently nonsense. The overwhelming numerical superiority of the Punjabis in Pakistan is so great that it cannot be redressed for decades through even the most severe differential fertility control programs.

There is, however, the fact that family planning remains a conjoint activity, and the governments of the Northwest and Baluchistan cannot but be influenced by the thinking of leaders of the socialist countries of the developing world that family planning is neo-colonial and anti-socialist (Amin, 1972). In addition, while population issues – the consequence of population growth on economic and social development – become important in the framework of a centrally planned economy, such issues loom less large at the provincial level. It would appear that population issues are largely viewed, and legitimately so, as important only at the level where economic planning takes place. An important question, therefore, is at what level family planning or population planning programs are controlled in Pakistan.

By maintaining family planning as a conjoint activity between the central government and the provincial governments, the political issues associated with conflicts among the provinces regarding population balance may be short-circuited. But since none of the provinces will have the responsibility for dealing with the issues of population pressure on social and economic development programs nor for dealing with the social and cultural conditions which support continuing high fertility levels, necessary support for population programs at the provincial levels may be difficult to organize.

REFERENCES

Ahmad, Wajihuddin
    1971   "Field Structures in Family Planning." Studies in Family planning 2 (January): 6–13.
Amin, Samir
    1972   "L'Afrique sous-peuplé." Development and Civilization 47–48 (March–June): 59–67.
Bean, Lee L.
    1967   "Demographic Aspects of Potential Labour Force Growth in Pakistan." International Union for the Scientific Study of Population, Sydney Conference, Contributed Papers (August): 87–97.
    1968   "Utilization of Human Resources: The Case of Women in Pakistan." International Labour Review 4 (April): 391–410.
——, and William Seltzer
    1968   "Couple Years of Protection and Births Prevented: A Methodological Examination." Demography, 2: 947–959.
——, et al.
    1968   Population Projections for Pakistan. Karachi: Pakistan Institute of Development Economics Monograph 17 (January).
——, and A. D. Bhatti
    1969   "Three Years of Pakistan's New National Family-Planning Programme." Pakistan Development Review 1 (Spring): 35–57.
Coale, A. J. and E. M. Hoover
    1958   Population and Economic Development in Low-Income Countries. New Jersey: Princeton University Press.
Coale, A. J.
    1965   "Factors Associated with Development of Low Fertility." United Nations: World Population Conference 2: 208.
Farooqui, M. N. I. and G. M. Farooq, eds.,
    1971   Final Report of the Population Growth Estimation Experiment. Dacca: Pakistan Institute of Development Economics (July).
Islam, Nurul
    1964   "Concepts and Measurement of Unemployment in Developing Economies." International Labour Review 3 (March): 240–256.

Khan, M. R.
    1967 "A Demographic Approach to Educational Planning in Pakistan." International Union for the Scientific Study of Population. Sydney Conference Contributed Papers (August): 192–200.
Kirk, Dudley
    1966 "Factors Affecting Moslem Natality." pp. 561–579 in Bernard Berelson (ed.) Family Planning and Population Program; A Review of World Developments. Chicago: University of Chicago Press.
Pakistan, (Ministry of Home and Kashmir Affairs) Census Commissioner.
    1964a Census of Pakistan Population 1961. Pakistan-1, Karachi: Manager of Publication (June): 5–9.
Pakistan, (Ministry of Home and Kashmir Affairs) Census Commissioner,
    1964b Census of Pakistan, Population: West Pakistan-3, Karachi: Manager of Publications (June) 2–78 to 2–93.
Pakistan, Institute of Development Economics
    1967 A Report on the Seminar on the Population Problems in the Economic Development of Pakistan. Karachi (September).
Pakistan, Government Finance Division Economic Advisors' Wing.
    1972a Pakistan Economic Survey 1971–72. Islamabad (June).
Pakistan, Central Statistical Office
    1972b 25 Years of Pakistan in Statistics 1947–72. Karachi: Manager of Publications (July).
Pakistan, Census Organization, Interior Division
    1973 Population Census of Pakistan, Census Bulletin-1, Provisional Tables (January): 1–4.
Sadiq, M. Nasim
    1965 "Estimation of Nuptiality and its Analysis from the Census Data." Pakistan Development Review 2 (Summer): 242.

Bhutto's Educational Reform

J. HENRY KORSON

University of Massachusetts, Amherst, U.S.A.

EVERY NEW ASPIRANT for political office in an election contest is expected to point out the failures of his predecessors in office, the inadequacy of his opponent(s), and to present to the electorate a more or less clearly defined program intended to cure the ills of his constituency. Such a program must be concerned with the basic needs of the electorate, and must demonstrate a realistic assessment of the feasibility of such a program. A candidate for office expects to appeal to the wishes, desires and ambitions of all the electorate, although he knows that not all will necessarily support him.

In an underdeveloped nation, aside from the political and economic issues which almost always hold center stage in a political campaign, perhaps no other item has as much appeal to the masses as that of universal and free education. Pakistan was left with few resources, economic or educational, at the time of independence in 1947, so that the building process for a complete and modern system of education necessarily had to be a slow one.[1]

Pakistan was founded as a new nation committed to a separate state based on Islamic ideology, but whose system of higher education was largely a replica of the British system, with its concern not with a religious philosophy, but with the arts, letters and sciences of western Europe. Many of the nation's leaders were products of either such institutions in British India or England. (Mr. Bhutto won his B.A. degree at the University of California and took his law training at Oxford. Two of his children are students at Harvard-Radcliffe, while two others are enrolled in the American School in Islamabad.) The ultimate purpose and goal of the educational system established by the British colonial government on the subcontinent was to train a cadre of junior administrators, most of whom could not hope to rise above the level of clerks.

---

1   When President Ayub Khan came to power in 1958, he proceeded to establish a number of Commissions to study diverse national problems. Among them was the National Commission on Education. In 1968, the Embassy of Pakistan in Washington, D.C., issued a pamphlet titled "Pakistan's Development Decade, 1958–68, Educational Reform," which proclaimed the educational advances that had been made during Ayub Khan's regime. "Of all the reforms introduced in Pakistan, I feel personally proud of our educational reforms." It boasted of the achievements of his regime, of which there were some, but played down the failure to achieve the goals set out in the Third Five Year Plan. There were many reasons for the latter, among them the rapid and unabated population increase.

And this sytem of education prevailed until 1947, when India and Pakistan won their independence.

Since Pakistan was founded on the basis of a religious ideology, but whose system of higher education depends so heavily on western educational experience and outlook, it would almost appear to some observers that in matters of education the nation has developed a schizoid personality. On the one hand the political leaders since independence have felt that they have had to maintain the confidence of the *mullahs*, yet on the other hand these leaders have also felt the heavy responsibility of leading the nation into the modern world with all its demands of contemporary technology equipped with an inadequate system of education for its people – not the least of which has been one of the highest rates of illiteracy in the world.

The results of the national election in December, 1970, saw not only the emergence of the Pakistan People's Party as the majority political party in West Pakistan, but Mr. Bhutto as the spokesman for the party and its program of reform in the political, economic and social spheres. Following the end of hostilities between Pakistan and India in December, 1971, the PPP was left as the majority party in the west, with the task of rebuilding a nation not only defeated in war, but with considerable self-doubt as to its future. Mr. Bhutto and his newly-named cabinet quickly rallied to the challenge, and within three months of assuming the office of president announced through his Minister of Education, Mr. Abdul Hafeez Pirzada, a short-range and long-range education plan for the nation for the period 1972–1980. This was termed *The Education Policy, 1972–1980,* and was accompanied by an appendix, *Martial Law Regulations, No. 118,* signed by Mr. Bhutto in his role as Chief Martial Law Administrator on March 29, 1972 (*Policy* 1972).

The permanent constitution was passed by the National Assembly on April 10th, 1973 and authenticated by President Bhutto two days later. Parts of two articles (37 and 38), clearly refer to the government's intentions in the field of education.

"Article 37.   The State shall—
   (a) promote, with special care, the educational and economic interests of backward classes or areas;
   (b) remove illiteracy and provide free and compulsory secondary education within the minimum possible period;
   (c) make technical and professional education generally available and higher education equally accessible to all on the basis of merit;
   (f) enable people of different areas, through education, training, agricultural and industrial development and other methods, to participate fully in all forms of national activities, including employment in the service of Pakistan...
"Article 38.   The State shall—
   (d) provide basic necessities of life, such as food, clothing, housing, education and medical relief for all such citizens, irrespective of sex, caste, creed or race, as are permanently or temporarily unable to earn their livelihood on account of infirmity, sickness or unemployment..."
   (*Constitution,* 1973: 17–18).

The Central government has also established the National Education Council with the Central Minister of Education as Chairman. The Council's purpose is to initiate and support research and disseminate its findings and mobilize the latest educational techniques and resources for the improvement of education. It will also maintain and develop cooperation with UNESCO. Ten basic committees will be established to conduct basic surveys and studies and to serve as a resource group to evaluate various programs (*Dawn* 12-3-72).

Reinforcement of the new education policy for the nation by a martial law edict was considered necessary because an important part of the plan called for the nationalization without compensation of all the privately owned and operated colleges beginning September 1, 1972, and all the privately owned and operated schools beginning October 1, 1972, but phased over a two-year period. Only those institutions that the government is fully satisfied are operated on a "genuinely benevolent, philanthropic and non-commercial basis" could be exempted from the application of nationalization.

Perhaps one of the most impressive aspects of the whole enterprise is the fact that the new policy was formulated and announced in a period of less than three months after Mr. Bhutto took office on December 20, 1971. Almost immediately after he assumed office, Mr. Bhutto met with the vice-chancellors of all the universities and requested suggestions for changes, while Mr. Pirzada on January 6th, 1972 met with teachers and students in Islamabad, followed by meetings with provincial officials and others who were invited to contribute their suggestions. Although President Bhutto's new education policy has not only been well received but highly praised in the press, no mention is made and insufficient credit is given to ex-President Yahya Khan in the field of education. Yahya Khan had asked Nurul Khan to develop a new education plan, which was done, but, unfortunately, it was never implemented. Bhutto's policy reflects much of the work that had already gone into Nurul Khan's plan. A sense of urgency pervades the whole policy and one cannot escape the feeling that the government is determined to implement its new program of education for the nation in the shortest possible time.

The new policy, or plan, itself is far-reaching and all-inclusive. It not only calls for the restructuring of the educational system from the primary through the graduate and professional school programs, but special emphasis is placed on the expansion and strengthening of technical training in a wide variety of fields. Although space does not permit a complete review of all the proposals in the plan, the major ones will be pointed up and explored.

Major Proposals

Free and Universal Education

The plan calls for a two-phase program to make education free and universal for all children up to Class X. Because of limited resources, the first phase, which began October 1, 1972, education up to Class VIII was made free for both boys and girls. With the second phase, beginning October 1, 1974, free education will be extended to Classes IX and X in all schools. Depending on response, the government anticipates that primary education will become *universal* up to Class V for boys by 1979 and for girls by 1984, and up to Class VIII in 1982 for boys and for girls in 1987. Some women's groups have already raised questions about the obvious discrimination against girls, but the protests have not been answered directly beyond the expected statements that limited resources would necessarily limit the desired ideal arrangements for the development of universal and free education. The question of making education compulsory has been stated to be the responsibility of the "parents to send their children to school on pain of punishment" (*Policy* 1972: 3). The government recognized the far-reaching implications, and has referred this problem to the provincial assemblies.

Ideological Goals

One of the basic objectives of the new plan will be the "Promotion of understanding and appreciation of the fundamentals of Islam and the basic ideology of Pakistan and their reflection in the code of personal and social life..." (*Weekly Commentary* June 1, 1973), and to achieve this goal the study of Islam will be required through Class X.

Throughout the text of the *Education Policy*, as well as from the periodic pronouncements by political leaders, the concept of useful service to the community and the nation is very apparent. The socialization of the young during the elementary school years is to be conducted by their teachers so that they will be motivated to perform productive service for the welfare of the community. Students will be organized into squads for a variety of tasks, and the dignity of labor will be emphasized. At the middle school level, students will be taught a variety of skills useful to their needs as future members of their communities. Furthermore, "...the People's Government was committed to restore the dignity of teachers so that they could act as guides, preachers and mentors for the moral training of the younger generation" (*Pakistan Times* May 24, 1973).

On May 4, 1973, the Punjab Minister of Education, Dr. Abdul Khaliq was reported in the *Pakistan Times* to have announced that beginning with the 1973–74 academic year, emphasis would be on agro-technical education subjects "to make education more purposeful and useful." He claimed that "there was no room for liberal education, and the major need was for ends-oriented programs and institutions to engage people in productive pursuits." A week later, in the same paper, Dr. Khaliq was quoted as stating that compulsory agricultural and technical education from the sixth class will be introduced in the boys' schools in the Punjab [beginning Sept., 1973], and home economics would be a compulsory subject for girls. This "move toward purposeful education has been taken in the light of the experience of countries like China, the Soviet Union, Cuba and Jugoslavia, in keeping with Pakistan's own conditions." Later in the same month, degrees other than technical and scientific were being referred to in the press as "worthless" (*Pakistan Times* May 12, 1973).

A massive attack will be made on illiteracy among the young through the universalization of elementary education and an equally massive attack will be made on adult illiteracy. For example, beginning September 1, 1973 the provincial government of Sind will launch a literacy program which is planned to reach 400,000 adults at a cost of Rs 8,000,000 (*Pakistan Affairs* August 14, 1973). Egalitarianism will be the keystone in educational opportunity, not only for women but for all underprivileged groups. Academic freedom for teachers and autonomony for institutions within the framework of the needs of the nation will be assured. It is hoped that students and parents, along with teachers and other members of the community will participate in educational affairs. And, finally, a nationwide motivational campaign will be instituted to help persuade parents not only to send their children to school, but to encourage them to participate in the community programs.

Elementary Education (Classes I-VIII)

Beginning October 1, 1972, elementary education was made free in all schools, both government-supported and privately managed. It is estimated that 70 percent of the boys and 25 percent of the girls in the primary school age cohort attend school while 30 percent of the boys and only 11 percent of the girls in the middle school cohort attend school. By 1980 these percentages are expected to increase to 100 percent of the boys and 70 percent of the girls at the primary level and 70 percent of the boys and 40 percent of the girls in the middle school level. These projections also call for the addition of 61,000 classrooms for these school levels, while priority will be given to rural areas and to the education of girls. Where feasible, other facilities will be put into use.

Secondary and Intermediate Education (Classes IX-XII)

Although only 8 percent of the secondary and intermediate school age cohort currently attend school, it is estimated that by 1980 the increase should see 15 percent of the youth in attendance. More important, perhaps, is the planned shift in emphasis of the kind of training offered. About two-thirds of all students are studying liberal arts subjects. The government plan calls for a "...massive shift in enrollment from the arts towards enrollment in science and technical subjects; from an aimless general education to a more purposeful agro-technical education" (*Policy* 1972: 10). This goal is to be achieved by 1980 by maintaining the number of student places in the arts at the present level while increasing the number of places in the science and technical/occupational fields. But since the arts fields largely attract students from the middle class while upward-mobile students from the lower class usually opt for technical training in greater numbers than they do the arts, this plan should not be a goal too difficult to meet. This writer predicts, however, that difficulties might well arise when the growing number of middle and upper-middle class students seek college and university training in the humanities and social science fields which they have traditionally elected in greatest numbers, only to be confronted by a "ceiling" on the numbers to be admitted. Since students from lower income families traditionally seek out the technical fields as the quickest path to occupational placement and upward mobility, it is possible that opportunities in higher education might become more readily available to the latter group than the former. Whether the government will find it necessary to revise the plan at some future date remains to be seen.

Higher Education

Although the announced goals of universal literacy and free education at the elementary levels can be expected to have very broad appeal to the masses, it is from the colleges and universities that a nation must expect to draw its trained staffs of educated men and women for administration, business and industry, and the professions. At the time of independence, there were only two universities in Pakistan, the University of the Punjab in Lahore, founded in 1882, and the University of Dacca in Dacca, founded in 1921. Following independence, the University of Sind in Hyderabad, was founded in 1947; Peshawar in 1950, and Karachi in 1951. Furthermore, before independence there was only one medical college and one engineering college, both located in Lahore. In the same light, only the Punjab and Dacca had law colleges. Since then, several more universities, medical, engineering and law colleges have been opened, all patterned after the British model. As might have been expected, the demand for seats has always been greater than the number available so that expansion of the university system has been quite steady, even though financial support by the central and provincial governments has not always been adequate for the development of the strongest programs. In addition, many students have sought graduate and professional training in established universities abroad, primarily in England, the United States, and Canada.

At present less than 2 percent of the relevant age cohort are enrolled in colleges and universities in Pakistan. Several of the institutions currently in existence are being expanded to full university status. A new University of Baluchistan is being established in Quetta, which includes a new medical school, while N.E.D. Engineering College in Karachi, and the Engineering and Agricultural Colleges in Peshawar, among others, will be raised to the status of universities. Even Azad Kashmir will shortly have its own university, as well as a Board of Secondary Education. A University Grants Commission will be organized to serve as a coordinating agency in order to avoid unnecessary duplication and waste, and, further, to serve as a buffer between the government and the university administrations. The Inter-University Board will serve as the nucleus of the University Grants Commission. Another new university is planned for D. I. Khan and by 1980 the number of universities will have doubled. It is also planned to add six new medical colleges, and to expand some of the existing ones.[1]

The University Ordinance

Long a bone of contention since the days of the Ayub regime, the PPP promised to revise the University Ordinance and rid it of those aspects most obnoxious to the academic community. For this reason it came as something of a shock that, instead of offering greater academic freedom, the control of the universities (in the eyes of the academic community) was to be politicized more than ever before.

Under the new ordinance, the provincial governor will again be the chancellor, while a new office of pro-chancellor has been created which will be filled by the provincial Minister of Education. It is considered by many that this will have an adverse effect on the autonomy of the university, and adds another step in the bureaucratic chain of command. Furthermore, since the provincial Minister of Education is a political appointee, and would serve as the pro-chancellor, he would serve in both the Syndicate and the Senate so that the "university could neither be autonomous nor democratic... he [would be] bound to interfere in the working of the university which would impair its autonomy. Being a politician himself he was sure to inject politics into the university which would vitiate its academic atmosphere" (Editorial, *Pakistan Times* April 24, 1973). The proponents of this measure feel that since the university is the creature of each provincial assembly, the latter is responsible for all agencies under its jurisdiction. Other proponents feel that it is well to have a high-level provincial administrator who is close to the university and participates in its deliberations, understands its problems and needs in such a post – someone who can, indeed, serve as a "friend in court" *vis-a-vis* the Assembly.

The vice-chancellor will be appointed by the chancellor and will serve at

---

1   M. L. Qureshi, Director of the Pakistan Institute of Development Economics, writing in the Pakistan Times (July 23, 1973), claims that the decision to open six new medical colleges cannot be defended. He claims there is no shortage of doctors in the nation, but, rather, a poor distribution of personnel [a common observation even in "modern" nations]. He claims that doctors are induced to leave the country because of higher salaries elsewhere. [Pakistan is a favorite nation for the recruitment of doctors by Arab nations.] In view of the great cost of building new medical facilities, as well as the number of years required to train doctors, Qureshi insists it would make for better government planning to change the system of health care delivery so that doctors would be available in rural areas, and otherwise to make it attractive for doctors to remain in Pakistan.

his pleasure, as will the acting vice-chancellor, who will serve in the absence of the vice-chancellor. In this ordinance, the Syndicate becomes more powerful than the Senate. A number of government servants, including five Members of the Provincial Assembly will be appointed by the government, as will the majority of the members of the Senate (*Dawn* November 24, 1972).

One of the reforms the new University Ordinance calls for is the rotation of department heads on a two-year basis among the three most senior members of each department. The stated purpose of this change is to avoid the solidification of too much power in the hands of one faculty member for long periods of time, and is considered to be an effort to establish a more egalitarian system of departmental governance. This has not been well received by the affected department heads at one university. At the University of Karachi it has been reported that a large number of full professors have applied for "study leave" abroad. "Among them are most of the recently dislodged heads of departments" (*Dawn* November 22, 1972). The vice-chancellor's response to this demonstrated unhappiness on the part of the senior professors was that they can now use their increased free time for research and scholarship! Since all the universities in Pakistan are government supported, they not only depend on the central and provincial governments for their budgets, but also for their administrative control.

At the college and university level, the student community has always been something less than peaceful, and all too frequently tumultuous, if not mercurial, depending on the political issue of the moment. Student groups have been used from time to time by political elements for their own purposes, and, apparently, this activity still continues on the campuses. But aside from this point, the students have always expected and demanded a degree of participatory democracy in the decision-making process of their institutions, and this opportunity has not been available to them in some years. The old university ordinance denied the students any degree of participation and little to the faculty. Under Ayub Khan, the University Senates were done away with. Students could be rusticated; student unions were abolished; graduates could lose their degrees, and faculty fired without due process for a variety of reasons. The new university ordinance does restore the Senate, the majority of which will be made up of elected faculty members as well as ex-officio members, students, and some legislators. The university Syndicate will be made up of elected faculty members, student union officers, government officials and other laymen, although this arrangement has not met universal support of the campuses. Student unions are once again functioning on the campuses. Since the students have always been an important constituency for every government leader, they will serve no less a role for Mr. Bhutto, and it is apparent that he has attempted to cultivate their support, and to use it.[1]

---

1   During the first year of the new University Ordinance (1972–73), it appears that neither the faculty nor the students are happy with it. The students want more representation in the Senate, while both the faculty and the students want more academic freedom and autonomy. There also appears to have been a shift of support by students and faculty

The new university ordinances appear to have been outlined or suggested in Islamabad, but the details were developed and finally approved by each Provincial Assembly for each of the universities. All of the ordinances were approved by their respective assemblies on September 30, 1972. Those of the University of Sind and the University of Karachi are precisely the same, while that of the University of the Punjab differs only in minor respects and is spelled out in greater detail. There are no significant differences. For example, in the composition of the Senate, the University of the Punjab calls for 15 elected faculty members, while the Universities of Sind and Karachi call for 12. It can be safely assumed that the ordinances of the other universities are similar in content.

Centers of Excellence

Another planned change at the university level is the development of Centers of Excellence. These centers will be developed by the University Grants Commission as the need is made apparent, and, from the earliest information available, the fields chosen will largely be in the scientific and technical fields. It is hoped that this development will reduce the nation's dependence on foreign training for its scientists and technicians. The centers will be financed by the central government and will be open to gifted students. The government has appropriated Rs 7,000,000 for this program for the current fiscal year. The University of the Punjab will have such a center in solid state physics; Karachi, marine biology; Sind, analytical chemistry; Peshawar, geology; and Baluchistan, mineralogy.[1]

---

from the PPP in 1970 to the Jamiat-e-Tulaba in 1972. At the first student elections at the University of the Punjab in the latter year, there were serious disruptions on campus when it appeared that the JeT would win handily. The JeT won a substantial victory when the second election was held. It has been reported that the elected president of the student union spends little time on campus, but travels about the province giving anti-government speeches. Since his political position is very anti-administration, he has been arrested twice and released. It should be noted that students and faculty members have always been politically active on the sub-continent.

1   That Bhutto is serious about the scientific and technological development of the nation can be seen from his State of the Republic Address of August 3, 1973. He announced the establishment of the Pakistan Science Foundation, whose major goals are to be:
   1) To make Pakistani society science and technology conscious
   2) To support scientific and technological research in the universities and other institutions which is relevant to the socio-economic needs of the nation
   3) To promote the utilization of such research, and
   4) To arrest the drain of talent from the country.
In order to implement the above program, the Pakistan Science Foundation Act of 1973 was passed and a budget of Rs 5,000,000 for the first year of operation was provided. Although the National Science Council was formed in 1961, it remained inactive and dormant because of the limitations of its charter and the lack of a full-time chairman. Bhutto has promised to meet with the Council periodically to check on its progress.

The government's emphasis on the shift toward science and technology in the colleges and universities becomes apparent when it is seen that 60 percent of all students enrolled in the nation's colleges and institutions of higher learning are enrolled in the arts programs. The shift in emphasis will be accomplished by holding the number of student places in the arts at the current level while increasing the number of places in science and technology so that the ratio by 1980 will be 30, 30 and 40 percent in the arts, sciences and the fields of technology respectively.

This plan is being supported by the government in spite of the fact that "about 5,000 diploma-holding engineers in the country are faced with starvation" because of a lack of employment, and another "600 have had their employment terminated in the last six months" (*Dawn* November 27, 1972). Yet *The Planning Commission Report* for 1970 claimed there was a need for 12,000 diploma-holding engineers. This kind of miscalculation is an additional aspect of the whole problem of the "educated unemployed" found in many underdeveloped nations, viz., a lack of accurate information on the country's labor force.

The Educated Unemployed

It is a commonly held view that modernizing nations suffer from a lack of scientists and technicians. More frequently found, however, is the paradox of considerable unemployment and underemployment among science and technology graduates. The "educated unemployed" appear to present a problem for many developing nations. One of the major aspects of the problem is the lack of accurate information concerning the numbers of unemployed or underemployed. The number of educated unemployed in Pakistan is estimated by some to be as high as 400,000, largely generalist degree/diploma holders. Recently, however, there has been a great increase in the unemployment of scientifically and technically qualified persons. The unemployment rate is claimed to be 52 percent for applied science M.Sc. degree holders, 44 percent for polytechnic graduates, and 31 percent for M.Sc. degree holders in Economics and Commerce. "The educated unemployed are the nerve-center and the most volatile section of our society. The feeling of being unwanted causes frustration.." (Pervez Tahir, *Pakistan Times* April 24, 1973). Even with the Literacy Corps and the export of trained manpower, Tahir sees no solution to the problem of producing degrees "which can't be marketed," and calls for a rethinking of the educational system and manpower planning. On the other hand, a rough estimate made by the government of Pakistan indicates that there are approximately 20,000 unemployed science graduates, plus an additional 5,000 graduates of the polytechnic institutions. One of the reasons put forth by the government is that private industry prefers to employ uneducated skilled labor at low wages and train them up to the level desired. Another reason offered is the lack of communication between the "industrial sector" and the institutions producing the science-polytechnic graduates.

Some quite consistent sources of employment for some groups of engineers, doctors and other trained specialists in the last decade have been some of the oil-producing Arab nations (as well as other countries). The Pakistan government has usually not discouraged the "export" of trained professionals, because, among other reasons, these people send considerable remittances to their families, and the government is happy to have this additional source of foreign exchange. It has been estimated in some quarters that about one-third of the nation's foreign exchange earnings came from this source in 1972. In fact, a front page item in the *Pakistan Times* (June 1, 1973) highlights the government's efforts to help place engineers as well as other educated unemployed "both inside and outside the country" by having the Manpower Division compile lists of available candidates.

In an additional effort to help alleviate the problem of the educated unemployed the central government has established the National Development Volunteer Program which will be limited to males between the ages of 25 and 40. Qualifications of the applicants will be matched with job opportunities, apprenticeship, or on-the-job training. The volunteers will be enrolled for a period of one year and be entitled to maintenance stipends (*Weekly Commentary* II, 18, pp. 4–5). On May 1, 1973, the central government announced the launching of the program with 1,000 engineers and other technicians to be appointed to the Volunteer program, which will eventually reach 2,500 in number (*Pakistan Affairs* XXVI, no 13, p. 3). Front page advertisements began to appear in the press urging scientists and engineers to enroll in the program, and inviting potential employers to make use of this new service.

The provincial government of Baluchistan is planning to institute a system of "unemployment allowance" for the educated unemployed who are *bona fide* residents of the province. The scale of allowances planned on a monthly basis is:

Rs 80/ for a matriculate
Rs 100/ for an intermediate
Rs 120/ for a graduate
Rs 150/ for a post-graduate

Since education up to matriculate will be free, and unemployed graduates will receive an unemployment allowance, it would appear that the provincial government of Baluchistan has embraced the ideology of the welfare state. It is also likely that the plan will call for registration of all those who wish to receive the allowance in the National Service Corps, or the National Development Volunteer Program.

In view of the planned expansion of higher education, and in view of the high level of unemployment among the educated group, serious questions must be raised concerning the long-range effects of the new education policy unless government intervention succeeds with its announced plans. Another aspect of the same problem is that women college and university graduates have even greater problems entering the labor force since they must largely conform to the norms of a traditional Muslim society. These norms severely limit their opportunities, and their relatively minor participation in the labor force of the nation contributes heavily to the high dependency ratio of the country (Korson 1970).

The Privately Managed Schools and Colleges. The development and spread of the private schools and colleges was largely a post-independence phenomenon in the large urban centers. Many were licensed as "charitable" institutions, but were, indeed, operated on a profit-making basis that sometimes reached scandalous proportions. Perhaps no other aspect of the new education policy has brought forth as much controversy as the nationalization of the privately managed colleges beginning September 1, 1972 and the privately managed schools over a period of two years, beginning October 1, 1972. It is interesting to note that no compensation was to be paid to the owners and operators of these schools and colleges, and that no property could be sold or transferred by the owners or managers following President Bhutto's announcement on March 15, 1972. The central government maintained the prerogative of exempting those schools and colleges which were located in the federal capital area, while the four provincial governments had the jurisdiction of those institutions in their respective provinces. However, each governmental unit had to be satisfied that such an exempted institution was being operated "on a genuinely benevolent, philanthropic and non-commercial basis" (*Policy* 1972: 19). For example, those non profit-making schools that have maintained high academic standards and good reputations for the treatment of their staffs have been exempted for expropriation. The American schools in Karachi, Lahore and Islamabad fall into this category. As of August 3, 1973, 3,693 schools and 178 colleges had been nationalized (*Pakistan Times*).

The major reasons offered by the government for the expropriation of the schools and colleges are 1) to do away with the profit-making aspect of an educational enterprise, 2) to make schooling more readily available to those children whose families could not afford private schooling, and 3) to bring the whole educational process of the poorer privately managed schools up to government standard. This includes the raising of teachers' salaries to the level of those in publicly supported schools. Many of the private institutions were notorious for underpaying teachers, withholding salaries, and other abuses. It should also be noted that many such teachers were less qualified, and therefore were open to exploitation by the owners and operators of such institutions.

In the course of the summer of 1972 there were numerous meetings between the bishops of the various Christian denominations and government officials. Before the school year opened it was decided to nationalize the colleges but to delay the nationalization of the mission schools to a later date. One of the problems has been the objections raised by the private Muslim schools, viz., that the government intended to delay the nationalization of the Christian schools, but planned to move against the Muslim institutions, – hardly a politically wise action in these unsettled times. In any case, the government's plans did not call for the *acquisition of the properties* of the churches or mosques, but the administration of the schools and colleges functioning within those institutions would be taken over by the nationalization scheme (*Pakistan Times* August 26, 1972; Sardar 1972: 6).

Many of the privately managed colleges and schools in Pakistan have performed a valuable service to the community and nation since they opened their doors, notably those operated by the several Christian missions. The latter, expecially, have established and maintained high academic standards and reputations. Since these institutions have offered essentially western-oriented curricula, they have provided the opportunity for many Pakistani students to pursue advanced degrees at both Pakistani and foreign universities. Since the missionary schools and colleges are English-medium institutions, their graduates have had distinct advantages in pursuing higher degrees whether in Pakistan or abroad. (Almost all teaching in Pakistani universities is done in English.) The administration and faculty of these institutions also have a commitment to provide higher education to their students at cost with no sense of personal gain but rather the satisfaction of serving the students and the community. (The "Government" colleges, as the name suggests, are supported by the provincial governments, and are usually considered the most prestigious among all the colleges.)

Some of the privately managed colleges and schools, however, were operated by their owners for the sole purpose of private gain. Their frequently low level of academic performance was often matched by a relatively weak financial situation which resulted in lower-than-average faculty salaries, and not infrequent payless pay days. The nationalization of the colleges without compensation, then, was designed as a corrective move by the central government. The provincial governments have appointed administrators who send periodic reports to the provincial ministries of education. It was planned to bring teachers' salaries into line with those of government college teachers, but many who had not been paid their salaries since March 15, 1972, were still waiting for redress in this matter in the spring of 1973. As government employees, they are now eligible for fringe benefits previously denied them, although there have been frequent complaints from some of the teachers that some of their basic needs were being overlooked, and that they were, indeed, being treated as second-class citizens.

As of May, 1973, some teachers of the nationalized schools had still not been paid their salaries, some even as far back as March 15, 1972. Another serious complaint was that some government officials considered that the eligibility for pension rights of these teachers from the nationalized schools and colleges began September 1, 1972. the date of nationalization – not the date of their original appointment.

After the announcement of nationalization on March 15, 1972 Prof. Shah F. Haque, Principal of Liaqat College, and a leader of the opposition in the Sind Assembly, claimed it would not be nationalization, but regimentation to place the private institutions under government bureaucracy (*Pakistan Times* August 23, 1972). On the other hand, some of the proponents of nationalization claimed that those elements of the Christian community that opposed nationalization were participating in a "foul conspiracy," and were being exploited by "mischief-mongers" determined to create problems for the government (*Ibid.*). It appears that some operators of private colleges did create problems. When the *Policy* announcing the nationalization of schools and colleges was made public on March 15, 1972, some owners stopped paying teachers' and other staff members' salaries, as well as other financial obligations.

As for the nationalization of the colleges, there is no private college in Baluchistan, while in N.W.F.P. only Edwards College has been temporarily exempted by the provincial government. But of the 135 private colleges in the Punjab and the Sind, all have been nationalized, including the eight colleges operated by various Christian missions, in spite of the fact that they could prove that they were "genuinely benevolent, philanthropic and non-commercial" institutions.

Although the government has not taken over the *properties* of the colleges, they have taken over their administration so that most of the college principals have been retained, but find themselves government employees, and all budget, personnel, administrative and academic matters are under the control of the government. Since the mandatory retirement age for teachers is 58, many teachers over that age have been forced into retirement without the government's willingness to support their pension claims. Many faculty openings have not been filled, while some of the openings at the English-medium Christian colleges have been filled by recent graduates of Urdu-medium institutions and are, therefore, unable to function properly. The missionary colleges have always used English as a medium of instruction, and these two factors have caused considerable unrest among college students.

Since many of the missionary colleges have maintained the highest academic standards, it is felt in many quarters that because of the lack of budgetary support from the government that the level of academic quality will be difficult to maintain. On the other hand, many of the private colleges with the poorest reputations are bound to be improved over the years (provided the government offers sufficient financial as well as other support), so that, in the long run there might well be a "leveling" of academic quality among the nation's colleges.

Schools

The first of the schools to be nationalized were those that catered to the low income groups so that immediate relief could be offered to such families, and also to "improve the lot of the teachers" working in those schools. As of May, 1973, 221 high-fee schools had been exempted, at least temporarily, on the condition that they reserve 20 percent of the seats in each class for outstanding students from low income families (*Pakistan Times* May 27, 1973).

Since the plan called for the nationalization of private schools over a two-year period beginning October 1, 1972, as of this writing many of the mission schools have been spared during the first round of nationalization. However, the threat of ultimate nationalization remains, and there is great anxiety among teachers, students, and their parents. Many of the non-missionary private schools have been nationalized, but it is felt that it is only a question of time (October 1, 1974) before the remaining private institutions will be nationalized. Since many of the missionary schools have always been considered centers of excellence, there is considerable apprehension among their staffs, students and their parents, because without proper financial support it is feared that academic standards will fall.

Many of the same problems faced by the former private colleges now confront the nationalized private schools. Teachers over age 58 have been retired, some with their pensions endangered, and since some of the poorer private schools employed teachers without proper credentials, these, too, have been forced out. Although the poorest schools, should they survive, are bound to gain and improve their performance, once again it is felt that the best of the private institutions will suffer since a "leveling" process will inevitably set in. The major problem, it appears, is that even though the new education plan has considerable support and great public appeal, too much has been attempted too soon, i.e., with insufficient planning and insufficient budget support. For example, many of the nationalized private schools have received little or no money for day-to-day supplies, and must manage with left-over stocks, or do without.

Schools for the Gifted and Talented

Some of the institutions to be taken over by the government will be developed as special schools for gifted students, regardless of their economic background. An example of such institutions is Aitchison College, in Lahore, where in the past only sons of the wealthiest families could hope to attend. In addition schools for the talented students in each district will be established, at first in newly expropriated institutions. Also, separate schools for talented girls will also be established. Each school will have residential facilities and will draw students from each area or district in which it is located.

Illiteracy

Aside from the expropriation of private schools and colleges perhaps no other aspect of the new education policy has received as much publicity as the announced plans for the eradication of illiteracy. This is a problem that many underdeveloped nations have been struggling with, and the results vary widely among these nations. Depending on the "baseline" or starting point, frequently beginning with political independence, and the kind and amount of resources available, some nations have had considerable success, while others have had relatively little. Unfortunately, Pakistan falls into the latter group.

The last census for which results are available in Pakistan (1961), the literacy rate was estimated to be about 20 percent, although the rates varied widely among sex and regional and rural-urban cohorts. The best estimates at the present time show a slight decline to approximately 18 percent, largely because of the continued high fertility rate and the lack of expansion of the educational facilities that had been planned by previous administrations. *Dawn* (December 7, 1972) reports a drop from 18 percent to 15 percent, although it mentioned no time span, or offered a source for this estimate. It is also estimated that there is an annual increase of about one million illiterates per year.

The Education Minister of Sind Province, Mr. Dur Mohammad Usto, has announced an appropriation of Rs 5,000,000 for its adult literacy program. A National Literacy Day was declared for October 1, 1972, and the opening of Education Week. It was celebrated by public appearances and speeches by Bhutto and Pirzada in Rawalpindi. They announced that the central government had budgeted Rs 903,000,000 for education for the current fiscal year, compared to Rs 630,000,000 for the previous year. They pleaded for peace in educational institutions and the avoidance of controversy so that the major goals could be achieved within the time limits set by the government. In Karachi, at least, Literacy Day received a "half-hearted" observance (*Dawn* October 1, 1972).

Although the present goal is to achieve universal primary education for boys by 1979 and for girls by 1984, the problem of adult illiteracy is also an important part of this announced program. It is planned that literacy centers will be established in all villages and towns, in "schools, factories, farms, union council halls, and community centers" (*Policy* 1972: 21). For literacy training alone, the plan calls for 276,000 centers by 1980, for an estimated 11 million illiterates. Short, intensive training courses for teachers are planned, to be supplemented by members of the National Literacy Corps, and other suitable persons. Although a National Literacy Corps was announced during Ayub Khan's regime, patterned after the corps in Iran, the plan was never implemented. Iran's success has been largely due to the use of army personnel in isolated rural and tribal areas, and with the help of college and university graduates who volunteer for a year of national service. Whether Pakistan's leaders would go so far as making a year of national service a requirement for all college and university graduates remains to be seen.

From the pronouncements in the press, as well as editorials in the major newspapers, it appears that the national and provincial leaders of the government are concerned with the problem of illiteracy. The President's wife, Begum Nusrat Bhutto, has been very active in this campaign by frequently appearing before women's groups urging "each one to teach one." How successful the government will be in meeting its targets in the projected time remains to be seen.

Teacher Training and Supply

It is planned that the training of teachers will be reorganized so that larger numbers will become available in a shorter period of time. The plan calls for the introduction of "innovative techniques," which are otherwise not defined.

In March, 1972, the estimated number of elementary and secondary teachers in the country was about 160,000. The estimated *additional* number needed to fulfill the program by 1980 is 235,000, not counting about 300,000 adult and continuing education teachers, both male and female. The 67 teacher training institutions now in operation can produce only 104,000 teachers in the next eight years at the different levels, so that Education as a subject will be introduced at the secondary level, as well as into all the general colleges in order that more teachers will become available in the national pool (*Policy* 1972: 23).

The proportion of women teachers at the primary level is only 30 percent (as against 75 percent in the United States). It is hoped to increase the number and proportion of women teachers in the primary levels so that parents will be encouraged to send their daughters to school. As a traditional Muslim society, this has been one of the major hurdles in any effort to increase the number and percentage of girls in school. It is also expected that with an increased number of women teachers coeducation can be introduced at the primary level. Segregation in schools is rarely ever equal, whether the variable is race or sex, and it is almost always more expensive.

The pay scales of teachers in expropriated schools will be brought up to par with those in the publicly-supported schools, and for those desiring further training, "sabbatical leave with full pay will be granted liberally to them" (*Policy* 1972: 24). One of the long-standing complaints of teachers has been the lack of low cost housing. The new policy calls for the construction of rent-free housing in the future, although no target date is set. One year after the announced education reforms, it was obvious that the planned reforms were not completely effective because college teachers in Lahore had drawn up a list of demands stating that teachers' salaries were being withheld, and that superannuation pensions were not being paid. They blamed "bureaucratic bottlenecks" (*Pakistan Times* March 22, 1973).

Student Welfare

In 1971–72, Rs 20,000,000 was available for scholarships to college and university students. This sum will be increased to Rs 80,000,000 by 1980. In addition, Rs 60,000,000 for interest-free loans will be available, although priority will be given to students in professional schools. In May, 1973, the central government announced that an additional Rs 2,500,000 was being made available for scholarship loans for poor students, the total sum to be divided among the seven universities (*Pakistan Affairs* XXVI, 12, p. 1). Loans will be repaid after students have become earning members in their occupations and professions. In addition, a comprehensive program for the construction of hostels to provide for 8,000 more school and college students at a cost of Rs 40,000,000 was approved by the central government. "Northern and federally-administered tribal areas would receive first priority," while other hostel facilities would be expanded (*Pakistan Times* July 3, 1973). Because of the high cost of books, book banks will be established in colleges and universities and will be available on loan. In addition, low-cost transportation is promised for all students who need such, as well as free medical check-ups. In an effort to reduce the social and economic disparity among students up to grade VIII, uniforms of modest cut and inexpensive materials will be designed. This program will be introduced gradually in various areas so that local sensibilities will not be offended.[1]

National Curriculum Bureau

The new *Policy* calls for the reorganization and strengthening of the National Curriculum Bureau, with Curriculum Centers for each province. It is expected that a wide variety of changes will be forthcoming in the training of teachers, the development of curricula, the development of new textbooks and resource materials. Radio and television will be introduced into the learning process wherever possible, and, by 1980, about 150,000 radio and 100,000 television sets will be distributed to schools and adult education centers, wherever the latter are organized. The use of these sets will be a boon to a wide variety of extension programs in "agriculture, health, education, family planning, and social reconstruction" (*Policy* 1972: 29).

Physical Education and Sports

It is planned that physical education will have parity with other fields of study in schools and colleges and that teachers in this field will have parity with other teachers. Physical education will become an integral part of primary school curricula, and that the field will be up-graded in the colleges. Special

---

1 The Government of Sind has already prescribed the uniforms for all students of the province from Classes I through VIII to become effective in the academic year 1973–74. Girls' frocks will be light blue, white shalwar or pyjama, and white dupatta. Boys will wear camel colored kurta with side pocket and tight collars, and camel colored shalwar or pyjama (*Dawn*, December 23, 1972). The motive for instituting uniform dress for students can be interpreted in various ways. The writer prefers, however, to believe that its major purpose is an effort on the part of the administration to further develop a sense of egalitarianism among students so that manifest differential expenditures for children's clothing are reduced to a minimum. Minister of Education Pirzada has also announced that free books as well as uniforms will be provided for poor students after October 1, 1974.

sports and recreation centers will be established for women, and, in an effort to develop the whole field of physical education, games and sports, a National Sports Trust will be established.

National Foundation for Book Production

For anyone who has taught in Pakistan, the shortage of text and reference books for students is a painful fact of life. It has not been unusual for syllabi distributed to univeristy students to include books that are not only many years out of date, are not even available in any bookstores in the country, and are frequently missing from library shelves. This shortage of text and resource materials has bordered on a national scandal, and, with the relatively limited number of highly qualified faculty members the total result has been seriously reflected in the quality of education that has been available to college and university students.

The new regime has evidently been very conscious of these glaring faults, and, even though the quality of the faculty has been improving over the years as more and more men and women trained abroad return to join the university faculties,[1] the problem of textbook and library resources has continued to plague the educational effort at all levels.[2]

In an effort to mount a frontal attack on the latter problem, the government plans to establish a National Foundation for Book Production to facilitate the production of books and other reading materials needed at all levels of this long-range effort. With the universalization of elementary education, reading materials will be produced locally at low cost by the Foundation which will write, edit, compile, translate, print and publish texts for all the schools, colleges and universities, as well as for the general public. The Ministry of Education's Pakistan Printing Corporation will become the nucleus of the Foundation. It has been announced that the government will no longer observe international copyright laws, and will be free to translate and print "expensive" foreign books. This measure will save much foreign exchange, and reduce the cost of books to the students.[3]

The new ordinance violates both the 1886 Berne (copyright) Convention

---

1 As of October 31, 1973, 3,669 Pakistani students were studying in various foreign countries. (*Pakistan Affairs*, XXVI, 5, February 16, 1973.)

2 Even though primary education was to be free, some schools have not been able to furnish books for their students, and many indigent parents do not send their children to school for lack of proper clothing. For this reason, demands are being made that school attendance should be made compulsory by statutory law.

3 According to *Weekly Commentary and Pakistan News Digest*, (*II*, 2, January 12, 1973) the domestic production of foreign textbooks has already begun, with the expected annual saving of Rs 5,000,000 to Rs 8,000,000 in foreign exchange. The new Textbook Ordinance states, "copyright shall not exist in respect to printing, translation, adaptation or publication ... of any book to be used as a textbook for teaching, study and research purposes in educational institutions" (*Weekly Commentary*, *I*, 29, December 8, 1972).

and UNESCO's more liberal Universal copyright convention of 1952. No official announcement of such action has appeared in government Gazette notifications. Moreover, under Article 35 of the Stockholm Copyright Act and Protocol, to which the government of Pakistan acceded on November 26, 1969, *one year* must elapse before withdrawal from the convention. A similar clause is found in the UNESCO convention. This appears to be an oversight on the part of the Pakistan government because Section 1(2) of the 1972 Amendment Ordinance states that it shall become effective "at once" (*Dawn* November 20, 1972).

Examinations

Perhaps no other aspect of the educational system in Pakistan has been as sensitive an issue to students at all levels as that of examinations. Mass student failure has been endemic on the subcontinent for years, so that almost any means to pass an examination (or do well) is considered justifiable in some quarters. In some areas of India, for example, students have demanded the right to copy from neighbors during examinations, while in Pakistan the problem of mass failure has been studied by faculty members in an effort to understand and get to the root of the problem (Mangalam 1960).[1]

The Education Policy states that "the existing system of examinations is one of the root causes of the general malaise in our educational system" (1972: 31). The current system offers annual internal examinations from Class I to IX on the basis of which students pass or fail. Mass failure causes many students to drop out and therefore creates an economic loss to the nation. The new plan calls for no annual examinations up to Class VIII. Instead, students will progress through the grades automatically, under a system of continuous evaluation by their teachers. From Class IX there will be a "combination of periodic-cum-annual examinations and a continuous, scientifically graded assessment of the student's achievement, general behavior and aptitude. Eventually, there will be no failures and no repetition of classes up to Class IX" (*Ibid*). In Classes X–XII the system of terminal examinations by the Boards of Intermediate and Secondary Education will be continued for the time being,

---

1   The problem of postponing final examinations upon the request of students so that more time can be allowed for preparation has been a continuing problem for university administrators. The latter wish to avoid any confrontation on what would appear to be purely an administrative matter, but when there is any degree of political unrest, a small group of students are inclined to seize upon this as an opportunity to request a delay for more preparation time. The result has been that the examinations scheduled for 1972, have now been postponed by nine months, which will cause a serious backlog. Students are not awarded their degrees until they have passed their final exams—not after they have completed their course work. According to the *Pakistan Times*, (March 12, 1973) final examinations were to be held April 10, 1973 for students who had completed their work in June, 1972.

although an effort will be made to eliminate long-standing malpractices. The number of Boards will be increased to handle the increased number of students so that there will be one Board for every 25,000 students.

The National Service Corps and Military Training

Next to the campaign to achieve universal literacy, and the nationalization of private schools and colleges, perhaps the most dramatic plan to be proposed by the national government is the creation of a National Service Corps as well as the progressive introduction of compulsory military training for all medically fit males between the ages of 13 to 17 years (Classes IX–XII).[1]

All those passing the Intermediate examination "will be encouraged" to serve one year in the Service Corps, either in one stretch, or consecutively in short intervals during summer vacations. In order to attract young men to serve in the Corps, the following incentives will be provided: a) a monthly stipend, b) uniform allowance, c) preference for selection into institutions of higher learning and/or employment in the private or public sector, and d) the time spent in the Corps will not be counted for purposes of age limit of entry in the services, etc. Although the sex of the volunteers is not mentioned, it is assumed that women will also be expected to volunteer (*Ibid.*).

The major purpose of organizing the Corps appears to be to lend support to the government's attack on illiteracy at all levels; the Ministry of Education will have over-all responsibility for the program, while the provincial governments' education administrations will implement the scheme and arrange for the necessary training. The combination of the two programs, National Service Corps and Military Training is expected to have a major impact on the morale and character of the nation's youth, and help meet the basic needs of achieving universal literacy at all levels as well as meeting military needs. No mention is made of those youths not in school, or who drop out of school before Class IX. It is recognized that a major motivational campaign will be needed to implement both programs.[2]

---

1 Students doing National Service in the Sind are demanding five points concession in their divisional standing for admission to college which the government has promised them. The drive against illiteracy was started in the Sind in December, 1972, with the aid of volunteers from the National Service Corps, and with the announced goal of producing 400,000 adult literates annually. Fifty "leader trainers" have been undergoing special training at the University of the Sind under the supervision of UNESCO specialists in adult education. It is planned to have 1,000 training centers where two leaders will train 200 adults over a two-month period. Special books and other equipment are being prepared for the program (*Dawn*, December 5, 1972).

2 The Vice-Chancellor of the University of the Punjab announced that he hopes to institute a "motivational plan" so that students will take their studies seriously, that would reduce their great interest in "instant gratification," and that teachers would "arouse young people from their sloth and indolence." To achieve this goal, he planned to establish a Counselling and Guidance Committee to determine students' aptitudes and suggest

Religious Education

For a nation that was founded on a religious ideology, it is not surprising that the Policy would call for the compulsory study of Islamiyat up to Class X; that such study will be carefully reviewed from time to time to assure that it will have its proper place in the curriculum and textbooks; that it will not become an isolated item, and that "the values and the spirit of Islam are woven into the warp and woof of our educational fabric" (*Policy* 1972: 37). Radio and television channels will devote substantial time to the recitation of the Quran and its translation.

Administrative Reorganization

Almost everyone who has had any experience with the educational process in Pakistan would agree that the administrative organization (as in so many nations) is cumbersome and unnecessarily complicated. In an effort to reorganize the bureaucratic machinery and, hopefully, to streamline the educational administration of the country and to make it more responsive to the needs of the people, it is planned that a series of Educational Councils will be set up at the national, provincial, district and institutional levels. Membership in the councils will be drawn from all walks of life, and will include representatives of teachers, students and relevant government departments and other agencies. The councils will have the following functions:

"1. to formulate and recommend changes and developments in educational policy
2. to oversee the implementation of the policies adopted from time to time
3. to assess and evaluate over-all educational progress in their respective spheres
4. to initiate and support educational research and disseminate the findings
5. to harness and mobilize the latest educational techniques and resources for the improvement of education" (*Plan* 1972: 39).

The councils will have 15 standing committees at the national level, 14 at the provincial level, 5 at the district/corporation/municipality/town level and two at the school and college level. Whether this planned major reorganization will prove successful remains to be seen.

Program Financing

From the time the new *Policy* was announced in mid-March, 1972, the first

courses of study for them. Students would also be urged to participate in the Peoples Works Program via manual labor on building roads and buildings on campus, as well as participating in the literacy program for adults (*Pakistan Times*, April 26, 1973).

question universally raised was "How will the program be financed"? And, as might be expected, many were skeptical that the program was nothing more than a propaganda ploy and would never be implemented.

The annual expenditure in 1971–72 in the public sector of education was about Rs 700,000,000 which represents less than 2 percent of the gross national product (*Policy* 1972: 41), one of the lowest in the world, even though UNESCO recommends that developing nations should spend at least a minimum of 4 percent of their GNP on publicly-supported education.[1] The proposed *Policy* calls for a 70 percent increase for the year 1972–73 over 1971–72. Thereafter it is expected that the annual rate of increase will be on the order of 15 percent, so that by 1980 the total expenditure on education will approximate the 4 percent level recommended by UNESCO. The *Policy* calls for the "mobilization of all resources" to meet this goal. To help finance the cost of universal education, the government has levied a tax of Rs 100 per year per worker on all employers who have 20 or more workers (*Pakistan Times*, July 6, 1973).

It is obvious that the heavy emphasis the current administration places on supporting the growth of elementary education is in direct contrast to that of earlier administrations. For example, the allocation for colleges and universities in the First Five Year Plan was more than 50 percent higher than for primary education. Furthermore, the question of allocation becomes somewhat academic when it is learned that of the Rs 580,700,000 appropriated, only 55 percent was actually spent on education (Curle 1966: 53).

Over the years the pattern has not improved noticeably; furthermore, the allocation of the education budget was felt to be disproportionately high for government-supported colleges and universities. For example, for the First Five Year Plan, 29.4 percent of the education allocation was devoted to government-supported colleges and universities, but only 18.0 percent and 26.7 percent for primary and secondary education respectively (*Ibid.*). (The writer is well aware that education costs rise sharply from the primary level upward.)

Another problem that confronts all governments of modernizing nations is the extraordinarily high drop-out rate, and Pakistan is no exception. For every 100 children in the entering Class I age cohort, only 44.6 percent actually enroll, and by Class V only 9 percent are still in attendance. These data are an average of the seven year period 1955–62 (Curle 1969: 52), although the situation has undoubtedly improved since that time. The sharpest drop in attendance occurs during and at the end of the first year. There are many reasons for the high drop-out rate, not the least of which is the poverty of the children's families. Nonetheless, the educational wastage is a challenge to any well intentioned government.

---

1   It had been the practice of previous administrations to allocate higher percentages of the national budget to education than were actually spent. For example, the Third Five Year Plan called for an expenditure of 5 percent for education, yet only about 1.5 percent of the budget was spent on education—one of the lowest in the world (Pakistan: *Basic Facts*, 1966: 115). In 1964, approximately 1.75 percent of Pakistan's Gross National Product was spent on education (Edding and Berstecher, 1969: 56).

Major Project Planning

Of the major projects planned, 14 will be financed exlusively by the central government. Among these are the National Education Council, Centers of Excellence, Centers of Area Studies, The National Book Foundation Scheme, The Peoples' Open University, The National College of Arts, The University Grants Commission, the granting of interest-free student loans, graded basic vocabularies and people libraries, Book Banks in the colleges and universities, including the import of textbooks, and the Councils of Professional Education.

Conclusion

The fact that President Bhutto and Minister of Education Pirzada were able to produce such a wide-ranging plan for educational reform in less than three months after taking office would seem to indicate that such an extensive reform had been uppermost in the president's mind even before he took office. Previous administrations had announced and promised a wide variety of educational reforms, and each five-year plan included projections for expanded educational services. But these goals were rarely ever fulfilled. It has been claimed in some quarters that President Yahya Khan had received an educational reform plan that bore some similarity to the current *Educational Policy, 1972-1980*, but it was never implemented.[1] The expansion of the universities, frequently undermanned and inadequately supported, matched by an actual decline in the literacy rate of the masses, struck many observers as an elitist approach to educational development in a modernizing nation.[2] This is not to say that the spread of primary and secondary schools was ignored. Rather, that a disproportionate amount of the education budget appeared to be spent on higher education.

The continued demand for more college and university places, of course, came from the middle class – undoubtedly more vocal than one would expect the illiterate masses to be. Over the years political agitation and student strikes have caused many colleges and universities to close from time to time, while little has been heard from the illiterate village peasants or the urban workers. The demand for more educational facilities at the primary, secondary and college levels, and the failure of preceding administrations to meet the demand led to the growth of the private schools and colleges. This unfilled need was

---

1 For example, a group of 14 university faculty members, with Dr. Mahmud Hussain, of the University of Karachi as chairman, was appointed in 1969 by the government of West Pakistan to examine the problems and status of the universities. This group issued its report on May 1, 1969, but its recommendations were never implemented (*Report of the Study Group on University Education, 1969*).

2 In April, 1973, the central government announced that new universities would be opened in Dera-Ismal-Khan, and at Saidu Sharif.

frequently met by entrepreneurs whose major goal frequently was a quick profit on little investment, and at the expense of both teachers and students.

There is little doubt that the new education policy has been widely acclaimed by all segments of the population. In terms of publicity, it has received a very good press, because hardly a day passes without news items reporting day-to-day developments, and almost all laudatory. The missionaries have probably received something less than a satisfactory compromise, but at least the government did not submit to the demands of the extremists who have long proclaimed that such institutions were used to "infect Muslim youth with foreign ideologies," and should be closed down. And few people will lament the losses of those entrepreneurs who operated sub-standard institutions. Such action was long overdue.

Compared to Bhutto's efforts in areas of political and economic reform, one must concede that there has been very little resistance to the new plan. After all, in a nation with such a weak educational base, there are no major organized power centers to oppose the kinds of reforms instituted by the government. Where opposition developed, e.g., from the missionary schools, the central and provincial governments have been sufficiently flexible to reach an accommodation and it is safe to predict that many more accommodations can be expected before 1980, in an effort to achieve the major goals Mr. Bhutto has set out in his new policy. The owners of the private institutions were neither well organized, nor did they enjoy much public support. The "foreign" schools, i.e., American and British, among others, were outside the purview of the new policy.

Not only is great emphasis being placed on achieving universal literacy in the shortest possible time, but universal and free education up to Class VIII beginning September, 1972, and up to Class X two years later is being promised to the people. The nationalization of the private schools may help reach this goal a little sooner than might have otherwise developed, but it is a safe assumption that the masses of the poor and illiterate will not be in a position to readily benefit from these measures overnight. After all, this is a long-term program, the goals of which are to be achieved over an eight-year period.

One can only speculate on the role of the new education policy in President Bhutto's over-all plan. There appears to be a radical reorientation of the educational enterprise, perhaps to facilitate his long-term goal of a more egalitarian society. At one level there appears to be a determined effort to respond to the perceived deprivation of the masses, and on another level a determination to hasten the process of modernization by increased emphasis on training in the technical and scientific fields. The administration probably hopes to see them work in tandem. Furthermore, government officials continue to convey the impression that since it will be funding education at all levels, that those who benefit from it should think in terms of repaying their debt to the nation by serving the people.

A major dilemma that has developed in recent years and undoubtedly continues to haunt the government is that of the educated unemployed. Other developing nations have also been confronted with this problem, and there does not appear to be a ready solution. On the one hand, higher education is the quickest means of gaining occupational placement in the white collar, business and professional occupations of a nation's labor force, and with it the achievement of higher social status. The demand for more seats in the nation's universities is being met by a rapid expansion of educational facilities, yet it appears that the economic organization of the nation cannot fully absorb, in either the private or the public sector, the increasing number of college and university graduates. Perhaps the introduction and expansion of the National Development Volunteer Program as well as the National Service Corps will have the necessary effect in providing the trained manpower needed to implement the government's plans for a more egalitarian society. The achievement of universal literacy in an underdeveloped nation is not only a popular political goal, but the economic value of education has been well established by scholars in the field.

There is no question but that the educational landscape of the nation has changed in the short time that the educational reform has been in force. And this reform might well become the key to the oft-proclaimed "Islamic Socialism" so often bandied about by various political figures in the last quarter century. Education, especially higher education will no longer be a monopoly of the middle and upper classes, because President Bhutto appears to have set the course of the educational enterprise in the direction of egalitarianism.[1]

The administration has made what appears to be remarkable progress in the first year the Policy has been in effect. But two major issues strike the writer as crucial in any effort to predict the success or failure of this new policy by the end of the decade. The first must obviously be financial support. Although it is still too early to make a final judgment on this point, it does appear that the government is making a determined effort in this regard. The allocation for education was increased by 50 percent in the first year, and the plan calls for a 15 percent annual increase.

The second will be far more difficult to assess, namely, fertility control. The first announcement of the census taken in September, 1972, claimed a population of 74,892,000 for what was formerly West Pakistan and is now known as Pakistan – an increase of 51.3 percent over the census count of 1961 (*Census*, 1972). This would indicate an average annual net increase of approximately 3.8 percent, which, if maintained, would indicate a doubling of the nations's population in less than 20 years from the census of 1961. If the first results of this census count are correct, it would undoubtedly have a disastrous effect on government plans for economic development.

For the last several years, family planning officials were claiming that the

---

1   "There are a number of issues being talked about now-a-days. But we are convinced that for us there is only one issue, namely, Islamic Socialism, which, in a nutshell, means that every person in this land has equal rights to be provided with food, shelter, clothing education and medical facilities." Liaqat Ali Khan, August, 1949. Quoted in *President Bhutto's Address to the National Assembly*, April, 1972, p. 42.

net reproduction rate had been reduced to 2.5 percent, an obviously gross miscalculation. The press has reacted to the dangers of the population "explosion," and called for government action to this threat to the nation's well-being. In March, 1972, the *Pakistan Times* carried a full-page advertisement proclaiming the advantages of family planning and stressing that a "small family is a happy family." Since then advertisements have daily carried the same and similar messages, such as "Use oral pills to ensure good health for mother and child," "Wise mothers space births of their children," on the front page of the same paper. In addition, smaller advertisements on inside pages have pointed up the ceiling prices that a consumer should expect to pay for a variety of contraceptives. It is obvious from the retail prices listed that these are highly subsidized by the government. The writer should like to point out that these are startling developments, because such advertisements have never appeared in the press before.[1] Although it has been the official policy of the government since the late 1950's to support fertility control programs, they were not as successful as the officials of the programs claimed.

Unless the government makes a far greater effort in this regard, and unless fertility control measures are more readily adopted than they have been in the past, there is a serious question whether the total effort in the field of education in the next decade will be more than an exercise in futility.

N.B. With the inauguration of the new Constitution on August 14, 1973, President Bhutto assumed the new office of Prime Minister.

REFERENCES

Curle, Adam
    1966   Planning for Education in Pakistan. Cambridge: Harvard Press.
    1969   Educational Problems of Developing Societies. New York: Praeger.
Dawn, Karachi, Pakistan
Edding, Friedrich and Dieter Berstecher
    1969   International Developments of Educational Expenditure, 1950–1965. Paris, U.N.E.S.C.O.
Embassy of Pakistan
    1968   "Pakistan's Development Decade, 1958–68, Educational Reform," Washington, D.C.
Government of Pakistan
    1957   Planning Board, The First Five Year Plan (1955–1960), Karachi.
    1966   Pakistan: Basic Facts, Department of Films and Publications, Fourth edition, Karachi.
    1970   Planning Commission Report, Karachi.
    1972   Education for the Masses, The New Policy, Department of Films and Publications, Karachi.

---

1   After about one month the advertisements disappeared from the *Pakistan Times* as suddenly as they had appeared. One can only speculate on the reasons for the abrupt change.

1972 President Bhutto's Address to the National Assembly, April, Islamabad.
1972 The Education Policy, 1972–1980, Ministry of Education, Islamabad.
1972 The Interim Constitution of the Islamic Republic of Pakistan (As Amended by Post Constitution P.O. No. 1 of 1972), Karachi.
1973 The Constitution of the Islamic Republic of Pakistan, Karachi.
1973 Population Census of Pakistan, 1972, Census Bulletin no. 1, P. no. 27. Islamabad, Census Organization, Interior Division.
Huq, Muhammad Shamsul
1965 Education and Development Strategy in South and Southeast Asia, Honolulu.
Korson, J. Henry
1970 "Career Constraints Among Women Graduate Students in a Developing Society," Journal of Comparative Family Studies, 1, 1, (Autumn): 82–100.
Mangalam, Joseph J.
1960 Study of Student Mass Failure, Study No. 2, Time Perspective and Academic Performance of Students. Lahore: Department of Sociology, University of the Punjab.
Pakistan Affairs, Washington, D. C.
Pakistan Times, Lahore
The New York Times, New York.
Report of the Study Group on University Education. Lahore (mimeo).
1969
Sarwar, Malik G.
1972 The Educational Institutions Take-over Regulations, 1972, (Martial Law Regulation No. 118), Lahore: Lahore Law Times Publications.
Weekly Commentary and Pakistan News Digest, Islamabad, Pakistan.

BIOGRAPHICAL NOTES

J. HENRY KORSON is a Professor of Sociology at the University of Massachusetts at Amherst. He has been a visiting professor at Mt. Holyoke and Smith Colleges; Kwansei Gakuin University in Japan, and a senior Fulbright Lecturer at the University of Karachi. He has had Ford and Asia Foundation research grants and is currently a consultant to H.E.W. for a family planning research project in Karachi. He is a member of the National Seminar on Pakistan/Bangladesh at Columbia University, and a trustee and the treasurer of the American Institute of Pakistan Studies. He has written numerous articles on the changing social structure of the family on Pakistan, and, in addition to editing this volume, he is preparing a book titled *Modernization and Social Change in the Family in Pakistan* to be published by Holt, Rinehart and Winston in 1974.

CRAIG BAXTER, an American Foreign Service Officer, is at present a visiting member of the faculty of the United States Military Academy, West Point. He has a doctorate in history from the University of Pennsylvania. His foreign service assignments have included Bombay, New Delhi and Lahore as well as Washington. He is the author of *The Jana Sangh, a Biography of an Indian Political Party* and *District Voting Trends in India* and several articles on South Asian history and politics.

Professor FAZLUR RAHMAN was born in North West Pakistan and graduated from the University of the Punjab. He received his Ph.D. from Oxford and has lectured at Durham University; The Central Institute of Islamic Studies, Karachi; The Institute of Islamic Studies at McGill University, and is currently a member of the Department of Near Eastern Languages and Civilizations at the University of Chicago. He has also been the Director of the Advisory Council of Islamic Ideology of the Government of Pakistan. Among his many publications are *Prophecy in Islam* (1958), and *Islam*, 1966.

HAFEEZ MALIK is Professor of History and Political Science at Villanova University. He received his higher degrees at Syracuse University and was for some time Lecturer at the Foreign Service Institute of the U. S. State Department. Among his writings are *Moslem Nationalism in India and Pakistan*, Washington, 1963, and *Iqbal's Poetry: Social and Political Themes*, New York, 1968.

LAWERENCE ZIRING is Professor of Political Science, Western Michigan University. He received his Ph.D. from Columbia University, and his major areas of scholarly interest are comparative government and political of South and Southwest Asia, and international politics and national security policy. He has taught at Dacca University in East Pakistan (now Bangladesh) in 1959–1960, and has served as Advisor to the Pakistan Aministrative Staff College, 1964–1966. He is the author of *The Ayub Khan Era: Politics in Pakistan, 1958–1969*, Syracuse, Syracuse University Press, 1971; and the forthcoming *Asia in Political Perspective*. He has also contributed articles to journals in the United States, Canada and Pakistan. Professor Ziring is a member of the National Seminar on Pakistan/Bangladesh at Columbia University as well as a trustee of the American Institute on Pakistan Studies.

W. ERIC GUSTAFSON is a Lecturer in Economics at the University of California, Davis. He has spent two years in Pakistan as a Research Advisor at the Pakistan Institute of Development Economics and one in India as a Faculty Fellow of the American Institute of Indian Studies. His major research interest is the economic history of irrigation in India and Pakistan. He is currently editing a volume of bibliographical essays on Pakistan and Bangladesh for the National Seminar on Pakistan and Bangladesh at Columbia University.

LEE L. BEAN was at the time of the writing of his paper the Associate Director, Demographic Division, The Population Council in New York. Currently he is Professor and Chairman, Department of Sociology, University of Utah. His Ph.D. is in Sociology from Yale University. A former advisor to the Demographic Section of the Pakistan Institute of Development Economics, his publications on Pakistant demography include the monographs *Population and Family Planning Manpower and Training* (with Richmond K. Anderson and Howard J. Tatum) and *The Population of Pakistan: 1960–2000* (with M. R. Khan and A. Razzaque Rukanuddin) as well as an article for *The Pakistan Development Review* entitled "Three Years of Pakistan's New National Family-Planning Programme" (with A. D. Bhatti). His earlier list of articles on the demography of Pakistan is quite extensive.

A. D. BHATTI is a research assitant with the Demographic Division of the Population Council. His M.A. is in Economics from the University of the Panjab, Pakistan. He was formerly a member of the Demographic Section at the Pakistant Institute of Development Economics. One of his publications is an article for the *Pakistan Development Review* entitled "The Three Years of Pakistan's New National Family-Planning Programme" (with Lee L. Bean). He is also the compiler of *A Bibliography of Pakistan Demography*.

INDEX

Administrative Reforms Commission, 96
Afghanistan, 64–8
Ahmad, Aziz, 78
Ahmadis, 42
American Schools, 130
Azad Pakistan Party, 21

Baghdad Pact (CENTO), 65
Baluchi independence movement, 73
Baluchistan, 65, 129
Bangladesh, 2, 73–4
Basic Democracies, 23
Batai, 87
Bhutto, Begum Nusrat, 134
Bhutto, Zulfikar Ali, 2–3, 6, 14, 30, 42–5, 51, 54, 56, 68–9, 96
Bizenjo, Mir Gaus Bakhsh, 36, 48, 54
Bogra, Mohammad Ali, 58
Book banks, 142
Burki, Shahid Javid, 25

Census Office, 114
Centers of Excellence, 121
Central Cartel Law Group, 83
Central Statistical Office, 100, 115
Civil Service of Pakistan, 1, 96
Civil service reform, 96
Coale, A. J., 90
Communal award, 116
Company Law Commission of 1961, 83
Congress Party, 75
Constitution, Interim, 3
    Permanent, 1, 3, 120
Convention League, 24
Copyright conventions, 137–8
Council of Common Interest, 54

Dais, 112
Daoud, Sardar, 65–8
Darbaris, 8
Dawood, Ahmad, 81
Despres, Emilio, 89
Devaluation, 89
Division of Population Planning, 112, 116
Dyarchy, 7, 16

Economic Reforms (Amendment)
    Ordinance (1973), 85
    Order (1972) ,81

Educated unemployed, 128–30
Education
    administrative reorganization, 140
    agro-technical, 122
    elementary (primary), 123
    free and universal, 121
    higher, 124
    ideological goal of, 122
    Ministry of, 137
    program financing, 140–1
    religious, 140
    secondary and intermediate, 123
Educational Policy, 1972–80, 3
Edwards College, 132
Egalitarianism, 2, 4, 33, 123, 144
Eisenhower-Dulles Administration, 72
Examinations, 138–9

Faiz, Ahmed Faiz, 86
Family Planning, 99
    division, 101
Faruq, Ghulam, 50
Feldman, Herbert, 12
Five Year Plans, 3

Gandhi, Indira, 47, 52
Geneva Accord, 72
Government Administrative Staff College, 1
Government of India Act, 1935, 16
"Green Revolution," 109

Haksar, P. M., 78
Haque, Shah F., 131
Hasan, Dr. Mubashir, 82, 93, 95
Hasan, Said, 102
Husain, Mian Sir Fazli, 9–10
Hussain, Mahmoud, 142

Illiteracy, 133–4
Indian Civil Service, 1
Industrial Employment (Standing Orders)
    Ordinance (1968), 85
International Court of Justice, 77
International Monetary Fund, 89
Iqbal, Muhammad, 18
Islamic Advisory Council, 37, 40–1, 43
Islamic Socialism, 1, 4, 31, 144

Jafar, Mohammad, 88
Jamiyat ul Ulama, 33

Jinnah, Mohammad Ali, 1, 18
Johnson Administration, 75

Kalabagh, Nawab of, 87
Kashmir, 69–70
Kasuri, Mahmoud Ali, 71
Khaliq, Abdul, 122
Khan, Abdul Wali, 45–8, 51, 54
Khan, Agha, 44
Khan, Liaqat Ali, 69
Khan, Mairaj Muhammad, 48
Khan, Mohammad Ayub, 2, 12–3, 23–4, 30,
     37, 40, 56, 83, 119, 126
Khan, Nurul, 121
Khan, Yahya, 2, 24, 30, 75, 89, 121, 142
Kissan, Mazdur Party, 46, 51
Kissinger, Henry, 75

Lahore Resolution, 18
Land Reform, 87
     Regulation, 88
Language riots, 104
"London Plot," 51–2

Madrassa, 38
Managing Agency and Election of Directors
     Order, 1972, 82
Mandot, 20–1
Martial Law Regulations No. 118, 120
Ministry of Health, 100
Ministry of Home and Kashmir Affairs, 100,
     114
Mirza, Iskander, 22
Modernist, 39
Montagu-Chelmsford Reforms, 7, 9
Moynihan, Daniel, 77
Mullahs, 120
Muslim League, 19–21
     Manifesto, 7, 11
Muslim Separaist Movement, 1

"Nankarshahi," 96
National Awami Party, 21, 33, 45
National Book Foundation Scheme, 142
National College of Arts, 142
National Credit Consultative Council, 93
National Curriculum Bureau, 136
National Development Volunteer Program,
     129, 144
National Education Council, 121
National Foundation for Book Production, 137
National Literacy Corps, 134
National Science Council, 127
National Service Corps and Military Train-
     ing, 139, 144
National Sports Trust, 137

Nationalization of schools and colleges, 121,
     130–3
Nixon administration, 75
North West Frontier Province, 65

Pakhtunistan, 48, 50, 65
Pakistan Democratic Party, 25
Pakistan Institute of Development Econo-
     mics, 100, 106
Pakistan Science Foundation, 127
Partition, 19–20
Payment of Wages Act, (1936) ,85
People's Party of Pakistan, 2, 6, 14, 24, 45, 86,
     95–6
People's Works Program, 140
Physical education and sports, 136–7
Pirzada, Abdul Hafeez, 54, 120
Pirzada, Syed Sharifuddin, 83
Planning Commission, 102, 105–6
Population Growth Estimate, 100
Population policy, 111
Provincial autonomy, 16
Public Demand Recovery Act, 93

Qayyum League, 25
Qureshi, M. L., 125

Rahim, J. A., 32
Rahman, Shaikh Mujib, 47, 52, 73
Rawalpindi Conspiracy, 69
Regional Cooperation for Development
     (RCD), 65, 70–1, 73
Repatriation, 76–9
Republican Party, 22
Repugnancy clause, 36
Riba, 35
Round Table conferences, 16

Singh, Hartirath, 73
Sialkot Program, 113
Schools for gifted and talented, 133
Shah, King Zahir, 65
Simla, 70
South East Asia Treaty Orgnization, 71–2
State Bank of Pakistan, 93
State Life Insurance Corporation, 92
Student loans, 135–6
Student hostels, 136
Student uniforms, 136
Student welfare, 135-6
Suhrawardy, H. S., 113

Teacher training and supply, 135
Tiwara, 19
Traditionalists, 39
Tumandars, 8, 16

Twenty two families, 4, 81, 86, 92–4

Unemployment allowance, 129
Unionist Party, 6, 10–1, 14, 19
United Democratic Front, 53
U.N.E.S.C.O., 121, 141
United Nations Fund for Population Activities, 114
United States Aid for International Development (A.I.D.), 114
United States Educational Foundation, 71
Universities, new, 124–5
University
    chancellor, 125
    Grants Commission, 124

Ordinance, 125–6
People's Open, 142
pro-chancellor, 125
Senate, 125–6
Syndicate, 125–6
vice-chancellor, 125

Valika, Fakhruddin, 81

West Pakistan Research and Evaluation Center, 101

Zakat, 35
Zamindars, 7